Macroeconomic Modeling and Policy Analysis for Less Developed Countries

Macroeconomic Modeling and Policy Analysis for Less Developed Countries

Mohammed F. Khayum

Routledge
Taylor & Francis Group
LONDON AND NEW YORK

First published 1991 by Westview Press

Published 2018 by Routledge
52 Vanderbilt Avenue, New York, NY 10017
2 Park Square, Milton Park, Abingdon, Oxon OX14 4RN

Routledge is an imprint of the Taylor & Francis Group, an informa business

Library of Congress Cataloging-in-Publication Data
Khayum, Mohammed F.
Macroeconomic modeling and policy analysis for less developed countries / by Mohammed F. Khayum.
p. cm.
Includes index.
ISBN 0-8133-8108-8
1. Guyana—Economic conditions—Econometric models. 2. Guyana—Economic policy—Econometric models. 3. Developing countries—Economic conditions—Econometric models. 4. Developing countries—Economic policy—Econometric models. I. Title.
HC207.K47 1991
330.9881'001'51—dc20 90-44540
CIP

ISBN 13: 978-0-367-01598-5 (hbk)
ISBN 13: 978-0-367-16585-7 (pbk)

To My Mother

Contents

Tables

Illustrations

Charts

Figures

Preface

The context for this study is the empirical fact that while the less developed countries (LDCs) as a group have experienced considerable improvements in output performance over the past three decades, there is an increasing number of countries within this group whose economic performance has not been encouraging. The poor results faced by many of the LDCs not only point to the ineffectiveness of adopted policies but also suggest the need for reformulations of existing approaches in order to provide insights and policies that are consistent with reality.

This study focuses on the need for greater relevance in theoretical frameworks and suggests that economic modeling for LDCs cannot ignore the behavior of the supply side of the economy and the role played by institutional factors in these countries. The conclusion derived from a case study based on Guyana is that short-term economic policies have limited potential for addressing contemporary economic problems unless there is success in the creation of a domestic capital goods sector.

I am grateful to Jay Mandle and James Sackey, who inspired me to pursue a career in economics. Thanks go to Fyodor Kushnirsky, who helped me to reformulate many of my ideas and to clarify their presentation. Special thanks to Dimitrios Diamantaras for introducing me to the typesetting package—TEX—that was used to produce this book. Finally, I wish to thank my wife, Desiree, and son, Omar, for their understanding as they endured prolonged periods of separation and emotional distance during the past three years.

Mohammed F. Khayum

1

Introduction

There is general recognition in the economic literature on Less Developed Countries (LDCs) that, despite some success in the growth in output for the group as a whole since the 1950s, the performance of many individual countries has not been consistent, particularly from the early 1970s onwards. Indeed, a large number of LDCs have failed over the past two decades to simultaneously achieve sustained economic growth, prolonged reductions in the rate of inflation, and a viable long-term balance of payments position.

The case of Guyana illustrates the experience of one of the LDCs that has faced severe economic crises for a major portion of the past two decades. The magnitude and persistence of poor economic performance are reflected in low growth in output, high rates of unemployment and inflation and macroeconomic imbalances in the form of severe external indebtedness and large trade and public sector deficits. Even though a wide range of policies including demand management adjustment measures as well as structural and institutional reforms were tried, there was little success in arresting the economic decline. To address the problem, this study proposes a model that can analyze the issues of external imbalance, inflation, and output performance with reference to the economic policies in Guyana.

The building blocks of the model presented are threefold: the IS-LM system which lays the foundation for aggregate demand analysis, an aggregate supply schedule in the neoclassical tradition which provides the basis for the supply side analysis, and the Keynesian formulation of the balance of payments for the analysis of the external sector. The model is tailored to the circumstances and structural characteristics of an economy such as Guyana's, with an emphasis on its open nature. Thus, on the aggregate demand side, the monetary consequences of the balance of payments are taken into account by adopting the open economy monetarist proposition stating that changes in the money stock can be usefully decomposed into changes in net domestic credit plus changes in net international reserves. On the supply side, the production function incorporates the role of external influences, through the inclusion of imported inputs as a factor of production.

Some of the important features of the model are as follows: First, it considers output, the price level, and the current account of the balance of payments in an integrated framework. Second, the model is able to link objectives of macroeconomic adjustment directly to a number of government policies in relation to the exchange rate, the money supply, and the public sector deficit. Third, the model can be used to quantify the effects of external shocks, such as changes in external demand, and in the import price level, on output and the current account balance.

The study is divided into seven chapters, covering an overview of macroeconometric modeling, the practice of macroeconometric modeling for LDCs, a description of the structure and performance of Guyana's economy, the formulation of a theoretical macromodel with the methodology for its estimation, an empirical testing of the model using annual data for Guyana between 1960 and 1984, and a simulation approach to policy evaluation.

Chapter 2 presents a survey and classification of the macroeconometric models in existence into certain types of macroeconometric systems. The basic features of each of these systems are identified and discussed. It is also shown that, although there are distinctions that separate each of these systems, there are some similarities in terms of analytical techniques, the critical aspects of economic behavior and economic structure emphasized, and the role of theoretical issues such as the formation of expectations. The emphasis on one particular system, the Keynes–Klein system, among the operational macroeconometric models that have been utilized for LDCs is made in Chapter 3. The reasons for the choice of this system given by the analysis are the lack of consolidation of other macroeconometric systems, problems of coverage in the available data, the complexity of the various economic and econometric problems involved, and the dichotomy between the implications and emphasis for policy in the other systems and the orientation within many LDCs for government intervention as a means of dealing with the problems of growth and adjustment.

Chapter 4 examines the circumstances surrounding the poor economic performance of Guyana's economy between 1960 and 1984. It identifies the close relationship between expansion of the public sector, with its acquisition of market power while crowding out the private sector, and the inertia that presently characterizes the official economy. The rise of parallel markets as a response to these conditions and the circumvention of policies enacted by the authorities has been shown to be a critical area for corrective measures if the economy is to become vibrant. The institutional structure and behavioral characteristics identified have been important considerations in the specification of the model in Chapter 5.

The model specification also seeks to address the growth oriented strategy in the context of balance of payments problems, severe external indebtedness, and inflation. The main implications from an analysis of the comparative static properties of the model are that policy measures involving changes in the exchange rate, or the public sector deficit, affect both the demand and supply sides of the economy so that in principle output and price level outcomes are ambiguous.

The feasibility of the approach and its potential for policy analyses, as well as empirical application to Guyana's economy is presented in Chapter 6. The model is estimated using both the Ordinary Least Squares (OLS) and Two Stage Least Squares (TSLS) techniques and the empirical results are commented upon. Besides the examination of parameter estimates, emphasis is placed on empirical results relevant for economic policy issues. The following are examples of these "policy oriented" findings:

- estimation of the actual multipliers which indicate the impact of policy induced shocks such as changes in the exchange rate, money supply, and the public sector deficit on output, the price level, and the current account balance.
- simulations of the path of output, the price level, and the current account of the balance of payments under different scenarios for policy variables, for example, the exchange rate.

The concluding chapter summarizes the main findings and highlights some of the directions in which the proposed framework can be extended and likely areas for future research. The study provides a quantified assessment of the elasticities of the aggregate demand and aggregate supply schedules which suggests that demand management policies would have a negligible impact on output but policies that can shift the aggregate supply schedule would have considerable impact on the level of output. However, based upon the existing supply side bottlenecks facing the economy this raises the alarming possibility of limited policy options extending beyond the short term unless a domestic capital goods sector is developed to ease production constraints.

One direction of improvement is to make the model dynamic so as to consider longer run issues in relation to growth rates and inflation rates.

Another area for further work concerns the issue of model stability, particularly when it is considered that in response to certain external shocks such as foreign price increases production may decline faster than absorption resulting in continued current account deficits. The model can also be elaborated through a greater degree of disaggregation and the disequilibrium aspects of the economy—in the sense that there are imbalances between demands and supplies in various sectors—needs to be investigated and modeled, perhaps within the framework of recent developments in disequilibrium macroeconometric modeling. Considerable scope also exists for further econometric work, particularly, in relation to issues such as non-linear estimation and the application of other system estimation methods such as three stage least squares. Finally, since the broader purpose of this study is the development of theoretically founded and operational macroeconometric models for LDCs, the suggested model can be tested for other LDCs that share structural and institutional characteristics similar to Guyana's using a larger data base.

2

Macroeconometric Modeling: An Overview

Background

Since the 1930s when Tinbergen first constructed a macroeconometric model with the purpose of analyzing the business cycle in the United States economy, macroeconometric modeling has emerged as one of the more widely used tools of quantitative economic analysis. Accompanying this trend has been the growth of a related literature encompassing developments in macroeconomics and in the econometric approach to economy-wide model building. Within the macroeconomic literature recent developments include the rational expectations theory, supply-side economic policy, and open economy macroeconomics.[1] In the econometric literature many of the related research areas bear some connection to the methodological issues surrounding structural estimation of an entire economy. Some of the issues cover problem areas such as exogeneity and model selection, and the use of appropriate models for data generation processes and policy analysis.[2]

These developments have raised theoretical and empirical questions that have placed macroeconometric modeling at a crossroads. From the theoretical standpoint there is a lack of consensus about the "true" structure of economies. The Keynesian-Monetarist debate, for instance, offering alternative visions of how the economy functions on the demand-side, currently overshadowed by the New Classical Macroeconomics and the focus on supply-side issues is indicative of the competing approaches that are in existence. In addition to the empirical questions specific to each approach such as making the models operational, there is the consideration that empirical results are a major avenue for testing the relevance of existing models. However, the empirical experience in the latter direction has been far from satisfactory since a number of plausible contending theories cannot be rejected on the basis of estimated results to date.[3] This problem of empirical model selection has led to divergent trends in macroeconometric modeling ranging from the rejection of structural estimation to the search for economic structure in the form of the parameters of preference and technology.[4]

This chapter presents an overview of the macroeconometric modeling literature. In order to conduct an exercise of this nature, the discussion will be based on a broad classification of the major types of macroeconometric systems with specific reference to two recurring themes in the evolution of this literature. This is followed by an indication of a trend towards rapprochement between some of the existing approaches in spite of the distinctions that appear to justify their separate existence. Finally, the discussion will be extended to consider the kind of research methodology that has grown in parallel with the problems of structural estimation. All of this will be setting the stage for an evaluation of macroeconometric modeling with specific reference to the less developed countries (LDCs).

Macroeconometric Systems

Amidst the huge growth in the volume of research on macroeconometric modeling two sets of issues have featured persistently in the evolution of this literature. The first involves the concern over the micro-foundations of macroeconomic relations and conditions for valid aggregation. The second pertains to the concerns of policy makers over a varying array of problems of an economy-wide nature.

The first aspect has consistently been an area of interest largely because it emanates from a perspective that has been highly favored within the economics profession, namely, that for macro propositions to be meaningful they must possess explicit micro-underpinnings. The basis of this position can be traced to the economic literature which predated the micro-macro distinction. However, its relevance for the evolution of the macroeconometric modeling literature was established with the outcome of an early methodological debate on aggregation. The favored position at the time was that held by one of the pioneering figures in macroeconometric modeling, who argued that a primary theoretical concern is to meet the challenges of making macroeconomic relations conformable with the postulate of rational behavior.[5]

The tradition set in train was one of a consistent concern with micro-theoretical detail on the part of macroeconomic modelers. It is not uncommon, therefore, to find the established theories of household and firm behavior highly visible in the macroeconomic specification of investment, production and consumption functions of large scale models currently in use—see Kmenta and Ramsey (1981) and Klein (1983). It should be noted, however, that recent research has raised questions about this predilection for micro-underpinnings in relation to macroeconomic propositions from a number of perspectives. Schlicht (1985), for example, resurrected from Pu (1946) and May (1946) the perspective that aggregation may proceed without detailed knowledge of micro behavior suggesting that it is feasible to have meaningful macro propositions without explicit micro-underpinnings. Here, a number of anomalies in making the transition from micro behavior to macro relationships are identified. These have been articulated in terms of differences in the qualitative relationships between microeconomic and macroeconomic laws because of the smoothing effect, the elimination effect and the system effect.[6]

Kalman (1979, 1980, 1983) has argued that, because system-theoretic questions come to the fore before the basic economic phenomena may have been understood, economic theory is of limited value to the process of building precise quantitative models for prediction or policy analysis.[7] Finally, there are the indications that even within the standard macroeconomic writings there is a growing skepticism about the feasibility and usefulness of building macro relations from micro perceptions (see Fisher 1983). At this stage, however, these perspectives have not had considerable impact on macroeconometric modeling and, while they are likely to exercise greater influence in the future, model formulation continues to portray a concern for an adequate micro-macro nexus.

The second major aspect that has had considerable impact on the evolution of macroeconometric modeling is the requirements of economic policy in the context of changing economic circumstances. The development of economics, in general, has been characterized by a symbiotic relationship between empirical trends and economic theory and economic policy.[8] The increased evidence of a widening and varied range of macroeconomic problems, therefore, witnessed considerable effort aimed at designing effective policies for changing an economic system and tests for selection among different economic theories. Accordingly, the macroeconometric literature witnessed enormous growth as the varied characteristics and experiences among economies led to a range of models characterized by differences in size, complexity, purpose, use of econometric techniques, and model design.

Many of these differences, however, emanate from the underlying paradigm chosen as the basis for analyzing the economy. Since the models tended to share the common perspective of seeking to provide a systematic understanding of the structure and operations of an economic system, it is the different points of departure about the functioning of the economy that are of fundamental significance in determining alternative specifications. As a consequence the vast literature on existing macroeconometric models can be reduced to manageable proportions through a consideration of the alternative frameworks that have been utilized in the construction of these models.

A useful taxonomy suggested by Challen and Hagger (1983) identifies five major systems under which the numerous macroeconometric models may fall. These systems, which are the KK (Keynes-Klein); the MS (Muth-Sargent); the PB (Phillips-Bergstrom); the WJ (Walras-Johansen); and the WL (Walras-Leontief), derive their names from two economists the first of whom produced the framework for analyzing the economy and the second produced the prototype macroeconometric model within this framework.[9] Although each of these systems has an extensive literature associated with it, the discussion of these systems will be far from exhaustive since the purpose is simply to identify the features that distinguish one system from another. Accordingly, an attempt is made to present specific examples which capture the salient features of each system, with a discussion of the modifications and details that have been incorporated over time.

One of the earliest examples of a KK macroeconometric model was one developed in the late 1940s by Klein (1950:84–122) for the United States economy. This system consists of sixteen relationships in forty-four variables. Of the forty-four variables, sixteen are classified as endogenous and twenty-eight as predetermined. Seven of the sixteen relationships deal with the product market—five in the form of behavioral relationships for components of aggregate demand, one an identity for private producers' investment, and the final one a market clearing condition for the goods market. Three of the other relationships pertain to money market variables, one deals with wages, three relationships focus on national income components, such as rent and private sector income, while another deals with a housing variable.

In a number of respects, this model differs from its theoretical antecedent which is the macro-analytical system put forward by Keynes (1936). The macro-analytical system incorporated a threefold categorization of aggregate demand in the goods market, combined with money market and labor market relationships. Additional features of Keynes's system include the treatment of government expenditure, the wage level, and the money supply as exogenous, the absence of open-economy relationships, lags in behavioral relationships, and any explicit expectational variables.

The Klein model, in its focus on a market clearing condition and behavioral relationships for expenditure categories in the goods market, has as its point of departure the core of the macro-analytical system. At the same time, however, it provided the basis for those features which have become essential characteristics of modern KK models but which no longer make it easy to detect their origin in Keynes's macro-analytical system. Aspects of the Klein model which have been influential in this regard are: the formulation of the model in dynamic terms by including lagged endogenous and lagged exogenous variables, the introduction of non-linear relationships, and the focus on the stochastic nature of relationships that were treated as deterministic.

In addition to these features, modern KK models are characterized by a greater degree of disaggregation of the expenditure categories, the endogenization of variables such as the money wage and the money supply, the presence of open-economy relationships, the inclusion of expectational variables, and an explicit treatment of the supply-side of the macro economy. These features not only serve to indicate the gap between existing models and their macro-analytical antecedent but also highlight the accommodation of new theoretical and empirical insights into the KK system.

The modern KK system, for instance, typically portrayed as a general equilibrium model of product markets, labor markets, government operations, and money and financial markets, draws heavily on neoclassical economics for theoretical backing. This has been a direct result of efforts aimed at showing that aggregate behavior portrayed through the IS-LM and AD-AS frameworks is consistent with individual optimization. Thus, Tobin (1956) demonstrated that the upward sloping LM curve is consistent with individual maximization of financial portfolios. Ando and Modigliani (1963) have used consumer theory to indicate that individual households maximizing their consumption over a lifetime can be reconciled with an aggregate consumption function. Jorgenson (1967) analyzing the behavior of individual firms showed how it is possible to determine the aggregate investment function. On the supply-side of the economy, the focus has been on the labor market with a search for the micro-foundations of the Phillips curve through the production and pricing behavior of firms (see Phelps 1967, 1970; Santomero and Seater 1978).

These developments have not gone uncontested.[10] However, they did much to improve the appeal of the KK system. Reinforced by the apparent success of its policy conclusions during the next two decades after the end of the second World War,[11] the KK system gained in prominence and became a critical component of applied and policy oriented model building.

Two policy implications in particular have been emphasized. The first is the notion that government could best minimize an economy's output fluctuations by systematically varying its own expenditures and monetary policy to offset fluctuations in private sector spending. The second, following from the first, is that stabilization policy was primarily about obtaining estimates from which the systematic government policy variation could be derived to best achieve full employment stability.

The very success of the KK system, however, has been regarded as a source of hindrance to its further development. Tobin has indicated, for instance, that Keynesians were not sufficiently challenged during the 1950s and 1960s to produce improvements that could have met the problem of the simultaneous occurrence of rising prices and rising unemployment in the 1970s.[12] Thus, even as the KK system became established as the dominant macroeconometric system, when it became apparent that policies derived from models within the KK system were ineffectual in dealing with the experience of stagflation, competing macroeconomic frameworks gained wider consideration.

Foremost, among the alternative perspectives on how the economy functions and the role for stabilization policy are the modern variants of two schools of thought formulated some time before the Keynesian paradigm. These are Monetarism, representing a reformulation of the old quantity theory, and the New Classical School, providing extensions to the classical model through the incorporation of rational expectations.

Monetarism, based on the quantity equation which states that the stock of money balances is proportional to the nominal value of transactions, is both a theory for explaining the impact of money supply on economic activity and inflation, and a prescription for specific policy action by the monetary authorities. Based on the interaction of a stable demand for money with an independently determined money supply, the key proposition of the modern quantity is that a change in the rate of growth of money will produce a corresponding but lagged change in the rate of growth of nominal income.[13] Linked to this, is the proposition that stabilization policy does not have a lasting impact on output and employment, hence the long run effect of changes in the money supply is on the price level.

The latter result is derived from the natural rate hypothesis outlined by Friedman (1968) which proceeds from the notion of an inherently stable private sector that forms its expectations adaptively. Starting from the position that workers are interested in their real wage, the argument is made that workers will know the value of the nominal wage that they are receiving, but would not know for certain what the prices of all goods will be when they come to buy them. In the short run an increase in aggregate spending may tend to raise prices and hence wages, but if workers do not accurately foresee the rise in prices then the nominal wage offer appears to imply higher real wages. More labor will be supplied and aggregate spending would have stimulated employment and output. In the long run, however, workers' expectations of the general price level will adjust leading to a reduction in hours worked and, therefore, a fall in employment and output.

Because there is only the possibility of short run minor deviations in employment and production, but not their permanent alteration through any deliberate economic policy, monetarism is characterized by an anti-activist attitude which opposes discretionary policy on the part of the government. In keeping with this view is the argument that if there are economic problems then they are the result of interventions by the government. These interventions may weaken the private sector through crowding-out by fiscal policies, accelerate inflation through expansionary monetary policy, or provoke unemployment through restrictive policies.

The New Classical School sharing an inference similar to the monetarists about the role of government in the economy provides added insights to the tenets of the Classical theory. According to the Classical view, there is no place for involuntary unemployment, overinvestment, underconsumption, and general crises. Furthermore, given the role of the price mechanism in achieving general market clearance, the tendency is for market economies to converge toward the general equilibrium. Also, the Classical School, while recognizing real economic problems, regarded them to be the result of specific disturbances to the market process, such as monopolies, cartels, unions, and state intervention.

In addition to the above, the New Classical School is identified by a vision of the economy in which rational expectations prevail. With this expectation formation process, individuals are assumed to know the correct economic model, use all information available, and thereby form subjective expectations about the probability distributions of future outcomes which on average coincide with the actual probability distributions. In this sense, as long as an economic variable is determined in line with a discernible process, rational people will form their expectation of the variable in accordance with that process using all the relevant information available at the time they form their expectation. To the extent that government policy is systematically applied to minimize output fluctuations, it becomes widely known and predictable. If in periods of recession people observe that government pursues expansionary policies and in periods of boom contractionary policies, then government policy could be inferred from the state of the economy in the current and previous periods. In such cases aggregate demand (AD) shifts become ineffective in changing the level of real output and employment since the price level changes will be foreseen, and the relevant short run aggregate supply (AS) curve would be that associated with the higher price level. Within this framework other notable propositions are that the business cycle and all other economic events can be considered as equilibrium phenomena, and that observable economic fluctuations can be traced to stochastic disturbances and changeable policy accompanied by imperfect foresight. If, for example economic agents mistakenly attribute price changes to relative demand shifts rather than to random demand shifts, then aggregate output will deviate from its natural level.

Accompanying the new directions in macroeconomics were revised perspectives on the relationship between money, prices, and output. These raised several questions pertaining to stabilization policy. The basic questions were: whether it was necessary to conduct stabilization policy, whether stabilization policy was theoretically possible, and whether stabilization policy could be carried out in practice. The answers to these questions by the different macroeconomic frameworks provide two distinct positions in terms of attitudes and political inferences about the role of government in the economy.

An attitude of economic liberalism shared by the Monetarist and New Classical Schools contends that there is no need to stabilize a market economy since the private sector is inherently stable. Further, both frameworks suggest that in the long run the effect of activist economic policy would only be a nominal one, since the price level would change but not real output. The theoretical possibility of an effective stabilization policy, however, is conceded in the short run by the monetarist position. Finally, these frameworks emphasize that there are limitations facing the government should it attempt to carry out stabilization policies. Monetarists emphasize policy and implementation lags which make it difficult for effective stabilization policies to be applied. The New Classical School argues that, should the government try, the result will be de-stabilization of the economy.

In contrast, there is an attitude of activism embodied in the Keynesian framework which suggests that the private sector is potentially unstable. This notion of a potentially unstable private sector can be traced to Keynes's belief that firms' expectations about the future profitability of their investment projects is highly volatile (Keynes 1936:161–162) and that interest rate expectations are inelastic.[14] These beliefs, incorporated within the IS-LM analytical framework in the form of volatile IS and relatively flat LM curves, indicate the possibility of sharp movements in aggregate demand originating in the private sector. It is this possibility which establishes a role for government in offsetting sharp undesirable fluctuations in the level of output and unemployment under the assumption that the government is able to perform effective stabilization in the face of short-term deficiencies in the economic process. Moreover, the success of stabilization policy in practice can be achieved by applying monetary and fiscal tools as well as direct controls.

One of the consequences of these alternative perspectives in macroeconomic theory was the emergence of other types of macroeconometric models aimed at testing the empirical relevance of the existing claims about the effectiveness of stabilization policies. An initial attempt at providing a macroeconometric model incorporating monetarist propositions was presented by Anderson and Carlson (1970). This model, subsequently referred to as the St. Louis model, is an eight-equation model with five behavioral relationships and three identities. The critical equation from the standpoint of the monetarist perspective is one which seeks to test the relationship between total spending and changes in the money supply as well as in high employment government expenditures. The other equations are concerned with determining the expected rate of price change, the rate of interest, and the level of unemployment.

The empirical results of the model supported the contention that changes in the money supply had a significant impact on changes in total spending. These results however, led to an overriding preoccupation in subsequent monetarist models over the issue of fiscal versus monetary policy as the more potent tool in stabilization policy. Much of the econometric work along these lines ended up as reduced-form equation estimations of the St. Louis type,[15] and as a result structural monetarist models failed to become an important class of contemporary macroeconometric models.

Another direction pursued in the context of the advances in macroeconomic analysis was the incorporation of rational expectations into structural estimation. This is not to say that expectations were not modeled in previous macroeconometric models. Rather, the approach was in line with the theory of rational expectations which does not limit expectation formation to the previous values of an economic variable. One of the recurring issues in these models is that there is no conclusive test of the rational expectations hypothesis separately since its inclusion hinges significantly on a particular model of how the economy works, namely, one that emphasizes speed with which equilibrium is achieved by price movements. In the taxonomy previously outlined these models fall within the MS system. Because of the contemporary significance of the concept of rational expectations a brief examination of this concept is in order before considering the prototype econometric version of the class of rational expectations models.

The basis for the rational expectations hypothesis (R.E.H) was provided by Muth (1961) as an outgrowth of efforts associated with the derivation of optimal policies in production scheduling and inventory management for the firm. Muth viewed expectations as an economic good, the quality of which could be judged by definite statistical criteria. The core proposition was that an optimal (in the sense of minimum squared error) forecast X_t should display the property:

$$X_t = X_t^e + u_t$$

where X_t^e denotes the expected future value of X as of the preceding period, and the forecast error u_t has zero mean, is serially uncorrelated, and has zero correlation with the forecast itself (X_t). The first condition implied unbiased forecasts, the second implied that systematic over-prediction and underprediction should not exist, and the third meant that all information through period $t-1$ useful in forecasting X_t would be utilized.

Muth's basic contention was that there was little reason to believe a priori that the expectational formulas in use at the time satisfied these conditions[16] since there was "little evidence to suggest that the presumed relations bear a resemblance to the way the economy works."[17] For Muth, "expectations, since they are informed predictions of future events,are essentially the same as the predictions of the relevant economic theory."[18] Accordingly, in a model designed to predict a variable X_t, the "rational" forecast must coincide with the prediction of the model itself. While Muth did not specifically apply the R.E.H. to macroeconomic analysis, it was not too long before it was recognized as having profound implications for macro modeling.

Critical questions were raised about the analyses contained in the Keynesian and Monetarist frameworks.[19] The limited emphasis on expectations, which in a highly interdependent system has been shown to have important consequences, is one deficiency highlighted in the Keynesian analysis. Another, is the effect rational expectations had on the nature of the Keynesian-Monetarist controversy. While challenging the core propositions of the Keynesian school, the development of the new classical non-interventionist logic forced monetarists into the dilemma of defending their position emanating from the Keynesian-Monetarist debate. In particular, the policy debate over gradualist versus sharp-shock monetary control and the effects on price and quantity dynamics was automatically precluded by the propositions of the new classical school. Both Keynesianism and Monetarism faced difficulties because of their demand side orientation as the new classical school re-emphasized the importance of the supply side. Monetarists critiqued Keynesian analysis on the basis of assumptions, such as the inherent stability of the private sector and its capacity for self-generating growth, the ultimate crowding out effect of fiscal policy, and the existence of a natural rate of unemployment. But it took the new classicals to pull these together in a supply side approach which, combined with the demand side, implied the ineffectiveness of demand management.

Sargent (1976) provided the first serious attempt to construct a macroeconometric model incorporating the notion of rational expectations. This model consists of five stochastic equations and one identity involving seventeen variables. Of the seventeen variables, five were classified as endogenous and the remaining twelve constituted the predetermined variables of the system. The five basic equations included a Phillips curve, a labor participation equation, a production function, an interest rate equation and a portfolio-balance equation. Through a process of substitution, the model is also capable of being represented as a two equation system comprised of aggregate demand and aggregate supply.

In this model Sargent explored the implications of rational expectations for contentions from both the Keynesian and Monetarist frameworks. He extended the Monetarist proposition of the absence of a long-run trade-off between inflation and unemployment to one which posited the possibility of no choice between unemployment and inflation even in the short-run. Forward-looking expectations in the labor market were therefore assumed not to be subject to any systematic forecast errors over any relevant time frame. Further, the

Keynesian proposition advocating scope for activist counter-cyclical policy was suggested to be non-existent, under the assumption of rational expectations and the adopted version of the natural rate of unemployment hypothesis.

In his attempt to establish whether quarterly data for the United States economy between 1951 and 1973 reject the basic contentions of the model, Sargent touched upon one of the main issues that characterize models in the MS system. This concerns the difficult econometric problems encountered in the task of testing for the validity of rational expectations within macroeconomic models. Analytically, a number of solution methods have been devised to determine expectation variables for which there are no observable data. These have shown that the rational expectation assumption imposes highly non-linear cross-equation restrictions in structural models. A variety of estimation methods ranging from single equation techniques (McCallum 1976) to full information methods (Taylor 1980 and Wickens 1982) now exist as possible options for testing macroeconometric models that involve rational expectations.

However, when Sargent developed his model, not much work had been done on the econometric estimation of rational expectation models. For this reason the estimation procedure he adopted has been viewed as very preliminary as well as not free of mistakes. Fair (1984), for example, states that Sargent made two econometric mistakes in estimating his model. The first was his use of variables outside the model in regressions to obtain values for the expected price level, as well as the values of instrumental variables for the endogenous explanatory variables. The second was his failure to note that the portfolio-balance equation was not identified. The implication of the latter is that it is not possible to deduce the values of the structural parameters of that equation, which would make the task of testing theoretical postulates concerning those structural parameters an impossible exercise.

Another aspect of rational expectations that has exercised some influence on macroeconometric modeling, but not discussed in the Sargent model, is the point made by Lucas (1976) about the practice of using macroeconometric models to evaluate different possible macroeconomic policies. According to Lucas, implicit in this practice is the assumption that the estimated model will remain unchanged in the face of different policies. He contends that, under alternative policies, the estimated coefficients which reflect existing decision rules and behavioral relationships within the economic system are likely to be different. This occurs with rational expectations because economic agents base their actions on all relevant information which includes altered economic circumstances emanating from different policies. Thus, the R.E.H. suggests that economic policy evaluation based on the estimated coefficients is likely to be misleading.

There have been a number of responses to this conclusion. One is a divergent trend in macroeconometric modeling which argues the case of the practical impossibility of policy evaluation (Sims 1982 and Wold 1982). Another is the emphasis on identifying the underlying structure of the economy by estimating parameters of preference and technology (Hansen and Sargent 1980) as one way of resolving the dilemma. A third response has been the case of modeling expectations explicitly (Taylor 1980).

With regard to the MS system, the third response has been the one most actively pursued. A contemporary example is the Liverpool model[20] in which expectations are separately identified and modeled by rational expectations methods. The model attempts to incorporate regime changes, by altering expectations through solving the model forwards in time, and treating the result as the expected one. This procedure, however, is still vulnerable to Lucas's argument since it is assumed that critical parameters in the model such as the coefficients of demand and supply curves were unchanged.

Difficulties of this nature have tended to slow the application of models in the MS system. Problems in the formalization of tests of rational expectations have led to a general recognition that the rational expectation approach is best tested in conjunction with the underlying economic model.[21] But, as major proponents of the New Classical School have indicated, there are deficiencies in the economic models that have been utilized in the MS system. Especially important in this regard are the comments by Sargent about the ad hoc nature of the theoretical specifications, as well as the recognition by Lucas that rational expectation models as developed are not geared to give concrete answers to questions of policy—see Minford and Peel (1983). All of these tendencies are indicative of a need for greater insight about how the economy functions and its structure beyond what has been generated from the MS class of models.

Another approach towards macroeconometric modeling that has established a place for itself in practice is the PB system. This system encompasses models with both theoretical insights from Keynesian and neo-Classical growth theory and a methodological focus on estimating the parameters of continuous models. Phillips (1954, 1957) provided the theoretical framework when he investigated the role of stabilization policy in the context of cyclical fluctuations in output and employment. His major argument was that the use of comparative static methods did not provide a firm basis for policy recommendations, since the time path of production and income during the process of adjustment was not revealed. Policies that give rise to greater fluctuations and instability may therefore be pursued between the initial and final equilibrium. Alternatively, Phillips suggested that stabilization policies must take cognisance of the continuous reaction of economic agents to changes in the circumstances confronting them. Accordingly, he utilized dynamic models to illustrate the operation of stabilization policy. This he argued required analysis of the time-forms of reactions in interdependent dynamic systems as desired values of economic variables deviated from actual values.

Bergstrom (1967) examined the difficulties of estimating the parameters of models formulated as systems of differential equations from discrete observations on the variables. He concluded that, in principle, techniques used for the estimation of parameters of discrete models could be utilized in the estimation of the parameters of continuous models. Thus, even without continuous observation of economic variables, it may be possible to derive predictions of continuous paths of the variables which may be relevant for policy and forecasting purposes.

Building upon a two relationship model[22] suggested by Phillips (1954), Bergstrom (1967) developed a prototype cyclical growth model with Keynesian feedback mechanisms as a system of differential equations capable of generating stable cyclical growth paths for plausible values of the parameters. Its major components include a liquidity preference function, an investment function, and wage and price adjustment relations. More sophisticated models have since emerged with extensions in the direction of external trade and production relationships. Bergstrom and Wymer (1976), for example, provide a quarterly model for the United Kingdom based on a single sector economy whose product can be used for consumption, capital formation, or be exported. It comprises a system of thirteen first-order differential equations, including ten behavioral relations and three identities. Economic theory is used to establish a priori restrictions limiting the number of parameters to be estimated to thirty-five, including sixteen long-run elasticities and propensities, sixteen speed adjustment parameters and three trend parameters. These results, indicative of the advances made in the operationalization of the PB system, also highlight some issues that are relevant to macroeconometric modeling as a whole.

With regard to model formulation, the feasibility of using the PB system raises a methodological question as to whether econometric models are to be formulated as systems of differential equations or difference equations. The adoption of the differential form of model equations has shown that considerable scope exists for the properties of the model to be studied mathematically, and for the derivation of the steady state and asymptotic stability properties of models. Also, because the endogenous variables can be assumed to adjust gradually rather than instantaneously, there is scope for the incorporation of policy reaction functions that specify the way in which policy-makers adjust a particular policy instrument in response to divergences between actual and desired values of variables of interest.[23] In this manner the PB type models offer another avenue for the formulation of automatic policy, without imposing rules as criteria for money supply and public spending growth. These corrective devices, which are activated on the basis of shortfalls or overshooting of target variables, provide the PB type models with a characteristic of being capable of formulating automatic policy, rather than purely discretionary or judgmental policy actions symptomatic of activist stabilization policy. Ultimately, however, the single most important aspect of the PB system, is its emphasis on estimating the structural parameters of stochastic economic models, in continuous time.

Thus far, single sector models of the economy have been emphasized. Not much attention has been placed on multi-sector models, which take account of the interactions between a large number of different sectors of the economy. There are two major macroeconometric systems which place considerable emphasis on this aspect of the economic system. These are the WJ and WL systems. Both of these systems are based on the framework provided by Walras

(1954) whose idea was that the economy could be described by a system of simultaneous equations given the endowments, factor supplies, knowledge, preferences, and tastes of economic decision makers and optimizers. In this framework, the economy constitutes a set of interdependent markets, and reaches a state of market clearing equilibrium through an adjustment process that results from the interplay of profit maximizing producers and utility maximizing consumers in competitive markets. In this way Walras's model has provided an explanation of allocation, production, and distribution in a market economy, with all resources fully employed and optimally allocated in a Pareto sense at any point in time.

The WJ system consists of those models that incorporate the basic notions of Walrasian general equilibrium theory into the context of macroeconomic planning and forecasting. The prototype model, referred to as the Multi-sector Growth Model (MSG) was presented by Johansen in 1960 and has since given impetus to extensive research efforts, particularly in the context of Norwegian economic planning (Norwegian Planning emphasizes the integration of sectoral analysis and decision making into the macroeconomic planning system and has developed a unique link between the academic community—the University of Oslo—the Central Bureau of Statistics and the ministry responsible for economic policy.)

The original Johansen model was produced in a study of the Norwegian economy aimed at analyzing the process of economic growth with an emphasis on explaining the differences in growth rates between various sectors in the economy. The model was disaggregated into twenty-three sectors, with twenty-two domestic production sectors, and one sector pertaining to the rest-of-the-world. Cobb-Douglas production functions were applied in modeling the substitution between labor and capital services, and neutral technical change was assumed by adding time trends to linear logarithmic production functions. Producer and household behavior were assumed to depend on relative prices, and the equilibrium solution was simultaneous in prices and quantities. The solution is determined where all product and factor markets clear simultaneously, and product prices equal the unit costs of production including a normal rate of return on capital.

A major accomplishment of this model was that, given the growth potential of the economy, it yielded insights into resource allocation patterns among different industries as a result of differential technical progress, changing domestic consumption patterns, or different trade policies. In this tradition subsequent models have been used to outline growth perspectives for as much as two decades ahead, so as to coordinate the development and policy issues of different sectors in a long term perspective. While the MSG model has been applied in Norway since the 1960s similar models have been developed for Sweden, Denmark, and Finland (Forsund et al. 1985). The operational possibility of the WJ system has also led to its extension into the area of "computable general equilibrium" (CGE) modeling which has been geared to specific analyses of issues such as economic structure and income distribution.[24] The WJ system, therefore, although not developed in stochastic terms, provides another avenue for the systematic study of macroeconomic phenomena.

Another sub-group of applied general equilibrium models, that has been even more widely used than WJ models, are input-output models. These have been categorized as belonging to the WL system. Based on the Walrasian notion of interdependence between sectors in an economy, Leontief (1941) developed a model that was capable of providing a picture of the inter-relationships between the inputs and outputs of industries in an economy. The input-output model traces the flow of goods and services from one sector to another recognizing that outputs can either be consumed or be used as intermediate goods in further productive activity.

The input-output analysis involves separating the economy into intermediate producers and consumers as well as primary producers and final purchasers. In the basic model, three matrix components are employed to indicate inter-industry transactions that arise from the demand for final products. The transactions matrix describes the flow of goods and services between buyers and sellers. A technological matrix—an input coefficient matrix—is derived from the transactions matrix showing the inputs required from suppliers by each intermediate purchaser per unit of output that is produced. The input coefficient matrix is then used to derive another matrix—the total requirements matrix—which shows the total purchases of direct and indirect inputs that are required by intermediate producers per unit of output sold to final purchasers.

In spite of great operational problems pertaining to the creation of the transactions matrix, the input-output method has been an attractive tool for quantitative economic analysis. It has been used to quantitatively assess the impact that compositional shifts in final demand have on output levels, assuming the input coefficients remain constant. In the context of binding resource limitations, the method has performed an important role in planning exercises with a focus on the linkages between sectoral issues and aggregate analysis, as well as between the demand side and production side of an economy.

The flexibility of input-output analysis has been further advanced with subsequent efforts in the direction of developing techniques to model the adjustment of input coefficients in response to changing prices and technology (Preston 1975). The importance of the WL system, therefore, is not limited to its description of the structure of an economy, but is in the creation of disaggregated general equilibrium framework which traces economic interplay between sectors while providing a vehicle for policy analysis of longer run issues.

This concludes the review of the major working macroeconometric systems. In light of the material presented above, some generalizations may be made about the nature of macroeconometric modeling. First of all, the various systems provide a menu of choices for those involved in the task of macroeconometric modeling. Secondly, the transition from theoretical macroeconomic frameworks to empirical models often poses difficulties which undermine the operational feasibility of certain models, for example models in the MS class. Thirdly, the evolution of the macroeconometric literature has witnessed a trend of changing concentration on issues of unemployment, inflation, and growth according to the prevailing circumstances, rather than the displacement of one theory by another. This has established the need to ascertain how and why these changes have occurred, instead of the ready acceptance that theories may somehow have been proved to be faulty in some definitive sense.

Prospects and Implications for Integration of Macroeconometric Systems

Several options exist with regard to the various dimensions of macroeconometric modeling. Model construction, for example, is possible under different visions of how the economic system functions. Model formulation and specification is further differentiated by methodological concerns which make a distinction between stochastic and deterministic models, discrete and continuous models, and static and dynamic models. Policy evaluation and analysis can also be conducted in relation to issues of allocation and accumulation, the short-run over the long-run responses of the economic system to exogenous changes, activist versus non-activist economic policies, and over political inferences about the role of government in the economy.

These possibilities underscore the diversity of macroeconomic frameworks that seek to provide explanations of the economic realities that characterize contemporary economies. They also point to the difficulties of creating a single or unified macroeconomic theory which would be capable of dealing with economic problems that vary over time and space. The existing macroeconometric systems not only highlight some theoretical deficiencies among the macroeconomic frameworks, but in the effort to understand observable economic phenomena of interest have tended to generate models less simplistic and even less extreme than the economic theories from which they were directly inspired. The modifications that have been made to each of the prototype models for the various systems provide ample indications of this.

The existence of these diverse models have also stimulated work aimed at some kind of reconciliation and integration among the macroeconometric systems. At one level, there is the claim of isomorphism with regard to world views and analytical technique. At another, there has been the consideration of an interface between some of these systems as well as a rapprochement between recent developments in macroeconomic theory and an existing macroeconometric system.

The phenomenon of isomorphism is related to the notion of distinct macroeconomic frameworks which have been categorized as Neo-Keynesian, Post-Keynesian, Monetarist, and the New Classical School. Included in the first category are the approaches of Tobin, Modigliani, and Samuelson, as well as those of Clower and Leijonhufvud who offer a different interpretation of Keynes's theory. The second category encompasses the approaches of Shackle, Davidson, and Kregel which stress the long term expectationist aspects of

Keynes's theory. This category also comprises a sub-group associated with the approaches of Robinson and Kalecki which focus on short period analyses. The third category includes the approaches of Friedman and Meltzer, in addition to the long-run approach advocated by Phelps. The final category incorporates the approaches of Lucas and Sargent with their focus on rational expectations.

Samuelson (1983) raised the issue of rapprochement among macroeconomic frameworks when he suggested that there exists "a complete isomorphism" of monetarist models associated with Friedman and Meltzer and those "written down by Keynesians like Tobin and Modigliani." This isomorphism pertained to the common technique of analysis, that is, IS-LM. This was also recognized by Tobin (1983) who viewed the Keynesian-Monetarist debate as one focused "on the slope of the Hicksian LM curve" and what affects it. Meltzer (1983) further noted that, while there is a difference between the Keynesian and Monetarist world views, there was strong similarity between Friedman's world view and that of the New Classical School.

Utilizing these insights as well as those of others who developed arguments along similar lines, Young (1987) identified two degrees of isomorphism—strong and weak—depending on how close macroeconometric systems are in terms of world views, the of analytical techniques utilized, and the role of expectations. In addition to the strong isomorphism of analytical technique between models in the Keynesian and Monetarist frameworks, he observes that Meltzer and Lucas stress a strong isomorphism between the world-views of Monetarists and the New Classicals. A weak degree of isomorphism was identified between the approaches of the Neo-Keynesians and Post-Keynesians, inspired by the Keynesian world-view but not sharing the same analytical technique. Leijonhufvud's contention that Keynes's view of short-term expectations implied perfect foresight is also used to suggest that there may be a weak degree of isomorphism between the Keynesian framework and that of the New Classical School.

Another dimension of the trend towards rapprochement was suggested by Klein (1983) in his interpretation of the contributions of monetarism, rational expectations, and supply side economics as possible extensions to the Keynesian system. With regard to the monetarist contribution, Klein contends that the critical consideration is that money matters, but that it is not the only thing that matters.

The implication is that there is need to fully incorporate the monetary sector in econometric models. Klein notes, however, that this development was under way in macroeconometric modeling before the ascendancy of monetarism.

The impact of rational expectations, according to Klein, lies in its contribution towards improving knowledge of the dynamics of expectation formation and the role of lag distributions in economic models. This, he regards, is especially useful since economic theory has been relatively empty in specifying these relationships. Supply side economics, in Klein's view, also does not invalidate Keynesian economics but provides a basis for a more balanced approach in understanding economic reality. This, he argues, is an extension of a process which was under way for some time involving a more detailed and systematic treatment of the production sector.

The incorporation of insights from supply side economics, rational expectations theory, and monetarism within the Keynesian system, in Klein's view, also had a major policy implication. This was the creation of an alternative to the activist—non-activist debate. This new viewpoint called for the "implementation of structural policy superimposed on well organized macro-demand policy."[25] Structural policy was suggested to be long to medium term policies, such as industrial policy aimed at raising productivity growth and improving the competitive position of the economy.

Apart from providing some kind of synthesis between existing macroeconomic theories, the above efforts have given strong support to the trend towards rapprochement among macroeconometric systems. Powell (1980), in examining the methodological feasibility of reconciliation among macroeconometric systems, concluded that the integration of small macromodels in the PB class with large applied general equilibrium models in the WJ class is feasible but the integration of models in the KK class with models of the WJ class does not seem feasible. It has been the work along the lines of the KK-WL integration, however, which has met with the greatest success at the operational level. Specific applications include the work of Preston (1975) which indicated the possibility of incorporating a flexible input-output table in a macro model framework.

The significance of the KK-WL interface resides in the claim that it can provide an adequate framework of analysis for dealing with contemporary economic problems such as stagflation, issues of competitiveness, and productivity increases (Klein (1983) Chapter 6). Through this framework, it becomes possible to trace the interplay between industrial sectors and changes in income and final demand within an economic system. Another advantage is that longer run issues pertaining to industrial policy, such as the impact of alternative policies at the sectoral level, are also capable of being addressed within this framework.

The possibility of integrating macroeconomic models at the theoretical and empirical levels has an important implication for macroeconometric modeling. This is, as a tool of economic analysis, it does not simply involve the estimation of theoretical relationships, nor is it a mechanism for establishing the "trueness" of economic theories. Rather, it involves the systematic effort to understand economic phenomena of interest using observed data with some underlying theory within a statistical framework.

There are methodological problems, however, that occur at two levels. First, at the level of exercising choice about the correct model of the economy. Second, at the level of determining the proper quantitative methods to be adopted. The problems at the first level have proven to be the most difficult to resolve.

The use of statistical tests as a guide for model selection was objected to as an inadequate way of discriminating among competing hypotheses since the early stages of econometric modeling. There were several responses to this criticism. One was that this problem could be resolved by adjustment to the size of significance tests, when the same data are used repeatedly for discriminating among hypotheses.[26] Another response was to dismiss the problem on the grounds that it is a problem of aggregation, since existing aggregation procedures often do not possess adequate economic foundations.

The more general response, however, was to stress multiple hypotheses as a purely statistical problem that could be solved by the accumulation of more data. The basis of this argument is that the true model would be revealed by the accumulation of more data because the coefficients of false models must asymptotically approach zero. Experience has shown, however, that statistical tests on aggregate economic data can fail to reject a number of seemingly incompatible theories.

These results have had the effect of strengthening the view that current models are generally too simple despite the large size of many of them. When examined closely, the credibility of current models as reflections of economic reality may become highly questionable. The identification of current models, for example, is often based on restrictions which are introduced without adequate explanation or proof in the structural equations—see Malinvaud (1981). Doubts have also been raised concerning the classification of variables as endogenous or exogenous and the kinds of constraints introduced. It is on the basis of these notions that there exists a strong case for greater theoretical realism on the part of those engaged in the analysis of macroeconomic activity.

Conclusion

The above considerations indicate that there are several modes of economic reasoning, based on alternative visions of the economic system or specific analytical techniques. The correctness of these approaches depends on the nature of existing economic circumstances. To date the aspiration for a single macroeconomic theory remains unrealized and, for technical and methodological reasons, seems likely to continue. Therefore, the task that faces any quantitative economic exercise at the macroeconomic level requires some choice about the model of the economy to be followed.

As the preceding discussion indicates, this raises the troublesome problem of model selection. At this stage, model selection seems incapable of being resolved as a purely statistical problem. This is so because statistical tests have not been definitive in rejecting economic theories, leading to a plausible conclusion that a number of models may be true and that different behavioral laws for the same phenomena can be in force at the same time.

It is also important to note that the reliability of econometric models in describing the consequences of alternative choices concerning economic policy will always remain in question because any model cannot be expected to be perfect. There will therefore be a permanent challenge to find formulations that are adequate for reality, in the relevant dimensions under investigation. These must also be operational from an econometric standpoint.

Along these lines there is growing recognition that macroeconometric modeling requires the construction of models that contain more historical and institutional structure than has been possible in traditional equational systems of macroeconometrics. In particular, this requires that econometric analyses be conducted at a level where institutional constraints and individual behavior are more clearly discernible. It is with this theme in mind that the lessons that may be gleaned from the practice of macroeconometric modeling for LDCs and the specific problems and circumstances of Guyana's economy will be examined in the next two chapters.

Notes

1. Each of these developments bear a close relationship to contemporary economic events, including economic policy, and have grown enormously to cover a wide range of issues in pure economic theory, econometrics, and economic policy. Recent contributions to the rational expectations literature are R. E. Lucas, *Models of Business Cycles* (Oxford: Basil Blackwell, 1987), and M. H. Pesaran, *The Limits to Rational Expectations* (Oxford: Basil Blackwell, 1987). A useful analysis of the basic issues in supply-side economics is provided by V. Canto, D. Joines, and A. Laffer, *Foundations of Supply-Side Economics* (New York: Academic Press, 1983). Introductory expositions on open economy macroeconomics are P. De Grauwe, *Macroeconomic Theory for the Open Economy* (Hampshire: Gower, 1983), and R. Dornbusch, *Open Economy Macroeconomics* (New York: Basic Books, 1980).

2. R. J. Epstein, *A History of Econometrics* (Amsterdam: North-Holland, 1987), for example, has shown that the statistical implications of exogenous variables within the simultaneous equations framework, and the selection of a model when estimation procedures use the same data to discriminate among plausible competing theories have posed endemic problems in the history of structural estimation. R. F. Engle, D. F. Hendry, and J. F. Richard, "Exogeneity," *Econometrica* 51 (1983):277–304, and M. H. Pesaran, "Comparison of Local Power of Alternative Tests of Non-Nested Regression Models," *Econometrica* 50 (1982):1287–1305, provide contributions on the exogeneity and model selection problems, respectively. A. Spanos, *Statistical Foundations of Econometric Modelling* (Cambridge: Cambridge University Press, 1986) provides a detailed account

of the implications of probability distributions surrounding the data used in econometric models for model design and specification. E. Malinvaud, "Econometrics Faced with the Needs of Macroeconomic Policy," *Econometrica* 49 (1981):1363–1375, and C. Sims, "Policy Analysis with Econometric Models," *Brookings Papers on Economic Activity* 1:82 (1982):107–164, provide useful analyses of the interface between policy issues, policy analysis and econometrics.

3. One of the difficulties encountered pertains to the choice of benchmark criteria in deciding which model out of a number best approximates the structure of an economy. Some of the more recent attempts aimed at evaluating and testing a variety of models with particular criteria include G. Adams, *The Business Forecasting Revolution* (Oxford: Oxford University Press, 1986), R. C. Fair, *Specification, Estimation, and Analysis of Macroeconometric Models* (Cambridge: Harvard University Press, 1984), and S. K. McNees, "The Recent Record of Thirteen Forecasts," *New England Economic Review* (September-October 1981):5–21. In addition, structural estimation has not been helped by the limited evidence that large macroeconometric models are consistently able to forecast out of sample better than very naive alternative models.

4. As R. C. Fair in *Specification, Estimation, and Analysis of Macroeconometric Models*, points out this methodological split is evident in the atheoretical approaches of C. Sims with vector autoregressions (VAR) and "soft modeling" by H. Wold which seek to move away from discovering underlying economic structure. In contrast there is the approach by L. P. Hansen and T. Sargent in, "Formulating and Estimating Dynamic Linear Rational Expectations Models," *Journal of Economic Dynamics and Control* 2 (1980):7–46, which emphasizes the need to estimate the parameters of the objective functions of decision-making units. In the middle ground there is the more traditional approach which recognizes a role for theory, but does not try to estimate the pure structural parameters. Rather the parameters estimated are those of derived decision equations which are functions of the objective functions.

5. This debate on the issue of aggregation involved L. R. Klein, "Remarks on the Theory of Aggregation," *Econometrica* 14 (1946):303–312—a pioneer in the field of applied econometrics—who saw the need for micro-underpinnings, K. May, "The Aggregation Problem for a One-Industry Model," *Econometrica* 14 (1946):285–298, and S. S. Pu, "A Note on Macroeconomics," *Econometrica* 14 (1946):299–302, who argued that aggregation may proceed without detailed knowledge of micro behavior.

6. The smoothing effect refers to the smoothing out of microeconomic discontinuities when microeconomic relations are put together to obtain a macroeconomic relation as in a macroeconomic variable proportions resulting from micro economic fixed proportions (see H. S. Houthakker, "The Pareto Distribution and the Cobb-Douglas Production Function in Activity Analysis," *Review of Economic Studies* 23 (1955/56):27–31, and L. Johansen, *Production Functions* (Amsterdam: North-Holland, 1972). The elimination effect is considered to occur when some microeconomic determinants cease to be of influence on the macro level as several microeconomic relations are combined, for instance, the elimination of aspiration levels in a representative utility function based on the aggregation of utility functions of households that have aspiration levels as an argument (e.g. the case of the Duesenberry household). The system effect refers to the diminution of influence of a variable at the aggregate level whereas it is of significance at the individual level. An example is the impact of the rate of interest on the aggregate savings ratio, whereas individual savings ratios are independent of the rate of interest in a variant of the distribution model by J. Stiglitz, "Distribution of Income and Wealth among Individuals," *Econometrica* 37 (1969):382–397.

7. Kalman's critique suggests that economic modeling cannot be seriously pursued if it is conducted without facts from system theory. His proposal is to proceed directly from data to model, and not to base economics on 'handed-down theory,' but to utilize the theory of modeling studied in system theory. However, E. J. Moore, "On System-Theoretic Methods and Econometric Modeling," *International Economic Review* 26 (February 1985):87–106, argues that since the problems are of an economic rather than system-theoretical origin, system theory is of limited use in overcoming present difficulties. But, he concedes that the methods of system theory can be of importance as economic theory and data on which models are based are improved.

8. There are some who hold the view, however, that specific pieces of theory may be difficult to justify on the basis of environmental relationships such as contemporary events and economic policy. In particular, the argument made is that since economics became a university discipline, it has often taken off on its own internal pressures, proceeding in isolation from the real world (see, for example, S. Hollander, *Classical Economics* (New York: Basil Blackwell, 1987).

9. As is common in most efforts to develop typologies, this characterization of macroeconometric systems is not complete, but is sufficient to

give an overview of the major types of working macroeconometric models in existence. A case can be made for an additional type of macroeconometric system which focuses on disequilibrium in the economy in terms of imbalances between demand and supply in markets. R. J. Barro, and H. I. Grossman, "A General Disequilibrium Model of Income and Employment," *American Economic Review* 61 (1971):82–93, are credited for developing the first theoretical macroeconomic disequilibrium model. The first efforts aimed at estimating macroeconomic disequilibrium models include the work by P. Kooiman, and T. Kloek, "An Empirical Two Market Disequilibrium Model for Dutch Manufacturing," *European Economic Review* 29 (1985):323–354, H. Sneessens, *Theory and estimation of Macroeconometric Rationing Models* (New York: Springer-Verlag, 1981), and P. Artus, G. Laroque, and G. Michael, "Estimation of a Quarterly Econometric Model with Quantity Rationing," *Econometrica* 52 (1984):1387–1414. Since then, there has been steady progress in overcoming some of the econometric problems posed by disequilibrium modeling (see, Jean-Paul Lambert, *Disequilibrium Macroeconomic Models* (Cambridge: Cambridge University Press, 1988), but at this stage the empirical versions are too sketchy to be appropriate for economic analysis. For this reason the disequilibrium macroeconometric system is not treated formally in this study.

10. There are alternative hypotheses in relation to consumption and investment for example, which do not stress the micro-foundations as much but which have met with empirical success. See D. Fisher, *Macroeconomic Theory: A Survey* (London: Macmillan, 1983).

11. The beginning of respectability along these lines dates back to economic expansion in World War II which coincided in the United States, for example, with the growth in government spending and the fall in the unemployment rate from 25 percent in 1933 to 2 percent in 1943, 1944, and 1945. These results were presumed to have been an important influence on the course of fiscal policies in the developed countries during the 1950s and the first half of the 1960s which were accompanied by relatively high growth rates.

12. L. R. Klein, *The Economics of Supply and Demand* (Baltimore: John Hopkins University Press, 1983), 91.

13. The transmission mechanism involved hinges on the notion that the relevant range of alternative assets to money includes financial and real assets and an increase in the money supply leads to an excess supply of money which will be eliminated by increased spending on other assets.

14. The slow adjustment of the expected future interest rate suggests that when the actual rate is above this level, then it is expected to fall, and if below this level it will be expected to rise. The liquidity trap notion suggests that this expected future rate is near constant and any deviations will result in large changes in the demand for money.

15. The St Louis equation is the central equation in the St. Louis model and the extent of subsequent research is evident in the studies by D. Batten, and R. Hafer, "The Relative Impact of Monetary and Fiscal Actions on Economic Activity: A Cross-Country Comparison," *Federal Reserve Bank of St. Louis Review* 65 (1983):5–12, and K. M. Carlson, "Inflation, Unemployment, and Money: Comparing the Evidence from Two Simple Models," *Federal Reserve Bank of St Louis Review* 60 (1978):2–6.

16. Because of this discrepancy there was likely to be extreme uncertainty in these cases regarding estimated parameters of expectations mechanisms, their potential inconsistency, their structural autonomy, and the extent to which the forecasts actually described the beliefs of economic agents.

17. J. F. Muth, "Rational Expectations and the Theory of Price Movements," *Econometrica* 29 (1961):315.

18. J. F. Muth, "Rational Expectations and the Theory of Price Movements," *Econometrica* 29 (1961):316.

19. See, for example, the discussion by J. Foster, *Evolutionary Macroeconomics* (London: Allen and Unwin, 1987) which traces the decline of the Keynesian consensus and the rise of the New Classical Macroeconomics.

20. This is a model that has been built by the Liverpool Research Group for the U.K. at Liverpool University since the late 1970s. A discussion of the model can be found in the work of two members, in P. Minford, and D. Peel, *Rational Expectations and the New Macroeconomics* (Oxford: Martin Robertson, 1983).

21. See P. Minford, and D. Peel, *Rational Expectations and the New Macroeconomics* (Oxford: Martin Robertson, 1983).

22. On the supply side the rate of flow of current production is adjusted after a time lag to the rate of flow of aggregate demand. On the demand side, aggregate demand varies with real income or production without significant time lag.

23. This possibility arises because there is often a pair of relationships associated with each endogenous variable. One of the pair explains the desired or long-run equilibrium value of the variable, while the other specifies the process by which the variable adjusts to its long-run value.

24. L. Bergman, "Extensions and Applications of the MSG Model: A Brief Survey," in *Production, Multi-Sectoral Growth and Planning*, edited by F. R. Førsund et al. (Amsterdam: North-Holland, 1985) discusses the linkages between the Johansen model and CGE model in the case of the Australian model developed in P. B. Dixon, B. Parmenter, C. Ryland, and J. Sutton, *ORANI: A Multisectoral Model of the Australian Economy* (Amsterdam, North-Holland, 1977).

25. L. R. Klein, *The Economics of Supply and Demand* (Baltimore: John Hopkins University Press, 1983), 109.

26. This was the view held by Marschak and still current in much of the contemporary research on model selection. See M. H. Pesaran, "Comparison of Local Power of Alternative Tests of Non-Nested Regression Models," *Econometrica* 50 (1982):1287–1305.

3

Macroeconometric Modeling for Less Developed Countries

Introduction

This chapter examines the role of macroeconometric modeling for LDCs. As a tool of economic analysis, its growing appeal within these economies is reminiscent of its halcyon days not so long ago within the developed economies. Several factors have dictated the contemporary preoccupation with macroeconometric modeling within LDCs.

One significant influence has been the failure of many of these countries to achieve the kinds of economic change envisaged over the past three to four decades. The major preoccupation was to promote economic development through structural changes in the economy. For many practitioners and theoreticians the problem of economic development was viewed to be closer to the concern over long term growth rather than short run stabilization. The time dimension associated with the corresponding economic policies, therefore, precluded great interest in the counter-cyclical policies that were the focal point of developments in macroeconomic theory.

A shift in focus occurred, however, as many LDCs witnessed limited success in attaining sustained economic growth. Instead, they experienced regular fluctuations in the level of output, increasing price levels, enormous debt burdens, as well as unmanageable trade and budget deficits. These events dictated the continued search within many of the LDCs for solutions to their endemic economic problems. Thus, notwithstanding the state of flux within the macroeconomic literature, there was considerable scope for the adoption of macroeconometric models which sought to address aspects of stabilization, structural adjustment, as well as longer run issues.

A source of contemporary interest in macroeconomic modeling for LDCs has also to do with the improved possibilities for its operationalization. This stems from some progress in the data generation process. Although still highly deficient in terms of length, comprehensiveness, and accuracy of coverage, the data which currently exist has now made it possible to conduct econometric exercises which could not be attempted for a lack of data two decades ago.

Certain advances that have occurred in the theory and practice of macroeconometric modeling have also made the adaptation of this mode of analysis amenable to the specific problems of LDCs. The variety of macroeconometric systems for instance offer a wider menu of choices to policy makers within LDCs. Some success in modeling qualitative information is also particularly important considering the concerns of LDCs with institutional and structural changes that in general are not easily quantifiable. Further, since existing models can accommodate the analysis of clusters of policies, then analysis of the design and implementation of development strategies has become much more feasible.

Another consideration has to do with the discernible lag in the adoption and application within LDCs of recent ideas and techniques in the economic literature. This often takes place because the issues and ideas are typically geared to the needs of developed economies. Even though recent research has been shown to have some relevance for some LDCs,[1] the adaptation of such research tends to be time consuming as well as costly. The latter tends to occur particularly if the utilization of new approaches and techniques requires a great deal of additional information and data.

Finally, the special place occupied by econometric models in the growing field of quantitative economic analysis cannot be ignored. These models have gained wider acceptance because they consider exogenous developments and policy, which are of vital importance especially in periods of uncertainty about the structure of the economy. Moreover, these models not only take account of an economy's structure and behavioral characteristics, but can consider the dynamics of movement over time and, perhaps most significantly, they provide detailed as well as structurally consistent forecasts which offer a forward view of the economy that is not available with other methods of analysis.

In considering the theory and practice of macroeconometric modeling for LDCs, this chapter firstly examines economic theorizing for LDCs with a focus on those aspects of development economics and the literature on macroeconomic stabilization for LDCs that have a bearing on model design and specification. The second section considers a sample of macroeconometric models for LDCs. An account of the major characteristics of these models will be given in order to provide some perspective of the purposes and design of these models. This will be followed by a review of the performance of the sample of models. Finally, the lessons derived from the assessment of the sample of models and implications for the model building process for an individual LDC will be discussed.

Theoretical Basis for Modeling LDCs

Since the 1940s, a special branch of economic literature known as development economics has paid special attention to the problems and economic analysis of LDCs. One of the primary motivations for this literature emanated from the perspective that LDCs shared some common economic characteristics which set them apart from the advanced industrial economies. Moreover, since economic analysis had traditionally been concentrated on the latter group of countries, the case was made for recasting prevailing economic analysis to deal with LDCs. Seers (1963) reflected the basic position shared by an increasing number of development economists when he attacked attempts to apply economic management policies in LDCs which were devised solely with the developed countries in mind. He also emphasized that there was a diversity of types of LDCs which would make it unlikely that few simple generalizations will be applicable to all of them simultaneously.

In general, three aspects stand out as important influences on the direction of research initially undertaken for LDCs. One, the argument that the economic objectives of LDCs were very different from those pertaining to the developed economies. Hence, policy measures had to be geared specifically to the issues of growth and equity which represented the primary concerns of policy makers in LDCs.[2] Two, the emergence of a theory of market failure developed in the context of the advanced economies which seemed capable of explaining some of the conditions within the LDCs and also offer suggestive insights in a setting of economic growth.[3] Three, the notion that government intervention and planning provided a viable means of achieving the desired objectives of economic development and equitable distribution within society.[4]

Within the framework of the ideas above, the literature on LDCs has become quite complex and extensive. It would be a formidable task, therefore, to attempt an adequate presentation of all facets of this literature. Instead, for purposes of this study a brief survey will be conducted in relation to some central themes that have featured consistently in this literature. These are the issues pertaining to description of the structure of these economies, analysis of their operational characteristics, and derivation of propositions to aid planners and policy makers. More recently an added dimension has been attempts to incorporate new ideas and issues in the economic literature that might have relevance for some LDCs.

The urgency attached to the objectives of economic and social transformation within LDCs dictated an early preoccupation with immediate policy measures. The critical problem was identified as one of capital accumulation. In the absence of systematic and detailed knowledge of the behavioral, structural, and institutional characteristics of many of these economies, there was strong reliance on theories of growth and accumulation based on the experiences and requirements of other countries. In this regard the Harrod-Domar growth model[5] and the Feldman model[6] were important forerunners of the development literature. While these models had different objectives and made alternative assumptions about different forms of investment, both emphasized the importance of investment in generating increases in total output. Because investment was generally regarded as the major limiting factor to the rate of economic growth in LDCs, the influence exercised by these models on early development theories and policies was considerable.

Many of the proposed economic strategies, for example, were often characterized by those aspects brought into sharp focus by the conclusions of the Harrod-Domar and Feldman models. In the case of the former the main proposition involved raising the savings-investment rate in order to promote economic growth, while the latter stressed the use of increased savings to develop the industrial sector, in particular, the production of capital goods. These proved to be important elements in the incipient literature on development. Thus, the models of development suggested by Rosenstein-Rodan (1943), Nurkse (1957), Lewis (1954), Mahalanobis (1953), Rostow (1960), Hirschman (1958), and Myint (1958) share the generalizable result that higher rates of investment will lead over time to higher levels of output.

The development strategies of these models, however, do differ in terms of emphasis on the pattern of investment allocation and the nature of investment incentives to be implemented. The big push and balanced growth theories of Rosenstein-Rodan and Nurkse respectively, for example, identified low income levels and the small size of the market as serious disincentives for investment. The Lewis model of surplus labor focused attention on the notion of the dual economy comprised of a modern (industrial) and a traditional (agricultural) sector within LDCs and the need for a shift of resources and income to the industrial sector to promote investment and growth. The Mahalanobis model as an elaboration of the Feldman model emphasized that investment across sectors is not equally productive and that optimal resource allocation requires an emphasis on heavy industry in development planning. Rostow's stages of growth typology classified LDCs at a stage that required establishing the preconditions for growth followed by a sharp increase in the overall rate of capital accumulation. Hirschman's theory of unbalanced growth recognized the limited decision-making capacity and resource availability within LDCs and suggested sectoral investment strategies with a focus on a leading sector. Myint analyzing the implications of population growth suggested the need for a "critical minimum effort" to offset the consequences of such increases.

These differences in policy emphasis emanate from diagnoses of the development process which identify various aspects of the less developed economies as critical dimensions of the development problem. Thus one notable contribution of early theorizing about development was the recognition given to certain distinctive features of LDCs and their influence over the process of capital accumulation. The following features in particular were identified as having a critical impact on how the LDCs functioned: (1) the existence of the agricultural sector as the largest economic sector in terms of employment and contribution to national output; (2) the importance of the external sector in accounting for economic performance; (3) the failure of many of these economies to generate sustained increases in output through productivity changes as opposed to greater use of resources; (4) the dominance of the monetary system in an otherwise undeveloped financial system. Although these were areas of relative neglect in the initial models of development, recognition of their importance was reflected in several attempts to incorporate them into the frameworks of the earlier development models.

Extensions and modifications of the dual economy theory undertaken by Ranis and Fei (1961) and Jorgenson (1961), for example, provided a greater focus on the role of agriculture in structural transformation. In this regard the major emphasis was on the importance of a marketed surplus of agricultural output and its generation through technical change particularly in the context of population growth.

Incorporation of the role of the external sector was attempted through the extension of the Harrod-Domar growth model (Bruton 1955) which suggested that the growth rate depended on the savings rate and the trade balance as a proportion of total output. Since an adverse trade balance is equivalent to a foreign capital transfer then the open economy version of the Harrod-Domar model indicated a growth generating role arising from additional investment through foreign assistance.[7] The problem with this approach, however, was that it implied that with a zero trade balance, foreign trade would appear to have no effect upon economic growth, which was contrary to the observed importance of imported inputs in production processes within LDCs.

A revised approach emphasizing domestic savings and import purchase capacity as two independent resource constraints on growth was provided by Chenery and Bruno (1962), McKinnon (1964), and Chenery and Strout (1966). This two-gap theory indicated that the achievement of a specific growth rate may be limited by the availability of domestic savings for investment or by the availability of foreign exchange to import specific commodities for current production or investment. Crucial issues, therefore, were raised as to which constraint was dominant and the implications for policy alternatives facing LDCs (Weisskopf 1972).

Attempts to ascertain the dominant constraint, however, have proved to be inconclusive and have yielded conclusions establishing the need for case studies and the recognition that different constraints on growth may be binding at different times. Moreover, accompanying the conjectures and econometric tests for the dominant constraint on investment within LDCs was the recognition that there were constraints other than savings or foreign exchange that might be binding. Gap analysis therefore, has provided a description of structural disequilibrium, emphasized a role for external resources,[8] and more recently has attempted to empirically accommodate constraints other than the traditional two gaps as potential limits to growth within LDCs (Gersovitz 1982).

With regard to the issue of endogenizing productivity Kuznets (1966) emphasized the possibility that output changes could occur without any readily measurable changes in capital or labor alone. Instead, sustained increases in output could be attributable to technological change. Based on an examination of the development process within the developed economies, Kuznets came to the conclusion that, while technological change embodied the utilization of modern technology, this was only feasible in the context of complementary institutional arrangements and a responsive social and political environment. By and large, however, the analysis of the causes and consequences of technological change has witnessed a concern over the role of technical change in production processes in improving the quality and quantity of output to the relative neglect of the other requirements suggested by Kuznets. Moreover, since advances in this direction invariably have been associated with improved machinery, changes in the machine-producing sector have become a critical area of focus in the process of technological change.[9]

Rosenberg (1976, 1982) who views the machine goods sector as playing a central role in the process of technical change emphasizes the dynamic relationship between the capital and consumption goods sectors with technical change at the center. For Rosenberg it is the capital goods sector, however, which provides innovations that have beneficial effects throughout the economy after an initial stimulus provided by the growth of demand in the capital-goods-using sector. The implication for LDCs is that in the absence of a capital goods sector a major source of technological change is pre-empted. Thus as Rosenberg (1976:147) states:

> underdeveloped countries with little or no organized domestic capital goods sector simply have not had the opportunity to make capital saving innovations because they have not had the capital goods industry necessary for them. Under these circumstances, such countries have typically imported their capital goods from abroad, but this has meant that they have not developed the technological base of skills, knowledge, facilities, and organization upon which further technical progress so largely depends.

Within this frame of reference one crucial aspect of a development strategy, therefore, would be the establishment of a capital goods sector within LDCs. Along these lines Mandle (1985) has argued that a viable strategy for technological change and development within LDCs centers on the modernization of the agricultural sector. This suggestion hinges on the idea that, because of the predominance of agricultural activity within LDCs, such a strategy would directly provide a dynamic relationship between the capital-goods-using-agricultural sector and a domestic capital goods sector with all the benefits that this relationship provides.

In contrast to the idea that the absence of a substantial capital goods sector is a serious development problem for LDCs, there is the argument that the beneficial effects of imported capital goods may be underestimated. Little (1982), for example, emphasizing the notion of comparative advantage suggests that modern technology can be acquired more cheaply from abroad than they can be developed or invented. In his view the task facing LDCs is more one of assimilating technology from abroad through improved knowledge of the range of world technology and better choice of techniques.

An alternative diagnosis of the development process which also considers the issue of technological change and its feasibility in terms of where it originates from, that is, within LDCs or from abroad, is provided by the theory of dependency and underdevelopment.

It is quite common to find in the development literature the characterization of LDCs as dependent economies encompassing features such as: (1) an economic structure dominated by production of primary commodities for export primarily to developed market economies, and a reliance on imports to meet domestic demand for consumer and industrial goods; (2) the influence of foreign economic interests in terms of the presence of transnational corporations; (3) a heavy dependence on imports of foreign technology; (4) and a general condition of cultural, social, and political dependence (Colman and Nixson 1986).

As O'Brien (1975) has shown, two basic strands of analysis constitute the dependency explanations of the lack of development within LDCs. One is in the tradition of the United Nations Commission for Latin America which highlights the absence of sustained economic growth as one of the implications of a longrun secular decline in the terms of trade between primary products and manufacturing goods considering the first feature outlined above. The other strand is one which contends that the historical and contemporary interaction between developed and less developed countries have resulted in capital accumulation for developed countries while creating the prevailing forms of economic, social, and political dependency (Baran 1957; Frank 1966, 1967, 1969; Dos Santos 1973).

To the extent that the interaction with developed countries leads to the underdevelopment of LDCs (see Frank 1966), a basic proposition within much of the dependency literature is that the development of the LDCs is directly related to the absence of such interaction. There is another view, however, which advances the argument that it is possible for development to occur even in the framework of dependency (Cardoso 1973). These contrasting positions of autonomous versus dependent development of course encompass the alternative strategies of developing an indigenous technological capability or maintaining a reliance on imported technology. They also bring to the fore the role of ideological orientation and political considerations in some crucial decisions that have to be made in LDCs.

Another dimension of less developed economies not explicitly treated in the early development literature was the nature and significance of the financial system within LDCs. However, given the concern over the process of capital accumulation the importance of the financial system was implicitly recognized. In one of the first detailed analyses of the financial system within LDCs, Goldsmith (1969) identified several notable characteristics based on a comparison between the financial structures of developed and less developed economies.

In keeping with the close association observed between development of the financial structure and overall economic development (Cameron 1972), it was observed that the LDCs tended to have a smaller financial superstructure[10] than the developed economies. In both the developed and less developed economies, however, the banking system, comprising commercial banks and a central bank, was relatively more important than other financial institutions in the structure of the financial system.

Some basic differences in the growth paths of financial institutions between developed and less developed economies were also identified. In terms of the share of their assets in the total assets for all financial institutions, the central banks in developed economies appear to experience a relatively sharper decline when compared with those in less developed countries. Further, there was evidence of a trend of an increased share for commercial banks in the distribution of the total assets in the case of LDCs compared with developed economies. Indications of a tendency for the share of mortgage banks, development banks, and insurance companies to increase more rapidly in the case of the developing countries was also observed. These trends of relatively rapid growth in the spread and use of a wider range of financial instruments within LDCs emphasized the growing importance of financial activities and its diverse implications for overall economic activity.

A basic model developed by Polak (1957/58) and Polak and Boissoneault (1959) hereafter referred to as the Polak model, was one of the earliest attempts to incorporate aspects of the financial system in the explanation of the economic performance, in particular, income and the balance of payments position of LDCs. Utilizing the notion of a circular flow of income and a unique relationship between the stock of money and flow of income implied by an assumed constant velocity of circulation, the central relationship emphasized was that income in the current period is equal to income of the previous period plus changes in the money supply. To explain changes in income, therefore, it was necessary to determine the sources of changes in the money supply. Considering certain characteristics of LDCs such as the undeveloped financial system and the open nature of the economies, domestic credit creation, exports, and capital inflows were identified as injections and imports as leakages in the determination of the quantity of money.

The Polak model highlighted several important issues for theoretical and policy analysis of LDCs. In contrast to the real sector emphases of the standard development approaches, this model emphasized the role of monetary forces and monetary policy in determining the behavior of critical economic aggregates in less developed economies. In relation to policy analysis the model addresses the implications of economic targets that exceed resource availability for the behavior of the price level and the balance of payments position. Moreover, the balance of payments constraint became identified as a serious obstacle to the continuity of economic policies.

These aspects of the economic performance of LDCs account for some major extensions to the literature dealing with LDCs. The failure to achieve desired changes in economic and social structures within LDCs has played a significant role in the upsurge of criticism and reevaluation of development economics (see, for example, Lal 1983). Further, the widespread occurrence of additional signs of poor and deteriorating economic performance within many LDCs has led to the view that contemporary problems such as a severe balance of payments constraint and enormous external debt burdens constitute serious obstacles to development. Accordingly, there has been a growing effort to bridge the gap between development economics and the conventional explanations of phenomena that have necessitated the practice of short term macroeconomic policies in LDCs. The areas in which there are indications of some strides in this direction include balance of payments theory, short run macroeconomic analysis, and the stabilization-structural adjustment debate in relation to LDCs.

With regard to balance of payments theory there are currently three approaches to the explanation of payments disequilibria within LDCs. The conventional absorption and monetary approaches stress the importance of expenditure and monetary influences, while the structural approach focuses on the effects of output changes and the implications of the types of goods produced and the efficiency with which they are produced for payments disequilibria. As Bird (1987) suggests, these approaches can be combined to form a general theory of the balance of payments which provides greater insights into the multiple and interdependent influences on payments disequilibria within LDCs. The notion that payments disequilibria reflect an imbalance between aggregate demand and aggregate supply, therefore, not only suggests that payments deficits originate with excess demand, but that this can arise from increases in aggregate demand (expenditure and monetary approaches) or from a fall in aggregate supply (structural influences).

Short term macroeconomic analysis in relation to LDCs is also characterized by several strands which focus on the implications of the special features within these economies. The motivation for these efforts has largely been one of providing a formal framework to address the short term problems facing LDCs and also analyze the standard policy packages agreed upon with international agencies such as the International Monetary Fund (IMF) and World Bank.

Cebula and Skogstad (1979), for instance, examining the implications of IMF favored monetary policy for LDCs demonstrated that, in the context of an open economy dominated by a few export commodities and the absence of a developed capital market, LDCs do not have the freedom to use fiscal and monetary policies as separate instruments. Rather, monetary and fiscal policy collapse to a single policy instrument that cannot be used to pursue simultaneously the dual objectives of internal and external balance. One implication is that, while monetary restraint may result in an improved balance of payments position, there is a trade off in terms of a loss of output and greater unemployment. Guitan (1973) emphasizing that LDCs are typically open economies operating under fixed exchange rates has shown that policy makers need to recognize that domestic credit rather than money supply becomes the appropriate policy controlled variable. Others such as Crockett (1981) make claims that lags, rigidities, and disequilibrium analysis are the essence of short term LDC macro understanding. Behrman and Hanson (1979) and Cline and Weintraub (1981) explore the implications of the "stylized facts" of LDCs for model design and procedures.

Porter and Ranney (1982) recognizing the diversity and significance of these insights suggested the need for an eclectic approach towards macroeconomic modeling for LDCs. Building upon the various strands of macroeconomic analysis for LDCs, these authors found that the standard developed country and LDC model differ not only because the slopes of the aggregate demand and aggregate supply curves are likely to be different, but also more importantly because the supply and demand sides of the economy interact more in the LDC's case. In particular, they emphasized that changes in labor market conditions have a direct impact on aggregate demand and changes in financial market conditions have a direct impact on aggregate supply. Considering the impact of monetary, fiscal, exchange rate, and incomes policies within this framework, one major conclusion was that "contractionary policy is likely to fuel, rather than dampen, inflationary tendencies."[11]

Perhaps the research area that comes closest to bridging the gap between development economics and conventional theorizing is that associated with the issues of stabilization and structural adjustment. In this literature stabilization issues are related to the process of restoring balance between supply and demand in the economy, with reference to foreign exchange or goods and services, while structural adjustment refers to the process encompassing substantial changes in the direction of an economy, its sectoral priorities, and its institutional make-up. For some time stabilization implied short run policy induced changes in the balance of payments, the rate of inflation, and other macro variables, with the principal emphasis being placed on domestic demand management and a secondary role given to supply stimulus.

More recently, however, stabilization efforts have been associated with the formulation of policies from medium-term and long-term perspectives as structural rigidities and heavy external debt obligations in many LDCs have become a focal point for discussion among researchers and practitioners. One strand of analysis emphasizes the need for far reaching changes in the "trade regimes" of LDCs, involving shifts in the structure of investment and production, decisions pertaining to an outward versus an inward orientation of the economy, as well as the balance between state control and the use of market incentives (see, for example, Krueger 1978). Another direction is associated with an expanding literature on growth oriented adjustment (see Khan and Montiel 1989) which emphasizes the design of policies that caters to the issues of economic growth and the correction of external imbalances simultaneously. These additional concerns have meant that stabilization efforts now encompass demand management policies, structural policies, exchange rate policies, and external financing policies (Khan 1987). When compared with the concerns and policies of structural adjustment, it becomes evident that the difference in the use of the two terms has become increasingly blurred over time. As Loxley (1986) suggests, if any difference exists, it lies not so much in objectives as in the range of tools, the relative emphasis given to different policy variables, and the time horizon over which policies are expected to take effect.

Much of this eclecticism and focus on the implications of the behavioral, institutional, technological, and market clearing potential within LDCs provide the foundation for of a formulation of fairly recent origin known as structuralist macroeconomics.[12] This approach recognizes that the specific characteristics within LDCs make some patterns of resource allocation and evolution more likely than others. Accordingly, there is no steadfast rule about the adjustment process to ensure macroeconomic balance in situations of disequilibrium. As Taylor (1983) points out, even though LDCs have many broad features in common whenever there is macroeconomic imbalance between aggregate demand and aggregate supply, then special factors may determine whether supply will adjust to meet demand, whether demand will adjust to meet supply, or whether components of these aggregates will freely adjust to correct the imbalance.

The message of the contemporary structuralist approach is not so much that the analysis of LDCs requires its own separate and distinct form of economic theory but that the foundation of this analysis must incorporate the influence exercised by aspects of economic structure and behavior on the way the economy functions. With an emphasis on the need to consider modifications in model design and appropriateness of tools of analysis in the model building process, the issue becomes largely one of degree rather than one of kind when comparing macroeconomic analysis for the developed and less developed countries. Yet, the distinctions are of considerable importance in discovering models for LDCs and deciding what features should be designed into these models.

Figure 3.1 summarizes a basic block organization that provides a description of the critical markets and sectors and possible linkages within LDCs. This bears a close resemblance to the model structures identified for developed economies.[13] The main distinction lies in the

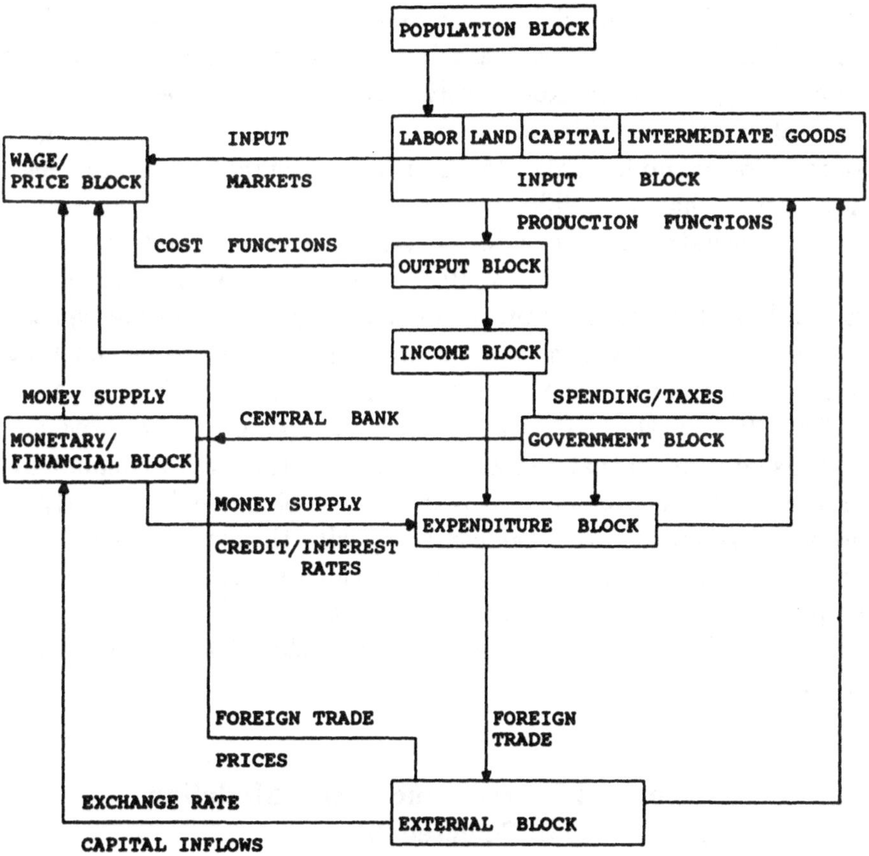

Figure 3.1 Generalized Flow Chart of the Economic System of LDCs

Source: S. Kinoshita, "On Macroeconometric Model Building in ASEAN countries – The Case of Thailand," in *Review of National Economies and Econometric Models in the ELSA Project: Vol. I* (Tokyo: Institute of Developing Economies, 1984), p. 497. Reprinted by permission.

emphasis on certain relationships within and across sectors which are the outcomes of the specific production, institutional, and behavioral patterns peculiar to the LDCs.

Another aspect of considerable importance has to do with unresolved issues surrounding the direction of causality between critical variables. Thus, model building tasks are further complicated by the indications of indeterminacy in the direction of effects resulting from changes in some exogenously determined variables. The influence of certain variables on both aggregate demand and aggregate supply, for example, makes the a priori determination of price level and output changes a difficult exercise.

The usual procedure under such circumstances would be to make use of *ceteris paribus* analysis. But, a detailed understanding of how fast or how slow economic processes do change is a major prerequisite for decisions as to which variables may be assumed to be constant. Very often it is the neglect of such considerations in the analysis of policy effects within LDCs which is at the root of the controversies and disagreements that characterize much of the macroeconomic literature for these economies. It is this notion of ambiguity underlying economic relationships, when combined with the experience of failed economic policies within many LDCs, which make a strong case for empirical work as a means of resolving theoretical debates and discovering which views of the economy are tenable at a particular point in time.

Empirical Macroeconometric Modeling in Selected LDCs

The earliest known macroeconometric models pertaining to the less developed countries were developed in the 1950s.[14] Since then, following the lead of the developed economies, macroeconometric models have spread to a large number of LDCs. Some of the earliest models emerged as a direct result of the need by the LDCs to obtain short and medium term macroeconomic forecasts, in order to negotiate financing arrangements with international organizations and other aid agencies.

In this context, the aid donors, especially international agencies played an active role. Thus, pioneers in macroeconometric modeling for a number of LDCs included agencies such as the Economic and Social Commission for Asia and the Pacific (ESCAP), the United Nations Conference on Trade and Development (UNCTAD), and the World Bank (IBRD). Subsequently, as the statistical systems strengthened and macroeconometric models increasingly came to be regarded as amenable to the specific problems of LDCs, central banks and government agencies within these countries began to play a more active role in their model building efforts. With this kind of institutional support, the number of models rapidly increased, and in retrospect some broad phases may be discerned.

The first phase consisted of the early models which were typically small and very often represented a simplistic transfer of the models developed in relation to the needs of the developed countries to the LDCs. These models, molded primarily in the then dominant Keynes-Klein tradition,[15] had a demand side emphasis, and tended to focus on narrow and specific objectives which generally served to delineate the nature of the economic processes underlying particular sectors. While not being comprehensive enough, the early models served to highlight weaknesses in the data and, more importantly, pinpointed areas for further research.

The second phase was comprised of those models which further developed and addressed the challenges arising from the first group of models. With the accumulation of data and a wider range of empirical studies to draw upon, the demands of policy analysis could more easily be accommodated. Accompanying this was an emphasis on the institutional characteristics of LDCs, particularly those which highlighted unique features in the economic structure. Klein (1965), for example, considered the following to be critical issues when constructing macroeconometric models for LDCs: (1) the limitation of output capacity rather than the shortage of effective demand; (2) the role of foreign capital inflows and direct investment; (3) the role of government policies; (4) the influence of the foreign trade sector and economic cooperation from international agencies; (5) the impact of environmental factors such as climate or political disturbances on economic activities. Additionally, in the attempt to be more comprehensive, there was a greater degree of disaggregation in combination with the tendency to incorporate lagged and more complex adjustment processes. As a result, the models of the second generation were typically larger and more varied than the earlier models.

A third phase can also be identified, comprising macroeconometric models which are extensions of the previous phases with a focus on contemporary economic problems within LDCs. A distinguishing feature of many of these models is the preoccupation with issues of macroeconomic adjustment. The areas of concern that have featured prominently in this regard pertain to stabilization and structural change in LDCs. Much greater attention was placed on modeling the supply side of the economy. In addition, the various mechanisms for macroeconomic adjustment have found expression in the consideration of a much wider range of policy instruments, such as government expenditure, monetary instruments, elements of the tax structure, and the exchange rates. One other significant feature has been the attempt to incorporate issues of a long run character in these models. This has taken the form of endogenization of variables that were previously treated as exogenous, such as the supply of labor services or even the formulation of behavioral relationships, so that there is a mechanism which leads to a long run adjustment level.[16] Invariably these extensions have led to much larger models, which display a variety of relationships and have simultaneously paved the way for a wider range of model specifications.

Several factors were taken into account when choosing the models in the sample considered here. First of all, the models had to be readily available from academic sources, government documentation, or from the publications of international agencies. Countries were then chosen so as to provide some geographic representation for the many countries that constitute the LDCs. It is recognized that every country possesses unique features of its own based on differences in endowments of natural resources, economic structure, stage of economic development, social structure, and political system. Nonetheless, this has not prevented economic analysis along the lines of regional groups of countries because of broad similarities in economic circumstances and economic structure among geographically close countries. Thus, in keeping with the grouping of countries into regions such as Latin America, the Caribbean, Asia, and Africa, found in the literature on LDCs, an effort was made to consider at least one model from each of these regions.

In those instances where more than one model had been built for a country, the most recent was chosen. Another objective was to include models that reflected a wide range of goals and also spanned the phases of model building outlined above.

The review thus focuses on the structure of a sample of sixteen models and on what they have to say about the functioning and characteristics of the respective economies in terms of adjustment mechanisms, linkage mechanisms, and policy analyses. A survey of the major characteristics of the sample is provided in Table 3.1. The first column identifies the country, the author, and the year of publication of the model under consideration. The second column indicates the methods of estimation, the period of estimation, and the frequency of the data utilized. The third column provides insights into the major areas of focus of the models. The size and structure of the model are summarized in terms of the total number of equations, and its decomposition into stochastic and non-stochastic equations with reference to the major categories in Figure 3.1. Next, the issue of output determination in the models is identified as demand determined, supply determined, or through the interaction of demand and supply. Finally, there is a consideration of critical features of each model paying special attention to the adjustment, linkage, and transmission mechanisms identified.

One of the evident features in Table 3.1 is the diversity that exists among these models. Model size, for example, ranges from a three equation system for Argentina (Maynard and Rijckeghem 1968) to a more elaborate system of sixty-seven equations for Indonesia (Central Bureau of Statistics 1984). Differences in model size further highlight the variation in the extent of sectoral coverage and sectoral disaggregation. A range of objectives can also be found, with differences in the way model builders view the functioning of the economy.

Models for Nicaragua (Downing and Solis 1979) and Malaysia (Imaoka and Meyanathan 1984), for instance, portray alternative ways of determining output. In studying adjustment mechanisms, wage, employment, and changes in inventory stock were stressed for Malaysia, whereas external resources were stressed for Nicaragua. In terms of linkage mechanisms, again there are significant dissimilarities. For Malaysia, there is no financial and real sector nexus,

TABLE 3.1 Major Characteristics of Selected Models of LDCs

COUNTRY AUTHOR YEAR	ESTIMATION METHOD SAMPLE PERIOD	OBJECTIVES OF MODEL	SIZE AND STRUCTURE TOTAL EQUATIONS EQUAL STOCHASTIC + NON-STOCHASTIC			OUTPUT	SPECIAL FEATURES ADJUSTMENT AND LINKAGE MECHANISMS
Thailand	OLS	Economic	1.	Population	1 = 1 + 0		Aggregate price level
Soonthornsima	Annual	Development	2.a.	Labor	0	Supply	equilibrates real output
1964	1952-1960	Policies	b.	Capital	0	determined	and nominal expenditure.
			c.	Land	0		
			3.	Output	1 = 1 + 0		
			4.	Income	2 = 0 + 2		
			5.	Government	3 = 2 + 1		
			6.	Expenditure	7 = 2 + 5		
			7.	External	3 = 2 + 1		
			8.	Price/wage	1 = 0 + 1		
			9.	Financial	1 = 1 + 0		
			10.	Total	19 = 9 + 10		
Argentina	OLS	Stabilization	1.	Population	0		Credit posited to be a
Maynard-Van	Annual	Policy	2.a.	Labor	0	Demand	critical determinant
Rijckeghem	1950-1965		b.	Capital	0	determined	of output changes.
1968			c.	Land	0		
			3.	Output	1 = 1 + 0		
			4.	Income	0		
			5.	Government	0		
			6.	Expenditure	0		
			7.	External	0		
			8.	Price/wage	2 = 2 + 0		
			9.	Financial	0		
			10.	Total	3 = 3 + 0		
Columbia	OLS	Economic	1.	Population	0		
Marwah	Annual	Structure	2.a.	Labor	0	Demand and	
1969	1951-1962		b.	Capital	0	Supply	
		Devaluation	c.	Land	0	determined	
			3.	Output	4 = 4 + 0		
		Policy	4.	Income	3 = 2 + 1		
		Analysis	5.	Government	1 = 1 + 0		
			6.	Expenditure	9 = 5 + 4		
			7.	External	10 = 7 + 3		
			8.	Price/wage	14 = 8 + 6		
			9.	Financial	3 = 1 + 2		
			10.	Total	44 = 28 + 16		

TABLE 3.1 (continued)

COUNTRY AUTHOR YEAR	ESTIMATION METHOD SAMPLE PERIOD	OBJECTIVES OF MODEL	SIZE AND STRUCTURE TOTAL EQUATIONS EQUAL STOCHASTIC + NON-STOCHASTIC		OUTPUT	SPECIAL FEATURES ADJUSTMENT AND LINKAGE MECHANISMS
Jamaica Carter 1970	OLS;IV Annual 1959-1966	Economic Structure	1. Population	0	Demand determined	Absence of financial sector.
			2.a. Labor	0		
			b. Capital	1 = 0 + 1		
			c. Land	0		
			3. Output	2 = 1 + 1		
			4. Income	9 = 5 + 4		
			5. Government	8 = 7 + 1		
			6. Expenditure	3 = 2 + 1		
			7. External	10 = 7 + 3		
			8. Price/wage	0		
			9. Financial	0		
			10. Total	33 = 22 + 11		
Nigeria UNCTAD 1973	OLS Annual 1955-1966	Economic Structure	1. Population	0	Supply determined	Absence of monetary sector. Investment critical in output determination.
			2.a. Labor	0		
			b. Capital	0		
			c. Land	0		
			3. Output	9 = 3 + 6		
			4. Income	1 = 0 + 1		
			5. Government	7 = 5 + 2		
			6. Expenditure	8 = 4 + 4		
			7. External	12 = 8 + 4		
			8. Price/wage	0		
			9. Financial	0		
			10. Total	37 = 20 + 17		
Trinidad and Tobago Persad 1975	OLS Annual 1960-1971	Economic Structure	1. Population	0	Demand determined	Absence of financial sector.
			2.a. Labor	0		
			b. Capital	0		
			c. Land	0		
			3. Output	0		
			4. Income	0		
			5. Government	1 = 0 + 1		
			6. Expenditure	3 = 2 + 1		
			7. External	11 = 9 + 2		
			8. Price/wage	0		
			9. Financial	0		
			10. Total	15 = 11 + 4		

TABLE 3.1 (continued)

COUNTRY AUTHOR YEAR	ESTIMATION METHOD SAMPLE PERIOD	OBJECTIVES OF MODEL	SIZE AND STRUCTURE TOTAL EQUATIONS EQUAL STOCHASTIC + NON-STOCHASTIC		OUTPUT	SPECIAL FEATURES ADJUSTMENT AND LINKAGE MECHANISMS
Philippines	OLS	Medium-term	1. Population	0		Absence of monetary
Velasco	Semi-Annual	Projections	2.a. Labor	1 = 1 + 0	Supply	sector.
1984	1967 I-1982 II		b. Capital	3 = 2 + 1	determined	
			c. Land	0		Critical role played
			3. Output	3 = 2 + 1		by capital formation.
			4. Income	1 = 0 + 1		
			5. Government	1 = 1 + 0		
			6. Expenditure	3 = 2 + 1		
			7. External	2 = 1 + 1		
			8. Price/wage	3 = 2 + 1		
			9. Financial	0		
			10. Total	17 = 11 + 6		
Singapore	OLS	Policy	1. Population	0		Monetarist small model
Toida	Annual	Analysis	2.a. Labor	0	Demand	framework.
1984	1967-1982		b. Capital	1 = 0 + 1	and	
		Evaluating	c. Land	0	Supply	
		external	3. Output	2 = 1 + 1	determined	
		impact	4. Income	0		
			5. Government	0		
		Stabilization	6. Expenditure	3 = 3 + 0		
		and	7. External	1 = 1 + 0		
		Economic	8. Price/wage	1 = 1 + 0		
		Growth	9. Financial	0		
			10. Total	8 = 6 + 2		
Indonesia	OLS	Economic	1. Population	0		
Central Bureau	Annual	Structure	2.a. Labor	17 = 11 + 6	Demand and	
Statistics	1960-1981		b. Capital	0	Supply	
1984			c. Land	0	determined	
			3. Output	24 = 17 + 7		
			4. Income	0		
			5. Government	9 = 4 + 5		
			6. Expenditure	4 = 3 + 1		
			7. External	7 = 4 + 3		
			8. Price/wage	0		
			9. Financial	6 = 4 + 2		
			10. Total	67 = 43 + 24		

TABLE 3.1 (continued)

COUNTRY AUTHOR YEAR	ESTIMATION METHOD SAMPLE PERIOD	OBJECTIVES OF MODEL	SIZE AND STRUCTURE TOTAL EQUATIONS EQUAL STOCHASTIC + NON-STOCHASTIC			OUTPUT	SPECIAL FEATURES ADJUSTMENT AND LINKAGE MECHANISMS
Taiwan	OLS	Forecasting	1.	Population	0		Price as adjustment
Yi-Chung Chiu	Semi-Annual		2.a.	Labor	0	Demand and	mechanism in product
1985	1960 II-1981 II	Policy	b.	Capital	0	Supply	market.
		Simulations	c.	Land	0	determined	
			3.	Output	4 = 2 + 2		
		Government	4.	Income	4 = 0 + 4		No financial sector.
		budget	5.	Government	4 = 4 + 0		
		compilation	6.	Expenditure	12 = 9 + 3		Investment determines
			7.	External	8 = 6 + 2		potential output.
			8.	Price/wage	9 = 6 + 3		
			9.	Financial	0		
			10.	Total	41 = 27 + 14		
Korea	2SLS	Inflationary	1.	Population	0		
Cheong and Kim	Quarterly	process	2.a.	Labor	0	Demand and	
1985	1973 I-1981 IV		b.	Capital	2 = 0 + 2	Supply	
		Simulation	c.	Land	0	determined	
		policies	3.	Output	3 = 0 + 3		
			4.	Income	0		
			5.	Government	1 = 0 + 1		
			6.	Expenditure	8 = 5 + 3		
			7.	External	8 = 4 + 4		
			8.	Price/wage	4 = 4 + 0		
			9.	Financial	8 = 5 + 3		
			10.	Total	34 = 18 + 16		
Guyana	OLS	Stabilization	1.	Population	0		Role of imports in macro
Paul	Annual	policies	2.a.	Labor	1 = 1 + 0	Demand and	adjustment emphasized.
1975	1960-1981		b.	Capital	0	Supply	
			c.	Land	0	determined	
			3.	Output	8 = 4 + 4		
			4.	Income	0		
			5.	Government	5 = 3 + 2		
			6.	Expenditure	7 = 4 + 3		
			7.	External	13 = 9 + 4		
			8.	Price/wage	2 = 2 + 0		
			9.	Financial	3 = 2 + 1		
			10.	Total	39 = 25 + 14		

TABLE 3.1 (continued)

COUNTRY AUTHOR YEAR	ESTIMATION METHOD SAMPLE PERIOD	OBJECTIVES OF MODEL	SIZE AND STRUCTURE TOTAL EQUATIONS EQUAL STOCHASTIC + NON-STOCHASTIC	OUTPUT	SPECIAL FEATURES ADJUSTMENT AND LINKAGE MECHANISMS
Nicaragua Downing and Solis 1979	OLS Annual 1960-1974	Economic Structure	1. Population 0 2.a. Labor 0 b. Capital 0 c. Land 0 3. Output 0 4. Income 3 = 0 + 3 5. Government 8 = 5 + 3 6. Expenditure 4 = 2 + 2 7. External 1 = 1 + 0 8. Price/wage 0 9. Financial 8 = 2 + 6 10. Total 24 = 10 + 14	Demand determined	Credit acts as a link between real and financial sectors. External resources fund capital expenditures.
Malaysia Imaoka and Meyanathan 1984	OLS Annual 1967-1982	Policy Analysis Simulation	1. Population 0 2.a. Labor 1 = 1 + 0 b. Capital 1 = 0 + 1 c. Land 0 3. Output 2 = 1 + 1 4. Income 0 5. Government 0 6. Expenditure 2 = 2 + 0 7. External 3 = 2 + 1 8. Price/wage 6 = 6 + 0 9. Financial 0 10. Total 15 = 12 + 3	Supply determined	Adjustment mechanisms are nominal wage, change in inventory stock, and employment.
Hong-Kong Tzong-biau Lin Win Lin Chou 1985	2SLS Annual 1962-1981	Short term Forecasting Policy Simulation	1. Population 0 2.a. Labor 2 = 1 + 1 b. Capital 2 = 0 + 2 c. Land 0 3. Output 7 = 2 + 5 4. Income 1 = 0 + 1 5. Government 2 = 2 + 0 6. Expenditure 4 = 4 + 0 7. External 12 = 8 + 4 8. Price/wage 7 = 7 + 0 9. Financial 6 = 4 + 2 10. Total 43 = 28 + 15	Demand determined	Keynesian framework Monetary-Real sector linkages through deposits and price level.

TABLE 3.1 (continued)

COUNTRY AUTHOR YEAR	ESTIMATION METHOD SAMPLE PERIOD	OBJECTIVES OF MODEL	SIZE AND STRUCTURE TOTAL EQUATIONS EQUAL STOCHASTIC + NON-STOCHASTIC			OUTPUT	SPECIAL FEATURES ADJUSTMENT AND LINKAGE MECHANISMS
India	OLS; 2SLS	Forecasting;	1.	Population	0		
Agarwala	Annual	Planning for	2.a.	Labor	1 = 1 + 0	Supply	Growth oriented model
1970	1948-1961	Growth	b.	Capital	2 = 0 + 2	determined	Emphasis on technological
			c.	Land	0		progress; Capital
			3.	Output	5 = 4 + 1		formation.
			4.	Income	0		
			5.	Government	1 = 0 + 1		
			6.	Expenditure	2 = 0 + 2		
			7.	External	4 = 3 + 1		
			8.	Price/wage	8 = 6 + 2		
			9.	Financial	1 = 1 + 0		
			10.	Total	24 = 17 + 7		

Sources:
Malaysia, Philippines, Singapore, Indonesia, and Thailand: Preliminary Results of Econometric Models in the ELSA Project: Vols I, II. Tokyo: Institute of Developing Economies, 1984.
Hong Kong, Korea, and Taiwan: S. Ichimura and M. Ezaki, Econometric Models of Asian LINK. Tokyo, Springer-Verlag, 1985.
Argentina: G. Maynard and V. Rijckegham, "Stabilization Policy in an Inflationary Economy." In Development Policy: Theory and Practice, edited by G. Papanek Cambridge: Harvard University Press, 1968.
Columbia: K. Marwah, "An Econometric Model of Columbia: A Prototype Devaluation View." Econometrica 37 (1969):228-251.
Jamaica: N. G. Carter, "A Macroeconometric Model of Jamaica 1959-1966." Social and Economic Studies 19 (1970):178-201.
Trinidad and Tobago: U. Persad, "An Econometric Model of Trinidad of Tobago 1960-1971." Social and Economic Studies 24 (1975):389-419.
Nicaragua: L. Downing and J. Solis, "An Econometric Model for Nicaragua." In Short-term Macroeconomic Policy in Latin America, edited by J. Behrman and J. Hanson. Cambridge: Ballinger, 1979.
India: R. A. Agarwala, An Econometric Model of India. London: Frank Cass, 1970.
Guyana: L. Paul, "Export Simulations of the Guyanese Economy." (PhD dissertation), Howard University, 1978.
Nigeria: UNCTAD, "Models for Developing Countries." In The International Linkage of National Economic Models, edited by R. Ball. Amsterdam: North-Holland, 1973.

whereas for the Nicaragua model, credit acts as the linkage mechanism between these sectors. In another model, for Indonesia, output links the monetary and real sectors.

Since economic problems, economic processes and economic structures are not homogeneous across countries, the disparities in adjustment and linkage mechanisms are to be expected. Broadly, three frameworks have been utilized in model specifications for the sample of countries considered in Table 3.1. The models for Hong Kong and Nicaragua, for example, were formulated with the notion that changes in aggregate demand are the main determinants of output change. On the other hand, for Thailand, the Philippines, India, Nigeria, and Malaysia, output was regarded as being primarily supply determined. The common perspectives shared by these models is the emphasis on capital formation. In this sense the focus on investment expenditures lies not so much with its income creating role as a component of aggregate demand, but with its output creating capacity and the potential for economic growth and dynamism with these economies.

The models for Indonesia, Guyana, Taiwan, Korea, and Singapore adopted the perspective that it is the interplay of demand side and supply side forces which determines output. Although in the cases of Guyana and Indonesia there is some semblance of conformity with the neo-Keynesian approach to the supply side of the economy, that is, through the operation of the labor market, the tendency has been for these models to adopt a mixture of Keynesian and development oriented approaches. Thus in all of these models, capital formation equations critical in determining aggregate supply represent the development approach, and behavioral equations used for the components of aggregate demand represent the Keynesian approach.

A significant point which emerges from the analysis is that, regardless of the analytical framework adopted, the central feature of the models is their focus on the behavior of aggregate output. For most of the models this concern is reflected in attention being placed on stabilization policies and short term forecasting in relation to output behavior. The issue of longer term growth is considered in the models for India and the Philippines. In general, however, the concern has been with the issues that have a bearing on short and medium term policy analysis. Preoccupation with the problem of inflation and unemployment is not much in evidence in these models, but many of them incorporate specifications for wage rates and the price level. One other notable feature is the modeling of the external sector for almost all of these models indicating the significance attached to the role of foreign trade in the functioning of these economies.

In relation to policy analysis, considerable attention has been placed on fiscal policy compared with other policy areas including monetary policy. While the treatment of the financial sector has been neglected in six of sixteen models, the government sector was incorporated in thirteen of the models. Another significant feature that should be mentioned is that, wherever the financial sector has been modeled, linkages with the real sector have not been through interest rates but through variables such as credit, output or the price level. This, of course, highlights the role of alternative linkage mechanisms in the real sector financial sector nexus.

Estimation Techniques and Model Performance

The frequent use of one particular estimation technique—ordinary least squares (OLS)—is characteristic of the sample of models. In only three cases was an estimation method other than OLS used, and in these instances the alternative chosen was the two stage least squares technique (TSLS). While model specification can influence the choice of estimation technique,[17] the use of OLS has been largely imposed by the availability of data. As Table 3.1 shows, apart from the models for Korea, the Philippines, and Taiwan, all of the other models described had less than twenty five observations in their series, and were annual models.

A direct consequence of the limited number of observations for most of these models was the necessity of employing the simplest estimation techniques available, since improved estimates through the use of alternative estimation methods (e.g. simultaneous equation) could not be assured.[18] Hence, even though the OLS method yields results that are theoretically biased in a simultaneous equation context, with observations as few as twenty, simultaneous equation methods were viewed as yielding estimates which would likewise be biased and not better than the OLS results. Apart from the TSLS method which possesses an additional property of being consistent, other limited and full information estimation methods have not been applied, particularly full information methods which are anticipated to yield estimators that are sensitive to specification errors.

With as diverse a group of models in terms of model specification, definition of variables, time periods, and consistency of data, any comparison between models is laden with difficulties. Nonetheless, in an effort to provide an overall picture of performance of macroeconometric models for LDCs and hence their usefulness in general terms, we will make an attempt to review the performance of a number of such models.

Typically, two broad groups of evaluation procedures for measuring whether a macroeconometric model achieves an acceptable level of performance are applied to either individual equations or the system as a whole. For the first group of procedures, evaluation is made with reference to the existence of disturbance autocorrelation, goodness of fit (measured by the coefficient of multiple correlation R^2), the right sign, size, and significance of parameter estimates. With regard to the second group of procedures, there are two streams of analysis: one aimed at assessing the tracking performance of the entire system, and the other aimed at assessing the plausibility of the dynamic properties of the system. It is the former, however, which is regarded by many as the more important of the evaluation procedures.[19]

Considering one of the commonly used measures of single equation evaluation, Table 3.2 illustrates the distribution of the size of R^2 for the equations in the models described in Table 3.1. Of these models, thirteen have more than seventy percent of their equations with an R^2 of 0.8 or more. However, when the OLS method is applied, sampling variances are more likely to be underestimated under positive autocorrelation than under zero autocorrelation. Therefore, the statistical significance of the estimates and the high R^2 may be partly attributable to the presence of disturbance autocorrelation. The tests for the presence of first order autocorrelation, the Durbin-Watson and Durbin-h tests, are normally used, with the latter being used when a lagged dependent variable is present in the equation under consideration.

TABLE 3.2
Percentage of Equations in Sample Models According to the Size of R^2

Country Model (Year)	Size of R^2 < 0.6	0.6 – 0.79	0.8 – 0.9	> 0.9
Argentina (1968)	0.0	0.0	100.0	0.0
Colombia (1969)	16.7	10.0	13.3	60.0
Guyana (1975)	12.0	24.0	20.0	44.0
Hong Kong (1985)	0.0	3.7	3.7	92.6
India (1970)	11.8	41.2	17.6	29.4
Indonesia (1984)	0.0	7.0	7.0	86.0
Jamaica (1970)	0.0	4.6	36.3	59.1
Korea (1985)	5.6	11.1	11.1	72.2
Malaysia (1984)	0.0	0.0	0.0	100.0
Nicaragua (1979)	0.0	10.0	10.0	80.0
Nigeria (1973)	10.0	20.0	40.0	30.0
Philippines (1984)	0.0	0.0	0.0	100.0
Singapore (1984)	0.0	0.0	0.0	100.0
Taiwan (1985)	11.1	3.7	11.1	72.2

Sources:

Malaysia, Philippines, Singapore, Indonesia: Preliminary Results of Econometric Models in the ELSA Project: Vols I, II Tokyo: Institute of Developing Economies, 1984.

Hong Kong, Korea, and Taiwan: S. Ichimura and M. Ezaki, Econometric Models of Asian LINK. Tokyo: Springer-Verlag, 1985.

Argentina: G. Maynard and V. Rijckegham, "Stabilization Policy in an Inflationary Economy." In Development Policy: Theory and Practice edited by G. Papanek Cambridge: Harvard University Press, 1968

Columbia: K. Marwah, "An Econometric Model of Columbia: A Prototype Devaluation View." Econometrica 37 (1969):228-251.

Jamaica: N. G. Carter, "A Macroeconometric Model of Jamaica 1959–1966." Social and Economic Studies 19 (1970):178-201.

Nicaragua: L. Downing and J. Solis, "An Econometric Model for Nicaragua In Short-term Macroeconomic Policy in Latin America, edited by J. Behrman and J. Hanson. Cambridge: Ballinger, 1979.

India: R. A. Agarwala, An Econometric Model of India. London: Frank Cass, 1970

Guyana: L. Paul, "Export Simulations of the Guyanese Economy." (PhD dissertation), Howard University, 1978.

Nigeria: UNCTAD, "Models for Developing Countries." In The International Linkage of National Economic Models, edited by R. Ball. Amsterdam: North-Holland, 1973.

Considering the sample of models, the size distribution of the stated Durbin-Watson (DW) statistic in Table 3.3 indicates the existence of positive first order autocorrelation. For example, the models by Marwah (1969), Lin and Chou (1985), Chiu (1985), and Imaoka and Mayanathan (1984) all have more than one third of their equations with a DW value of less than 1.5. While this indication of considerable positive autocorrelation is not totally unexpected since the time series data for macro aggregates are generally trending, there has not been evidence of effort to adjust the equations, for instance through the transformation of variables. In addition, the usefulness of the DW statistic is often questionable because of the presence of lagged endogenous variables in many of the equations.

If evaluation has to be based primarily on the basis of R^2 and tests of significance, then not much can be said about the properties of these models simply because the very evaluation procedures are often conducted with the development of individual stochastic equations. This overlap between validation and the search for the most appropriate specification therefore undermines the validity of procedures applied to individual equations. A further limitation of the evaluation procedures for individual equations arises whenever a stochastic equation performs adequately, yet the system as a whole gives a poor representation of the real economy in which the historical time paths of the endogenous variables were generated. Under these circumstances, the case for evaluation procedures applied to the system as a whole becomes stronger.

In most of the models contained in Table 3.1, the emphasis has been placed on within sample tracking performance, that is, comparing simulated values for endogenous variables with their historical values. Model evaluation along these lines has involved the use of two measures, the root mean square percentage error (RMSPE) and the mean absolute percentage error (MAPE).[20] To evaluate the performance of LDCs' models in terms of these summary measures, several points about system evaluation should be mentioned.

It is often argued that, because of the nature of structural change, LDCs are not amenable to the methods of economic analysis based on stable economic relationships.[21] This notion of dynamic changes is sometimes stated explicitly, as in the models by Agarwala (1970) and Lin and Chou (1985), but is more often implied in models

TABLE 3.3
Percentage of Equations in Sample Models According to the Size of D. W. Statistics

Country Model (Year)	Value of D.W. statistic < 1.5	1.5 – 2.5	> 2.5
Argentina (1968)	0.0	100.0	0.0
Colombia (1969)	43.3	53.3	3.4
Guyana (1975)	20.0	80.0	0.0
Hong Kong (1985)	48.1	51.9	0.0
India (1970)	29.4	64.7	5.9
Indonesia (1984)	9.3	37.2	53.5
Jamaica (1970)	4.5	68.2	27.3
Korea (1985)	16.7	83.3	0.0
Malaysia (1984)	50.0	33.3	16.7
Nicaragua (1979)	20.0	60.0	20.0
Nigeria (1973)	50.0	50.0	0.0
Philippines (1984)	27.3	72.7	0.0
Singapore (1984)	33.3	66.7	0.0
Taiwan (1985)	40.6	51.8	7.4

Sources:

Malaysia, Philippines, Singapore, Indonesia: Preliminary Results of Econometric Models in the ELSA Project: Vols I, II Tokyo: Institute of Developing Economies, 1984.

Hong Kong, Korea, and Taiwan: S. Ichimura and M. Ezaki, Econometric Models of Asian LINK. Tokyo: Springer-Verlag, 1985.

Argentina: G. Maynard and V. Rijckegham, "Stabilization Policy in an Inflationary Economy." In Development Policy: Theory and Practice edited by G. Papanek Cambridge: Harvard University Press, 1968

Columbia: K. Marwah, "An Econometric Model of Columbia: A Prototype Devaluation View." Econometrica 37 (1969):228-251.

Jamaica: N. G. Carter, "A Macroeconometric Model of Jamaica 1959–1966." Social and Economic Studies 19 (1970):178-201.

Nicaragua: L. Downing and J. Solis, "An Econometric Model for Nicaragua In Short-term Macroeconomic Policy in Latin America, edited by J. Behrman and J. Hanson. Cambridge: Ballinger, 1979.

India: R. A. Agarwala, An Econometric Model of India. London: Frank Cass, 1970

Guyana: L. Paul, "Export Simulations of the Guyanese Economy." (PhD dissertation), Howard University, 1978.

Nigeria: UNCTAD, "Models for Developing Countries." In The International Linkage of National Economic Models, edited by R. Ball. Amsterdam: North-Holland, 1973.

of LDCs. In this regard, for most of the models considered in Table 3.1 limited attention has been placed on evaluating the dynamic properties of these models. Thus, while policy analyses are often conducted, an examination of whether the models respond sensibly in terms of sign and magnitude to a given exogenous change or whether these responses are transmitted suitably within the structure of the model is often neglected. The only instance of this type of evaluation can be found in the models of the Philippines and Nicaragua.

Furthermore, the RMSPE and MAPE, while possessing the advantages of being simple to calculate and straightforward to interpret across equations, tend to obscure very useful information about system tracking performance. However, it is only in the models for Malaysia and the Philippines that an attempt was made to use an alternative evaluation procedure. This involved an analysis of the ability of the system to predict correctly turning points in the historical time paths of the endogenous variables.

One final consideration involves the limited use of a much stiffer test for the whole system, that is, the ability of the model to track the historical time paths of the endogenous variables over a period which lies entirely outside the estimating period. The fact that this form of evaluation has hardly been used, however, is a direct result of the relatively short time series available for the variables in most of the models.

The basic form of system evaluation that has generally been used in many of the macroeconometric models for LDCs is tied to the within sample simulation errors for endogenous variables. As Table 3.4 shows, the evaluation measures that have featured prominently have been the RMSPE and the MAPE which, as unit free measures, make the task of interpretation across models somewhat easier relative to the absolute versions of these measures. From an examination of Table 3.4 the following general statements can be made:

1. The within sample tracking performance across models shows considerable variability for the same endogenous variables. The MAPE/(RMSPE),[22] which measures the percentage deviation of the simulated from the actual value for a variable, was as high as 37.4 percent for real output for Argentina and as low as 1.4 percent for Singapore.

TABLE 3.4 Forecasting Accuracy of a Sample of LDC Models

VARIABLE/ SUMMARY MEASURE	HONG KONG	THAILAND	INDIA	NICARAGUA
REAL OUTPUT				
RMSPE	4.74%	...	...	7.72%
MAPE	...	2.8%	4.68%	...
NOMINAL OUTPUT				
RMSPE	...	...	...	...
MAPE	...	...	...	...
PRICE LEVEL				
RMSPE	3.36%	...	...	...
MAPE	...	5.1%	4.76%	...
INVESTMENT				
RMSPE	9.35%	...	...	13.85%
MAPE	...	5.3%	12.60%	...
FINANCIAL				
RMSPE	11.22%	...	...	5.74%
MAPE	...	...	2.07%	...
TRADE				
RMSPE	1.78%	...	...	5.02%
MAPE	...	7.0%	6.23%	...
SIMULATION PERIOD	1963-81	1965-80	1949-60	1960-74

TABLE 3.4 (continued)

VARIABLE/ SUMMARY MEASURE	ARGENTINA	MALAYSIA	SINGAPORE	INDONESIA	PHILIPPINES
REAL OUTPUT					
RMSPE	...	3.72%	1.4%	2.8%	3.42%
MAPE	37.40%	...	...	...	...
NOMINAL OUTPUT					
RMSPE	...	...	3.1%	7.0%	...
MAPE	...	...	...	...	...
PRICE LEVEL					
RMSPE	...	10.31%	2.7%	7.0%	41.82%
MAPE	21.37%	...	...	...	...
INVESTMENT					
RMSPE	...	8.09%	3.3%	7.2%	12.67%
MAPE	...	...	...	...	...
FINANCIAL					
RMSPE	...	...	4.3%	15.5%	...
MAPE	...	...	...	...	...
TRADE					
RMSPE	...	12.68%	...	...	21.75%
MAPE	...	...	...	...	...
SIMULATION PERIOD	1958-65	1969-82	1973-80	1972-80	1960-81

Sources:
Argentina: G. Maynard and V. Rijckegham, "Stabilization Policy in an Inflationary Economy." In Development Policy: Theory and Practice, edited by G. Papanek Cambridge: Harvard University Press, 1968.
India: R. A. Agarwala, An Econometric Model of India. London: Frank Cass, 1970.
Nicaragua: L. Downing and J. Solis, "An Econometric Model for Nicaragua." In Short-term Macroeconomic Policy in Latin America, edited by J. Behrman and J. Hanson. Cambridge: Ballinger, 1979.
Hong Kong, Indonesia, Singapore, and Thailand: S. Ichimura and M. Ezaki, Econometric Models of Asian LINK. Tokyo: Springer-Verlag, 1985.
Malaysia and Philippines: Preliminary Results of Econometric Models in the ELSA Project: Vols I, II. Tokyo: Institute of Developing Economies, 1984.

2. There is a general pattern of relative ranking based on the magnitude of the errors for a number of endogenous variables in many of the model considered. In all of the models where investment is forecasted, there is a tendency for this variable's errors to be high relative to those for other variables. Similarly, the forecast errors for the price level and nominal output show a tendency to be high compared with the errors for real output in almost all of the models.

3. There is general evidence of higher forecasting errors for nominal variables than for real variables, particularly when the price level variable is modeled in detail.

4. Wherever financial variables are modeled, the forecasting errors are also found to be relatively high.

5. In the few cases where variables are determined as residuals or as a rate of change, the simulation errors are extremely high.

6. Some models, for example, for Argentina and the Philippines, portray more variation in the summary measures for a larger number of variables than others.

In relation to these considerations, a number of comments can be made. Firstly, because of differences in model specification, linkage and adjustment mechanisms, and time periods, the notion of direct comparison from one model to another has to be viewed with caution, and the inferences made in this context cannot be regarded as definitive conclusions. Secondly, the simple averaging which is undertaken in the RMSPE and MAPE may not be appropriate to the extent that the endogenous variable under consideration may vary over time. Thirdly, the use of the percentage form of the forecasting error measures is not always appropriate, especially when the observed values of the endogenous variable may be relatively small, as in the case of the rate of change of inflation, or when the observed values frequently switch between positive and negative values, as in the case of trade balances. (The problem with the percentage measure is that a small error can be associated with a large value of the RMSPE or MAPE.) Hence, the results in Table 3.4 pertaining to the inflation rate and trade balances must be viewed with caution.

In spite of these inherent difficulties in making generalizations, it is a characteristic of almost all of the sample models that the authors view the results of model validation with optimism. But, in all cases it is a qualified optimism since large forecasting errors for "problem variables" have been an accompanying feature in all of these models.

The issue of forecasting accuracy, therefore, is an important consideration in the assessment of the performance of macroeconometric models for LDCs. Numerous studies which have attempted to deal with this issue, particularly for models of the advanced countries, have shown that this issue is not a straightforward one (Stekler 1968; Sims 1967; Fair 1984; McNees 1973, 1974, 1981). The critical consideration centers on what kind of benchmark to use when judging the forecasting accuracy of macroeconometric models. This involves, for example, some decision on how close to zero is an acceptable value for a typical summary measure used.

While many judgmental considerations may enter these decisions, those usually called upon are formed from the experience of a model builder, knowledge of the performance of other macroeconometric models, the results of previous attempts, and the performance of other forecasting methods. In many of these aspects, builders of LDCs' models have benefited from the experience of macroeconometric modeling for advanced countries. Based on the considerations just mentioned, some broad conclusions have been made in the literature on advanced economies with regard to forecasting performance and on some benchmarks for certain economic aggregates which may have some relevance for LDCs. For example, Adams (1986) pinpointed a number of generalities based on a comparison of the forecasting performance of some major econometric groups for the U.S. economy (Chase, DRI, and Wharton) over the period between the second quarter of 1976 and the second quarter of 1983. The forecasts considered were those for major economic aggregates such as real GNP, nominal GNP, the GNP deflator, the unemployment rate, net exports, and fixed investment. The forecast error statistics based on the average absolute error were converted to show the percentage difference between the forecast and the actual value observed. The forecast horizons were mainly short term ranging from one quarter to eight quarters. Assessing the record, Adams concluded:

1. The average absolute forecast errors with regard to the selected indicators were relatively large for the major forecasting groups.

2. As the forecast horizon extended into the future (up to eight quarters) the magnitude of the errors have shown a tendency to rise. It must be noted, however, that this observation may be trivial. It makes a difference as to whether a forecast is monthly or say a 2-year one since a small error in a monthly forecast can be as serious as a larger percentage error in a 2-year forecast.

3. The accuracy of model forecasts varied considerably among the different variables in the case of each of the major forecasting groups.

4. Forecast performance varied among the different forecasting groups, with no group having superior performance over the others with regard to all the variables under consideration. Thus, the Wharton model performed better than the DRI model in terms of real personal consumption, but not real GNP over a four quarter forecast horizon.

It is significant to note that the above findings are equally applicable to the sample of LDCs' models considered in Table 3.4. Furthermore, there is a striking similarity between the general consistency of the ranking of forecast accuracy for specific variables in terms of the relative size of the RMSPE. Thus, the forecasting error for real GNP was smaller than that for nominal GNP. The trade variable, net exports, was characterized by a relatively high forecast error as well as the investment variable. These results are also typical for many of the LDC models considered.

A distinct difference exists, however, when a comparison is made between what is regarded as feasible benchmarks for model selection (see Challen and Hagger 1983) and the results obtained in the LDCs' models. An example is real aggregates such as private consumption expenditure and national product for which a RMSPE of between 1 and 2 percent is regarded as highly satisfact- ory. Yet for most of the models described in Table 3.4 this range was exceeded. For the price level, a RMSPE of less than 1 percent and a range of 1 and 2 percent for the rate of price change is viewed as possible, but has proved hard to achieve in the LDCs' models. For nominal aggregates from the monetary and financial sectors, a 6 to 8 percent range regarded as tolerable, again, has not been consistently met in a number of the LDC models.

Two critical issues arise from the above pattern of forecasting accuracy by macroeconometric models for LDCs: (1) whether, the record of macroeconometric forecasting to date is sufficiently good for the forecasts to be useful, and (2) whether the forecasts can be improved.

In connection with the first issue, the fact that macroeconometric forecasting is currently being used in LDCs more than ever in the past attests to its perceived usefulness in spite of imperfect forecasts. This in turn can be largely ascribed to the ability of macroeconometric models to provide numerical answers to a wide range of questions which have fundamental significance for economic policy. Additionally, to the extent that forecasts can reduce the uncertainty facing policy makers, they would appear to be useful. There are those, however, who argue that the emphasis on absolute measures of performance as standards for measuring forecasting accuracy might be too restrictive. McNees (1981:10) articulates this point in an extreme way when he states:

> to adopt perfection as the appropriate standard for forecast evaluation would not only be naive, but counterproductive—naive because we know that the future cannot be foretold perfectly, and counterproductive because experience has shown that even less than perfect forecasts provide valuable information about the future.

It is the case however that striving for perfection can certainly be helpful rather than counterproductive, particularly in the case of LDCs. Improvements can come from a number of directions. Thus, improvements in the underlying data can be made. More detailed information on specific sectors, and better national account statistics would, for example, assist in the better specification of models as well as reduce the measurement error in data which would narrow the error band around the forecasts. Further, through a greater understanding of the data generation process the design of macroeconometric models can only become better representations of the real world. At another level, with a larger and better understood data set, a wider range of estimation methods may be applied. Model performance can also improve as better use can be made of available information. This may take the form of constraints on certain coefficients in line with theoretical and empirical considerations. Finally, restructuring of the models may be a way to obtain improved model specification for understanding the economic processes within LDCs.

Although forecasting ability has tended to vary, where success has been attained, the credibility of macroeconometric modeling has been sustained. But, where forecasts have been poor, renewed efforts have occurred largely because of: (a) existing deficiencies in model construction; (b) existence of alternative specifications which in turn emanate from various streams of macroeconometric systems, different purposes which motivate model construction, and different emphases which arise in the context of a number of potential mechanisms depending on a country's specific circumstances; (c) the continued search within many LDCs for solutions to their endemic economic problems and the promise offered by macroeconometric models, which have sought to address aspects of the stabilization and structural adjustment perspectives as well as long run issues; and (d) the increased theoretical support for the use of macroeconometric models, particularly with recent developments in terms of the interface between existing econometric systems.

The lessons derived for model specification and selection for a LDC can be summarized in terms of the following guidelines. Firstly, the quest for procedures which involve generating answers to four basic questions:

- Does the economy consist of interdependent markets or sectors?
- What are the critical markets or sectors with reference to the structure and performance of the economy?
- What links exist within and between the markets or sectors?
- What mechanisms form these links? For example, are there feedback, spiralling, or stabilizing effects?

Underscoring these questions is the notion of discovering a model that is congruent with the available evidence pertaining to theory, measurement, and sample information.

Secondly, the selection of the econometric methodology by observing the criteria suggested by Hendry and Richard (1983). This entails ensuring that: (1) the model is data admissible, that is, it is logically possible for the data to have been generated from the model. Variables must therefore be specified so that they may not lie outside the range over which economic variables are defined; (2) the model is consistent with theory meaning that the parameters are interpretable in terms of economic theory; (3) the model exhibits reasonable parameter constancy, to be useful for forecasting or policy simulation; (4) the model is data coherent, that is, the differences between the fitted values and the actuals should be random and not predictable from their own past history; (5) the model has regressors that are at least weakly exogenous. (In a simultaneous context this requirement would refer to the regressor variables in the reduced form.) Finally, the model should encompass a range of rival models[23] in the sense that it is able to explain the successes and failures of rival models in accounting for the same data.

Notes

1. M. Corden, *The Relevance for Developing Countries of Recent Developments in Macroeconomic Theory* (Cambridge, Massachusetts: Harvard University, 1985), for instance suggests that certain Keynesian effects, aspects of public choice theory, and some insights from the rational expectations theory have relevance for the economic analysis of LDCs.

2. These concerns, shaped by the existing conditions were focal points in the movement for political independence in many of the new nation states and were extended as important pillars in pronouncements of economic strategy in the initial stages of domestic economic management.

3. Early attempts to apply the arguments for market failure to development theories can be found in T. Scitovsky, "Two Concepts of External Economies," *Journal of Political Economy* LXII (April 1954):143–151, M. Fleming, "External Economies and the Doctrine of Balanced Growth," *Economic Journal* 65 (June 1955):241–256, and W. Fellner, "Individual Investment Projects in Growing Economies," in *Investment Criteria and Economic Growth, Proceedings of a Conference: Center of International Studies* (Cambridge: Massachusetts Institute of Technology, 1955).

4. The rationale for this view was provided by the detailed indications of poverty, economic stagnation, and inequality within LDCs associated with relatively unregulated economic behavior and dominance by foreign economic interests.

5. This model represents essentially the same theory independently produced by R. F. Harrod, "An Essay in Dynamic Theory," *Economic*

Journal 49 (1939):14–33, and E. D. Domar, "Capital Expansion, Rate of Growth, and Employment," *Econometrica* (April 1946):137–147.

6. This model which had its origin in the Soviet industrialization debates of the 1920s is discussed in the secondary literature including contributions by F. Stewart, *Technology and Underdevelopment* (London: Macmillan, 1977) and L. Taylor, *Macro Models for Developing Countries* (New York: McGraw-Hill, 1979), Ch.8.

7. This could take the form of foreign aid, credit, or foreign investment.

8. Since external resources could act to cover both a savings gap and a foreign exchange gap the theory was an important contribution to the analysis of the role of foreign assistance in economic development.

9. M. Fransman (ed.), *Machinery and Economic Development* (London: Macmillan, 1986), traces a continued interest on this aspect of economic development from the time of Adam Smith to contemporary concerns with technological change.

10. This terminology has been suggested by Goldsmith to refer to the range of financial institutions, financial instruments, and magnitude of financial assets/liabilities within an economy.

11. R. C. Porter, and S. I. Ranney, "An Eclectic Model of Recent LDC Macroeconomic Policy Analysis," *World Development* 10 (1982):762.

12. L. Taylor, *Structuralist Macroeconomics: Applicable Models for the Third World* (New York: Basic Books, 1983), provides an insightful introduction to this perspective and its application towards model building and analysis of the problems of stabilization and growth in LDCs.

13. An examination of the flow chart of the U.S. economy provided by the Wharton group for instance is built around the same sectoral blocks, albeit with a greater degree of disaggregation and clear cut directions of causality.

14. Perhaps, the first such model was constructed for India under the guidance of Tinbergen, one of the pioneers of macroeconometric modeling. See N. V. A. Narasimham, *Short-term Planning Model for India* (Amsterdam: North-Holland, 1956).

15. It should be pointed out that initially it was models in the Walras-Leontief tradition that were more popular in LDCs. This popularity was based on the perceived advantages of the WL over the KK system in relation to the promotion of economic development.

16. This occurs for instance when behavioral relationships are formulated in two distinct phases. First, specifying a relationship showing the determinants of the desired or long run level of the variable concerned followed by a relationship showing the mechanism by which the actual level of the variable adjusts to its desired level.

17. In the case of single equation estimation as well as recursive models, OLS is used whereas in the case of simultaneous equation models TSLS and Three Stage Least Squares techniques have been used.

18. See J. Johnston, *Econometric Methods* (New York: McGraw-Hill, 1972), 408–420, and C. Christ, *Econometric Models and Methods* (New York: Wiley, 1966), 477–481.

19. See D. W. Challen, and A. J. Hagger, *Macroeconometric Systems, Constructions, Validations, and Applications* (New York: St. Martin's Press, 1983).

20. The RMSPE is defined as:

$$100 \cdot [\frac{1}{N}\sum_{t=1}^{N}(X_t^F - X_t^A)/X_t^A)^2]^{\frac{1}{2}}.$$

and MAPE as:

$$100 \cdot [\frac{1}{N}\sum_{t-1}^{N}(X_t^F - X_t^A)/X_t^A].$$

where N is the number of observations, X_t^A is the actual value of the variable in period t, and X_t^F is the corresponding predicted value.

21. This is a position that Behrman identifies as a basic rationale for the exclusion of econometric exercises in analyses such as those conducted by L. Taylor, *Structuralist Macroeconomics: Applicable Models for the Third World* (New York: Basic Books, 1983).

22. In some models the MAPE was used while in others the RMSPE was chosen.

23. The suggested synthesis of the Monetarist and Keynesian orientations to the balance of payments by J. Frenkel, T. Gylfason, and J. Helliwell, "A Synthesis of Monetary and Keynesian Approaches to Short-run Balance of Payments Theories," *Economic Journal* 90 (1980):582–592, for example, allows empirical testing of their respective hypotheses within the same model.

4

The Economy of Guyana

The purpose of this chapter is to provide an account of the economic system of Guyana covering the period 1960 to 1984. The discussion will focus on the major characteristics of the economy, the way it has functioned, and on the basic patterns of economic arrangements, relationships, and behavior during the period. The first section puts the evolution of the economy in historical perspective and identifies the major aspects of the socio-economic structure that prevailed by 1960. Section 2 considers the performance of the economy during the period under study. In section 3 the major trends in economic policy are discussed, focusing on the interaction and interrelationships between economic structure, economic performance, policy responses, and policy outcomes. Finally, a concluding section highlights those aspects of economic policy and economic behavior that have serious implications for model construction, policy analysis, and policy design.

Socio-economic and Historic Background

Guyana's status as a settled colony began in the early seventeenth century under Dutch influence and after several interludes of French and English control was ceded by the French to Great Britain in 1814. British control was uninterrupted from that time until Guyana gained political independence in 1966. Located 2 to 8 degrees north of the equator on the northeast coast of the South American continent, Guyana has a coastline along the Atlantic ocean of 270 miles, a land area of about 83,000 square miles, and has an equatorial climate with two rainy and two dry seasons a year that extends over most of the country.

The resource base of the country is conditioned by its location, proximity to an ocean, and the existence of four natural regions: the highland region, the hilly sand and clay area, the interior savannas, and the coastal plain. The first two regions are densely forested, and account for over 75 percent of the country's surface area. In general, the soils in these two regions are poor in nutrients and do not support intensive agriculture. Both of these regions, however, have shown evidence of exploitable mineral resources. The hilly sand and clay region is best known for the extraction of bauxite deposits which lie below the topsoil while the highland region which is inaccessible by land and water transport and yet virtually untapped is known to have resources such as uranium and iron ore.

The interior savannas which account for over one tenth of the land area are poorly drained and of low fertility with limited potential for agriculture. The available grasslands, however, provide some pasturage to encourage cattle rearing. The coastal plain which ranges from ten to thirty miles wide accounts for about 4 percent of the landspace and possesses a variety of soils that can sustain intensive agriculture. A depth of 5 to 8 miles of the coastal zone, however, lies below sea level and requires extensive drainage and irrigation facilities as well as sea defenses as some of the preconditions for agricultural success.

Colonization efforts proceeded with an emphasis on agriculture and a concentration of inhabitants on the 5 to 8 mile coastal strip. The predominance of commercial agriculture under private initiative geared towards external markets featured large scale production, vulnerability to changing international market conditions, and crop specific input and infrastructural requirements. From the mid-seventeenth century when sugar cane cultivation superseded coffee and cocoa as the major crop, the plantation became the dominant form of economic organization. The production techniques utilized by the plantations generated substantial labor requirements which were met largely through the importation of labor.

African slaves were brought first to be followed by indentured servants from China, Portugal, and India. As a consequence, a distinctive social structure evolved with the laboring population playing a subordinate role to the planters and wealthy merchants in a highly stratified society. The political dominance of planters and merchants was gradually eroded through a number of constitutional changes enacted in the first half of the twentieth century. The introduction of adult suffrage without income or property requirements in 1953 proved to be an important turning point as the majority of the population was given the opportunity to elect their government representatives. At the same time, however, these political developments did not lessen the challenges generated by colonial economic arrangements which confronted those responsible for conducting economic policy.

Against this background, by 1960, the economy was characterized by several aspects that had considerable bearing upon economic performance and the formulation of economic policy. Foremost among these were the following 7 factors:

One, a limited domestic technological capability. This was manifested in the predominantly foreign origin of technological activity, the virtual nonexistence of a domestic capital goods sector, and consequently, a critical dependence on imports of capital goods. Thus, between 1903 and 1960 while 498 patents were granted in Guyana, 452 of them, or 91 percent, originated in other countries, particularly Britain and the United States.[1] By 1960 domestic production of machinery accounted for 5 percent of gross capital formation while imports of capital goods constituted 75 percent of the machinery and equipment component of fixed investment. This pattern of externally induced changes in technology was paralleled by the significance of foreign direct investment which in 1960 accounted for 43 percent of net domestic capital formation.[2]

Two, the economy was dominated by the production of a few primary products for export. Table 4.1 provides information on various categories in the national income accounts highlighting the significance of export production and the importance of imports in the total supply of goods and services. In 1960, as the table indicates, the extraction of bauxite and the cultivation of sugar and rice alone accounted for about 26 percent of total value added and for 73 percent of exports of goods and services. The small share of these products in world output defined a price taking role which made the economy highly vulnerable to external economic developments.

Three, serious problems were posed for effective internal decision making since foreign economic interests had an entrenched position in the productive and financial apparatus of the colony. Sugar cane

TABLE 4.1 Aggregate Demand and Aggregate Supply Data for Guyana, 1960–1984 (G$ Mn)

	1960	1961	1962	1963	1964	1965	1966	1967	1968	1969	1970	1971	1972	1973
Total Expenditures on Goods and Services	460.0	487.4	482.2	440.3	512.6	574.8	622.7	679.6	712.9	764.0	848.8	872.6	951.3	1089.2
Domestic Expenditures	316.5	321.5	294.9	250.7	321.9	372.7	408.9	435.3	445.3	468.6	538.4	543.1	606.9	752.7
Private Consumption	200.7	207.2	200.7	162.7	221.7	237.7	256.7	259.2	273.5	297.0	325.7	336.3	371.1	417.5
Public Consumption	33.4	38.0	38.6	36.6	46.6	54.4	59.1	66.6	69.9	79.1	90.9	101.7	116.9	159.7
Investment[a]	82.4	76.4	55.6	50.9	53.6	80.6	92.8	109.8	102.3	103.8	121.8	105.1	118.9	175.5
Exports of Goods and Services	145.3	165.9	189.3	189.6	190.7	202.1	213.8	244.3	267.6	295.4	302.4	329.5	344.4	336.5
Bauxite exports	29.5	40.6	53.8	50.9	56.9	70.7	84.0	86.1	101.6	120.2	138.5	136.4	132.2	137.4
Sugar exports	60.2	59.5	62.3	79.2	57.9	46.0	51.3	59.2	66.1	81.7	77.6	92.2	101.8	75.9
Rice exports	15.4	22.6	20.5	20.1	21.8	23.0	24.9	25.2	26.1	19.7	18.3	21.3	25.3	25.0
Total Supply of Goods and Services	460.0	487.4	484.2	440.3	512.6	574.8	622.7	679.6	712.9	764.0	848.8	872.6	951.3	1089.2
Imports of Goods and Services	168.3	168.8	150.0	139.0	178.7	212.6	233.9	254.3	253.4	275.4	305.3	308.5	352.2	444.2
Consumer imports	56.0	56.1	50.6	46.8	56.2	70.7	76.4	75.2	81.0	92.3	92.7	101.4	106.3	115.3
Intermediate goods	38.9	43.7	40.8	43.3	50.0	55.9	60.8	62.3	66.4	72.2	79.0	86.3	100.7	144.0
Capital goods	52.5	46.9	34.9	28.3	45.0	54.4	65.6	81.4	65.9	70.7	96.6	78.3	90.1	106.9
GDP at Market Prices	291.7	318.6	334.2	301.3	333.9	362.2	388.8	425.3	459.5	498.6	535.57	564.1	599.1	645.0
Per cent of GDP														
Factor cost:														
Sugar output	13.4	12.5	11.5	15.3	10.7	10.7	9.1	10.1	8.7	10.2	9.1	10.8	10.6	8.6
Rice output	4.4	4.5	4.2	3.6	5.1	4.8	4.3	3.1	3.1	2.3	2.8	2.2	1.7	2.2
Bauxite output	8.1	9.9	12.9	10.8	15.1	13.1	14.3	15.1	18.1	18.7	19.3	17.2	15.9	13.2
Manufacturing	10.3	10.9	11.6	14.5	12.3	13.1	12.4	12.4	12.0	11.9	12.1	12.2	12.0	11.1
Services	52.3	49.7	46.2	45.3	45.4	46.2	48.6	48.4	48.6	47.9	40.5	41.3	43.3	48.3
of which: Government	10.0	10.5	9.9	10.2	10.7	12.3	12.7	13.3	12.8	12.6	13.7	14.6	16.5	21.0

Continues

TABLE 4.1 (continued)

	1974	1975	1976	1977	1978	1979	1980	1981	1982	1983	1984
Total Expenditures on Goods and Services	1588.8	2077.0	2169.7	2010.5	2067.5	2244.0	2708.3	2979.1	2459.4	2416.0	2789.2
Domestic Expenditures	936.3	1187.8	1419.0	1299.6	1267.8	1450.9	1666.4	1947.2	1665.0	1740.7	1846.9
Private Consumption	522.0	562.3	673.7	682.7	711.9	692.0	781.4	1012.3	923.0	973.7	842.9
Public Consumption	162.2	232.9	320.1	290.0	296.0	348.0	436.0	464.0	392.0	458.0	566.0
Investment*	252.1	392.6	425.2	326.8	260.0	411.0	449.0	471.0	350.0	309.0	438.0
Exports of Goods and Services	652.5	889.2	750.7	710.9	799.7	793.1	1041.9	1031.9	794.4	675.3	942.3
Bauxite exports	205.8	272.8	288.7	331.2	332.1	326.8	479.3	429.8	313.1	218.8	349.9
Sugar exports	284.8	413.1	259.0	185.7	234.1	230.6	307.6	305.9	263.1	214.5	271.5
Rice exports	49.0	84.8	73.6	66.8	96.0	80.8	87.5	110.0	60.7	64.9	81.6
Total Supply of Goods and Services	1588.8	2077.0	2169.7	2010.5	2067.5	2244.0	2708.3	2979.1	2459.4	2416.0	2789.2
Imports of Goods and Services	634.1	889.5	1033.5	885.9	799.9	918.0	1200.3	1382.1	1013.4	948.0	1089.2
Consumer imports	106.6	131.6	165.2	143.0	130.8	147.3	130.0	160.9	108.0	75.0	83.0
Intermediate goods	307.8	413.9	450.0	410.5	420.9	511.6	424.4	851.2	584.7	519.9	611.0
Capital goods	146.2	260.6	303.0	226.4	153.6	146.0	193.4	216.0	140.7	144.0	117.0
GDP at Market Prices	954.7	1187.5	1136.2	1124.6	1267.6	1326.0	1508.0	1597.0	1446.0	1468.0	1700.0
Per cent of GDP											
Factor cost:											
Sugar output	21.5	22.3	13.6	7.5	10.7	10.4	11.1	8.8	6.7	6.3	7.3
Rice output	2.9	3.2	2.4	4.8	3.6	2.8	3.0	3.1	3.6	3.3	3.4
Bauxite output	12.7	12.3	13.2	15.1	14.5	13.4	15.7	6.2	5.6	0.1	3.1
Manufacturing	13.8	14.7	12.9	12.0	12.1	12.3	12.1	14.8	14.3	13.1	12.9
Services	36.5	34.5	42.1	43.6	42.9	43.6	40.8	47.2	47.6	53.0	50.7
of which: Government	14.5	14.5	18.6	19.6	20.2	19.8	18.7	20.4	19.0	21.2	22.3

*Gross Domestic Investment

Sources: Central Bank of Guyana, Annual Reports; Statistical Bureau, Ministry of Economic Development Economic Surveys of Guyana.

cultivation and processing were in the hands of Bookers McConnel and Jessels holdings, two subsidiaries of foreign corporations. Bauxite-alumina production by the Demerara Bauxite Company and the Berbice Bauxite Company was also under the control of a Canadian and an American firm respectively. The financial system dominated by a duopolistic banking structure was also dominated by foreign interests in the form of branches of a British and a Canadian bank.

Four, the widespread existence of social and economic inequality which predisposed the majority of the population to the exercise of political authority over economic decision making as a way of eliminating these differences. One indication of inequality was the existence of a skewed distribution of income, with the lowest 20 percent of households receiving 4.3 percent of the income and the highest 5 percent of households receiving 18.8 percent of income in 1960.[3] This was compounded by an estimated unemployment rate of 8 percent combined with a high degree of underemployment, particularly in the seasonal agricultural activities.[4]

Five, the presence of underlying social and political tensions and cleavages between the two major racial groups—the descendants of African slaves, who constituted about 32 percent of the population, and the descendants of Indian indentured immigrants, who accounted for about 48 percent of the population. These groups had become polarized in terms of their allegiance to separate political parties along racial lines by the end of the 1950s. This was paralleled by a broad rural urban distinction between these groups as the majority of the Indians lived in the countryside and engaged in agriculture while the majority of Africans were concentrated in the urban centers and engaged primarily in non-agricultural activities.

Six, an agrarian structure in which the majority of farmers were engaged in small scale farming under land tenure arrangements which granted long term leases but not ownership of land. In 1960, 76.2 percent of all farms were less than 10 acres in size and in the case of rice farming 81 percent of rice farmers accounted for 42 percent of all rice lands.[5] The agricultural sector was also unable to absorb the growth of rural labor and did not cater to domestic needs since food imports constituted a major share of total consumer imports.

Seven, a relatively small government sector which functioned traditionally to provide social and economic infrastructure with the major portion of expenditures spent on administration. Fiscal and monetary policy for developmental or stabilization purposes was secondary to redistribution goals incorporated in minimum wage and price controls. Thus, price controls which have had a tradition since the late nineteenth century continued to be implemented particularly during and after World War II, officially, to protect consumers.

The high specialization in trade represented by export and import to GNP ratios of 53.5 percent and 62.8 percent, respectively, in 1960, characterized Guyana as a very open economy. While there were indications of internal and external imbalance in the form of a relatively high level of unemployment and a balance of payments deficit, these did not gain the undivided attention of policy makers.

Economic Performance

Charts 4.1 through 4.8 provide an overview of the behavior of major macroeconomic variables for Guyana during the period 1960 to 1984. The choice of 1960 as the beginning of the period was dictated largely by the limited availability of data on the variables of interest before this year. At the same time it provides an opportunity for the comparison of economic performance and structure in a period preceding the independent status of the country in 1966 with the changes that occurred with the practice of domestic economic management.

Chart 4.1 records inflation in Guyana between 1960 and 1984. The cross-hatched area identify periods of decline in real gross national product (GNP). In the period 1961 to 1971 inflation was relatively stable, though since 1971 there was greater variability and a more sustained inflation trend. To an extent, import prices play a role in this development thus, a close relationship between import prices and inflation behavior is indicated by a correlation coefficient of 0.97 between these two variables. The other proximate source of domestic price level changes is the behavior of prices in the non-tradeable sector. However, a definite relationship between consumer prices and non-tradeable prices, has been more difficult to detect.

Chart 4.2 plots the real GNP growth rate. The observable feature is the frequency of turning points as output fluctuated regularly. Before 1971, however, real GNP growth averaged 3.2 percent a year.

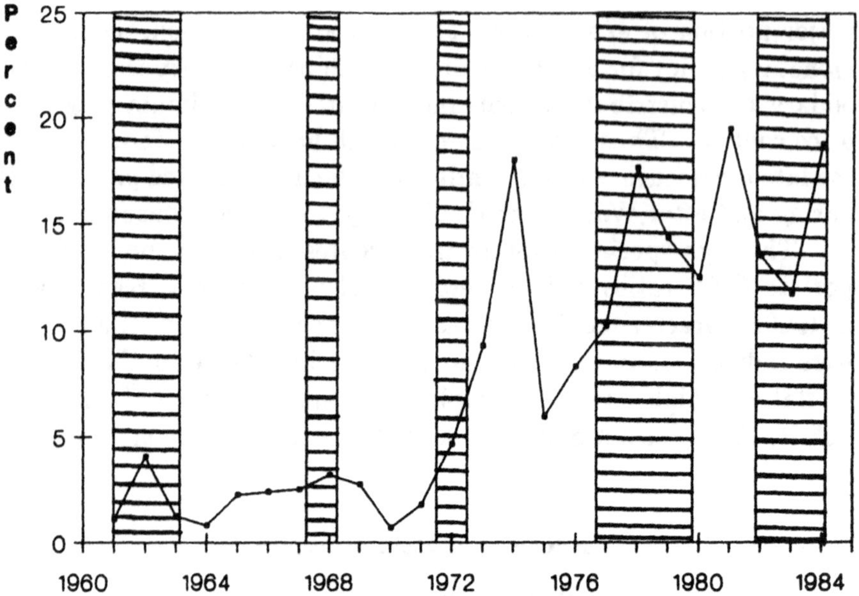

Chart 4.1 Inflation Rate in Guyana: 1960-1984

Source: Bank of Guyana Annual Reports.

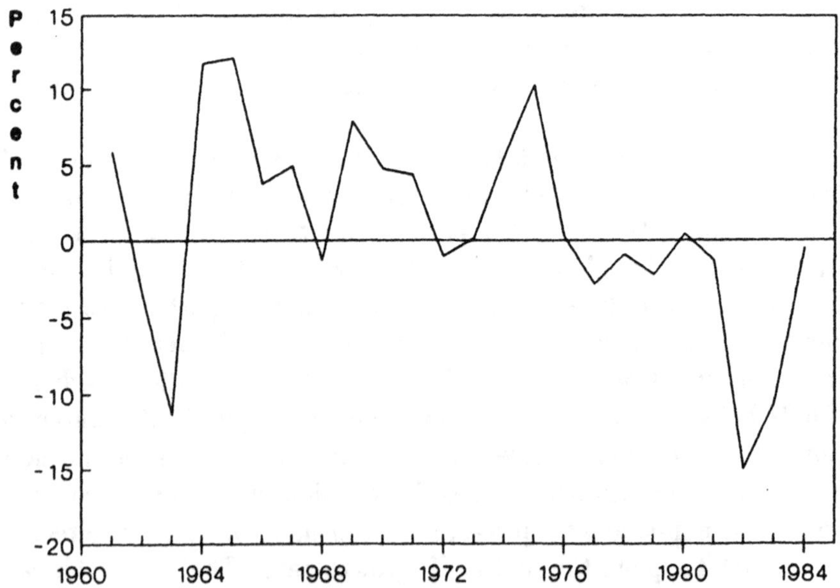

Chart 4.2 Real GNP Growth in Guyana: 1960-1984

Source: Bank of Guyana Annual Reports.

Real growth averaged much less in the period after 1971, and the inflation uptrend associated with this period needs to be investigated as both an aggregate demand and an aggregate supply phenomenon.

The nominal GNP growth rate is presented in Chart 4.3. Though most values are positive, there also are negatives. Some of them coincide with periods of decline in real GNP; in other periods of decline in real GNP, nominal GNP had grown due to considerable inflation. The evidence would seem to indicate, therefore, that variability of real GNP growth was not the only factor influencing the behavior of nominal GNP.

Chart 4.4 plots the ratio of the public sector deficit to nominal GNP. An increase in the deficit to GNP ratio reflects the real deficit rising faster than real growth. The record shows that real deficit growth did not consistently exceed real output growth for much of the 1960s but this was altered from the early 1970s as the deficit to GNP ratio rose appreciably in twice as many years as it fell. Since big deficits occurred and were sustained while nominal GNP growth accelerated and decelerated, there is an absence of a systematic correlation between government spending policies and GNP growth.

The gap between domestic production and domestic spending is presented in Chart 4.5. The difference between expenditures and domestic availability of goods and services is reflected in the current account position of the balance of payments. Since 1972, except 1974, 1975, and 1978, a definite upward trend in the gap representing periods of decline in domestic production as well as sustained increases in overall domestic demand was in evidence. This widening gap between domestic demand and domestic production placed great pressure on available international reserves since, inevitably, imports were relied upon to supplement domestic production of goods and services.

Chart 4.6 plots the data on the country's net international reserves. As could be expected in periods of increased balance of payments difficulties the international reserve position experienced significant declines. Moreover, from 1976 as the foreign exchange reserves became depleted, the growth of external debt and external payment arrears took up the slack.

The annual percentage changes in the narrow (M1) and relatively broad (M2) versions of the money stock are shown in Chart 4.7. Both measures of the money supply follow a similar pattern of

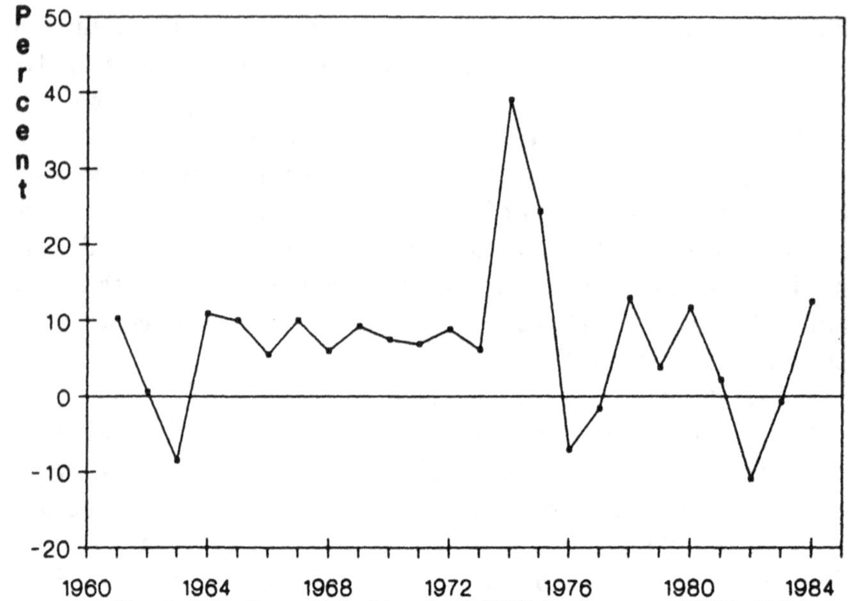

Chart 4.3 Growth in Nominal GNP in Guyana: 1960-1984

Source: Bank of Guyana Annual Reports.

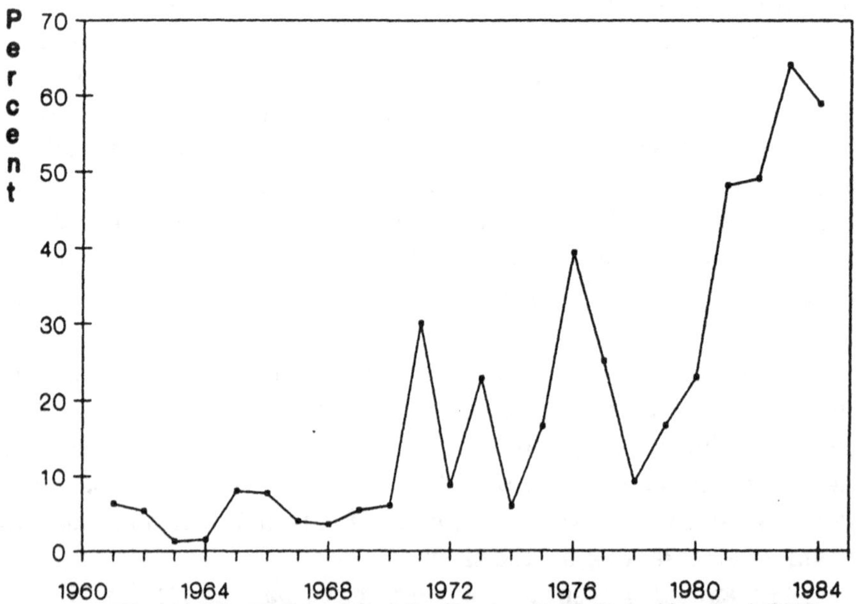

Chart 4.4 Ratio of Public Sector Deficit to Nominal GNP

Source: Bank of Guyana Annual Reports.

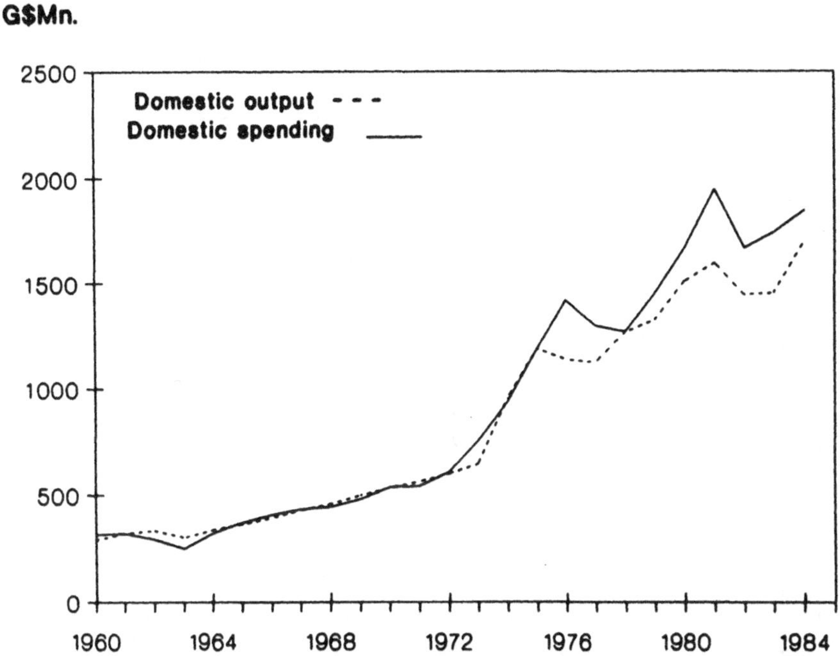

Chart 4.5 Domestic Output and Spending in Guyana: 1960-1984

Source: Bank of Guyana Annual Reports.

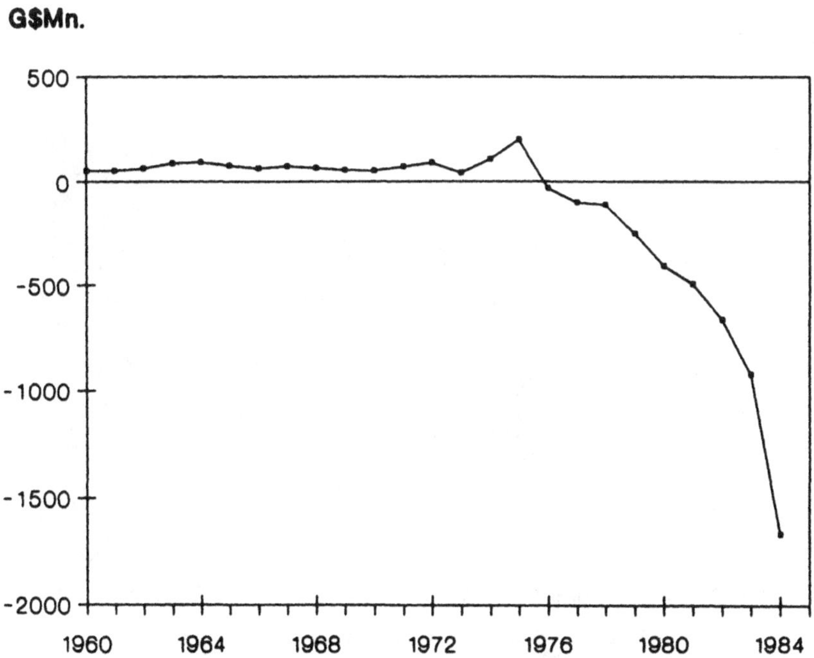

Chart 4.6 Net International Reserves in Guyana: 1960-1984

Source: Bank of Guyana Annual Reports.

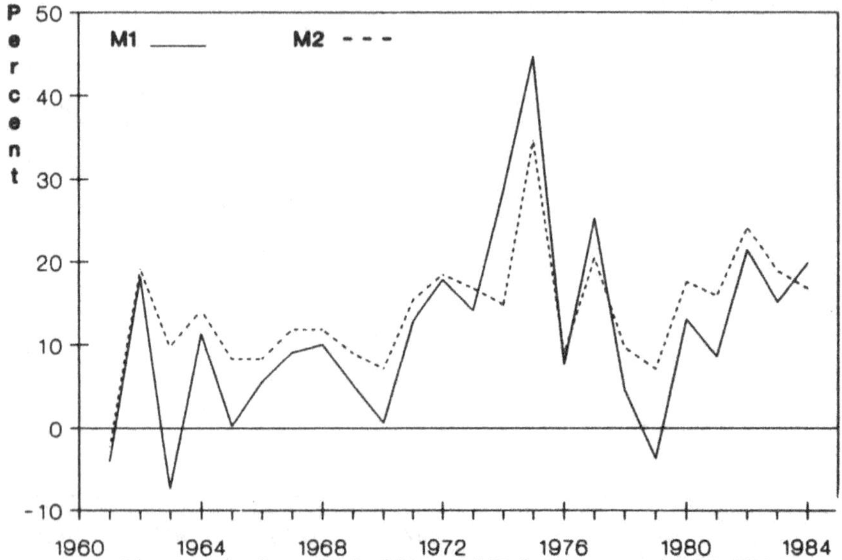

Chart 4.7 Growth in M1 and M2 in Guyana: 1960-1984

Source: Bank of Guyana Annual Reports.

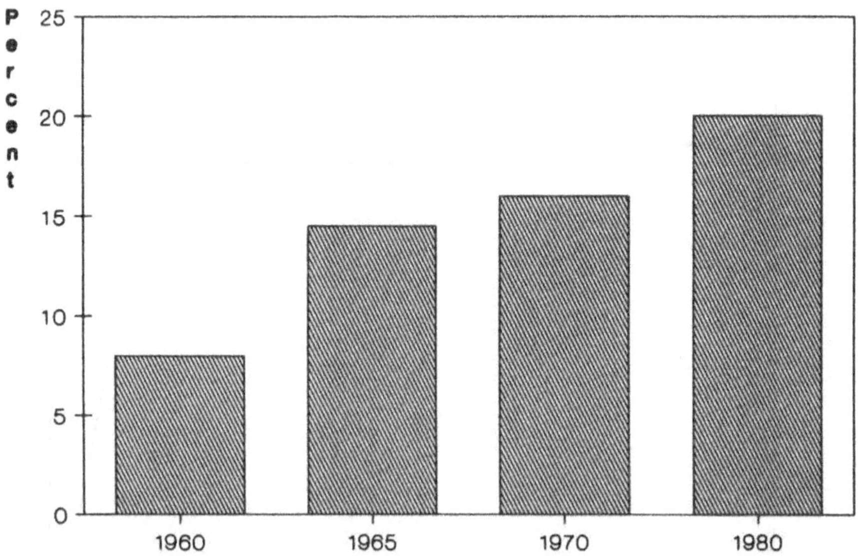

Chart 4.8 Unemployment Rate for Selected Years in Guyana

Source: Bank of Guyana Annual Reports.

fluctuation with no distinct trend. When the money supply-to-GNP ratio is considered in relation to the public sector deficit-to-GNP ratio, there are indications that fiscal and monetary actions often moved in the same direction, particularly as credit expansion occurred to accommodate fiscal expansion.

Chart 4.8 indicates the behavior of unemployment. This has been one of the persistent problems facing Guyana's economy as the unemployment rate continued to rise over the period. There was a conscious effort on the part of the government to utilize the public sector as a vehicle for employment creation, especially between 1970 and 1982, though this did not have a significant impact as the record shows. The magnitude of the problem is further highlighted when it is considered that, with a population of just over three quarters of 1 million, official statistics indicate emigration rising from a yearly average of 3,284 persons during the decade of the 1960s to 11,671 persons between 1970 and 1984.[6]

These empirical trends indicate the emergence of a prolonged economic crisis with symptoms that reflected severe internal and external imbalances and much greater obstacles to sustained economic growth than those that prevailed around 1960. The extent of the decline and the close association between internal and external imbalances are illustrated in Table 4.2 for the periods 1960 to 1969, 1970 to 1979, and 1980 to 1984.

Though Table 4.2 indicates a consistent trend of economic deterioration in terms of a variety of performance indicators, there were some years of growth and improvements in external balance within the periods examined. These usually coincided with the favorable performance of the bauxite, sugar, and rice producing sectors. The occurrence of major turning points and some of the events that had an impact on economic policies and outcomes are indicated in following description of the behavior of the economy between 1960 and 1984.

The early years of the period, 1960 and 1961, witnessed substantial growth in nominal and real output and in per capita income. For example, the gross domestic product (GDP) at current market prices rose by about 15 percent per year. Over these two years the inflation rate averaged 0.98 percent, there was some relief to the unemployment situation, and the balance of payments position was a favorable

TABLE 4.2
Internal and External Imbalance in Selected Periods

Indicators of:	Periods		
Internal Imbalance	1960 – 69	1970 – 79	1980 – 89
Growth in government deficit	7.9%	21.4%	21.5%
Internal debt(G$ Mn)	43.4	527.1	2964.6
Growth in money supply	9.4%	15.8%	16.0%
Growth in the price level	1.9%	9.4%	13.4%
Unemployment rate	16.0%	20.0%	n.a.
Growth in real GNP	3.0%	1.4%	–4.2%
External Imbalance			
External debt (G$ Mn)	108.0	677.1	2005.7
Payments arrears (G$ Mn)	0.0	7.0	364.9
Balance of trade[a] (G$ Mn)	15.1	–33.5	–105.4
International reserves[b]	68.3	6.6	–830.7
Net capital inflows (G$ Mn)	29.6	79.9	10.1

Note: Growth figures are calculated as average annual rates. The inflation rate is the average of annual changes and the unemployment rates are end of period figures.
[a]Negative sign indicates trade deficits.
[b]Negative sign indicates net foreign liabilities.

Source: Central Bank of Guyana.

one. External debt amounted to 29.4 percent of GNP, with maturities of a long term nature and a high concessionary component.

In 1962 and 1963 social strife involving the major ethnic groups in the country erupted as the Indian based political party in government met with violent protest from a coalition of opposition groups over the economic policies and philosophy of the government. Production was affected by supply disruptions due to the destruction of production and infrastructural facilities and to strikes which led to the loss of about 502,000 mandays in the two years.[7] The seriousness of the situation, which led to the establishment of a state of emergency, was a major factor in the creation of an uncertain economic climate to which the private sector responded by reducing investment expenditures. As a result, there was a slowing down of nominal GDP growth, to 4.8 percent in 1962 followed by a decline of 9.8 percent in 1963. Imports of goods and services declined absolutely in both years, and the value of exports rose in 1962 but remained constant in 1963 even though the terms of trade improved considerably in the latter year.

In the aftermath of the civil unrest, the economy showed signs of improvement. From 1964 to 1967 output grew rapidly as production in both the sugar and bauxite industries increased. The GDP at market prices increased on average by 8.4 percent per year. Price level increases were moderate, averaging 3 percent per year. A major policy measure introduced in 1967 in response to a devaluation of the British pound, to which the Guyana dollar was pegged, was a 17 percent devaluation of the Guyana dollar. The immediate impact was to cause a significant reduction in the foreign balances held by the commercial banks as they now faced exchange rate risks associated with the large share of foreign financial assets in their portfolios.

In 1968 even though nominal GDP grew by 8.4 percent, real output was stagnant. A significant development was a sharp decline of private investment of about 30 percent as the bauxite industry completed an expansion program initiated in 1966. In addition, unfavorable weather and a heightening of labor unrest played an important role in accounting for shortfalls in rice, bauxite and sugar production. In 1969, GDP at market prices grew by about 8 percent and exports rose by 9 percent. The number of strikes and mandays lost were at their lowest since the early 1960s. Though investment outlays lagged, there was an increase in domestic demand, but with domestic production keeping pace there was no appreciable widening of the resource gap.

In 1970 and 1971 GDP grew by 6.3 percent even though labor unrest had again emerged as a serious problem. The number of strikes had increased from 126 in 1969 to 159 in 1970 and as much as 199 in 1971 most of which occurred in the traditionally strike prone sugar industry. The balance of payments position improved in spite of the lower output and export receipts in 1970 when compared to the preceding year because of the introduction of import controls.

Real output contracted during 1972 and 1973 due largely to unfavorable weather conditions which reduced yields in the sugar and rice industries and affected physical output in the bauxite industry. Fiscal expansion occurred and the ensuing fiscal deficit was partly financed through monetary expansion. In 1973 wages for government workers were increased, and a public sector investment program was launched, coinciding with the release of a draft development plan for 1972-76. The annual inflation rate rose by about 8 percent during these two years.

In an effort to correct the balance of payments situation that existed at the end of 1973, the government sought to control expenditure in 1974, by administrative means, limiting certain luxury purchases from abroad, suspending allowances for tourism and emigration and reduced borrowing from domestic banks by foreign companies. The import bill had risen considerably because of the oil price increase in 1973, but, with an improved terms of trade resulting from favorable sugar and bauxite prices, in 1974 and 1975 the balance of payments position improved. In 1976, as sugar prices fell and the bauxite sector continued to experience production problems, GDP at market prices declined by 4 percent. The use of foreign exchange reserves to purchase foreign owned firms led to a decline in the international reserves, and, with a decline in merchandise exports, a balance of payments problem again became evident.

In 1977 a fall in domestic sugar production accompanied by declining international sugar prices led to a 5.5 percent decline in real GDP and a further weakening of the balance of payments position. Price controls which were in effect for much of the 1970s were revised in 1977 and controls on foreign spending were tightened in 1977. The limited access to foreign exchange resulted in the emergence of black markets for foreign currency as well as the limited supply of imported items that could now be obtained. As these activities mushroomed, a multiple exchange rate system came into effect.

The period from 1978 to 1984 was one of ongoing economic difficulty. A deepened foreign exchange crisis and ineffectiveness of policies to ameliorate the situation led to a proliferation of unofficial markets, smuggling, and the existence of an informal economy capable of conducting activities outside of the control of the government. While there are no official estimates of the size of the informal economy, there are suggestions that it ranges from anywhere between 25 to 100 percent of GDP at market prices.

Table 4.3 compares the estimated black market rates of Guyana dollars to the US dollar against the official exchange rate between these two currencies from 1981 to 1984. As the table indicates, over this period the gap widened between the official exchange rate and the black market rate and when adjustments were made to the official rates, the absolute change in the black market rate was larger. The implied excess demand for black market foreign exchange reinforces the idea of an expanding informal sector as the performance of the official sector deteriorated from the late 1970s. Under these circumstances there were indications of considerable shift in policy focus as measures were introduced to cope with the immediate problems of macroeconomic imbalance, particularly, in relation to the budget position of the public sector and the balance of payments. The nature of these changes are charted in the following discussion of policy formulation and implementation between 1960 and 1984.

TABLE 4.3
Official and Black Market Exchange Rates: $ G to $ US (1981-84)

Year	Official Rate	Black Market Rate
1981	3.00	6.50
1982	3.00	8.00
1983	3.00	12.50
1984 Jan 11-Oct 5	3.75	
1984 Oct 6-Oct 12	4.12	
1984 Oct 13-Oct 19	4.15	
1984 Oct 20-Oct 26	4.25	
1984 Dec	4.25	14.00

Data from: C. Y. Thomas, "Foreign Currency Blackmarkets: Lessons from Guyana," *Social and Economic Studies* 38 (1988).

Policy Framework and Policy Measures

The formulation of development plans with an emphasis on the allocation of investment expenditures provided a framework for economic strategies from 1960 to the late 1970s. The 1960–64 development plan, for example, projected investment spending of G$110 million with an emphasis on employment and output expansion through the agricultural sector.

The advent of a new government in 1964 resulted in the formulation of a new development plan in 1965 for the 1966–72 period. This plan emphasized an alternative strategy of industrial growth which was reflected in a shift in the distribution of projected spending away from agriculture toward infrastructure and public works that would support industrial activity. After two revisions this plan was subsequently abandoned because of a new policy orientation adopted by the government in 1970.

In February 1970, Guyana was declared a Cooperative Socialist Republic, with the stated objective of establishing an economic system based on the existence of the cooperative, public and private sectors. A new plan for the period 1972–76 was released in draft form in 1973 with an emphasis on expanding the role of the cooperative and public sectors in the economy. The economic strategy was one of self-reliant growth to be achieved through increased productivity in agricultural and mining activities and the exploitation of other natural resources, especially in the interior of the country. This strategy was expected to resolve two basic problems facing the economy, the geographical imbalance in economic activity and unemployment.

After the expiry of the 1972–76 plan period, two years elapsed before another plan document was issued. This plan covered the period 1978–81 and included greater detail on the policy measures and targets that were to be pursued. Specific targets included a real GDP growth rate of 17 percent for the four year period, a high domestic savings rate reaching 16 percent of GDP in 1980–81, and the maintenance of a tax revenue/GDP ratio of more than 30 percent. The latter targets represented the growing concern over the uncertainty faced in financing the investment program which made the realistic formulation of subsequent development plans a difficult exercise. In fact since 1981 no formal plan has been released though a capital expenditure and investment program of over G$1.3 billion was outlined for 1981-83.

The significance of the financial constraint facing the implementation of the plans is indicated by the general pattern of actual expenditures falling below projected spending in all of the plans. In the 1960–64 plan the difficulty experienced was in relation to both domestic and external financing. In the 1966–72 plan the problem was not so much the unavailability of financing, but the inability to follow the guidelines of the plan. A problem faced in implementing the 1972–76 plan was the occurrence of significant shortfalls in external financing, while the expenditures of the 1978–81 plan were difficult to achieve because of the economic decline and corresponding shift in attention to stabilization policies.

All of these plans shared some common characteristics. In particular, they have had little positive impact on the economy being generally overly optimistic. Further, the plans neglected to explicitly include the private sector in the development process. Finally, they were inadequate in terms of providing a consistent framework for an analysis of the impact of the investment strategies on various macro indicators such as unemployment, the budget deficit, and the public debt.

In the 1966–72 period a number of incentives were offered to encourage foreign investment such as income tax holidays for 2 year and 5–10 year periods, tax allowances for investment based upon the amounted invested in fixed assets, and duty free importation of raw materials, building materials, machinery, and appliances. The response was not overwhelming, however, as foreign direct investment declined from 1968 to the end of the period indicating the importance of other considerations such as wages and labor relations and an official policy position on the role of the private sector.

Though the 1972–76 plan was an improvement on the previous plans in terms of coverage and identification of macroeconomic targets there was still limited discussion of the kinds of measures that would be utilized. From 1970 to 1977 a systematic policy of public sector expansion was promoted through a mix of legal and administrative measures which led to a substantial transfer of ownership of assets from the private sector to the public sector. These measures included nationalizations, joint ventures between the public and private sectors, regulations governing the private sector, and the involvement of public sector agencies in new areas of economic activity. These measures led to a process of economic withdrawal and reduced levels of activity by the local and foreign private sector, more so as the public sector appeared to have preferential access to scarce foreign exchange and financial resources.

Table 4.4 indicates the growth in the public sector through the acquisition of existing assets and to a lesser extent the creation of new entities. In 1970 the number of public sector entities was 15, and by 1978 the number had increased to 42. As Table 4.5 indicates, crowding out of the private sector was evident in the changed distribution of banking system credit and capital inflows between the public sector and private sector. This pattern was paralleled by the shrinking access of the private sector to available physical resources as the displacement of private investment by public sector investment also shown in Table 4.5 reflected reduced access to capital imports which had been a major component of fixed investment.

Accompanying the growth in the public sector was the emergence of an expanded administrative framework which sought to coordinate the activities of the various public sector agencies. Up to 1970, areas of responsibility, authority, and accountability of public corporations were defined by the Public Corporation Ordinance of 1962. This decree made the council of government ministers (Cabinet), that was accountable to the legislative body (Parliament) responsible for the formation, policy making, and performance of public corporations. Specifically, the Cabinet could direct policy to each corporation in terms of its orientation, capital investment and borrowing operations. In practice these functions were dispersed as each corporation was attached to a specific ministry which selected a Board of Directors and left much to the discretion of the Board in relation to the conduct and performance of each corporation.

These arrangements were altered in 1971 with the passing of the Public Corporations Act which transferred the statutory powers of the Cabinet pertaining to public corporations to a newly created agency, the Guyana State Corporation (Guystac). The intention was aimed at making the management of corporations more accountable, reinforcing the objectives of economic and commercial efficiency, and ensuring that corporations function within the political and ideological framework of the government.

TABLE 4.4 The number of Public Sector Agencies by Sector[a] 1960–1978

	Sectors								
	Agriculture	Fishing	Forestry	Mining	Commerce	Finance	Services	Industry	Total
1960	1	-	-	-	1	1	2	-	5
1961	1	-	-	-	1	1	2	-	5
1962	1	-	-	-	1	1	2	-	5
1963	1	-	-	-	1	1	3	-	6
1964	1	-	-	-	2	2	3	-	8
1965	1	-	-	-	2	2	3	-	8
1966	1	-	-	-	2	2	3	-	8
1967	1	-	-	-	2	2	4	-	9
1968	1	-	-	-	2	2	4	-	9
1969	1	-	-	-	2	3	4	-	10
1970	1	-	-	-	4	4	6	-	15
1971	1	1	1	1	4	4	8	-	20
1972	1	1	2	1	5	4	8	-	22
1973	1	1	2	1	4	6	8	1	24
1974	1	1	2	1	4	7	8	2	26
1975	1	1	2	2	5	5	8	2	26
1976	2	3	2	1	7	5	10	9	39
1977	2	3	2	1	7	6	12	10	43
1978	2	3	2	1	6	5	12	11	42

[a]The Services sector includes infrastructure and Industry includes processing and manufacturing.

Source: Central Bank of Guyana.

TABLE 4.5
Public and Private Sector Shares of Credit, Investment, and Capital Flows

	Fixed Investment % of GDP		% of Net Domestic Credit		Capital Inflows $ US Million	
	Public	Private	Public	Private	Public	Private
1960	5.6	21.6	15.8	84.2	7.3	17.8
1961	7.3	16.9	19.5	80.5	8.2	4.7
1962	6.0	11.1	20.0	80.5	8.5	−0.9
1963	4.1	9.1	16.4	83.6	6.2	4.8
1964	2.8	13.0	15.7	84.3	4.3	5.2
1965	4.5	14.8	38.1	61.9	7.9	9.9
1966	6.7	15.4	42.9	57.1	7.5	15.3
1967	6.3	18.3	38.5	61.5	8.0	20.4
1968	8.1	12.7	40.1	59.9	7.3	10.2
1969	7.8	11.8	42.5	47.5	9.8	7.5
1970	10.2	10.8	43.4	46.6	8.3	4.3
1971	11.7	6.5	49.4	40.6	14.8	−0.1
1972	12.2	5.8	51.8	48.2	10.9	4.6
1973	16.5	7.5	64.0	36.0	17.3	23.5
1974	14.0	6.7	58.2	41.8	29.7	16.3
1975	23.5	5.9	64.8	35.2	88.2	−31.0
1976	27.3	6.2	80.0	20.0	56.9	−6.7
1977	20.4	5.3	86.6	13.4	30.5	38.6
1978	15.3	3.7	86.3	13.7	27.3	−7.8
1979	19.6	4.9	87.8	12.2	31.6	−6.5
1980	22.1	4.6	89.8	10.2	52.2	−40.9
1981	22.6	5.0	89.6	10.4	115.6	36.3
1982	20.0	4.2	93.1	6.9	40.8	−14.6
1983	16.9	4.1	93.5	6.5	0.5	−17.7
1984	21.0	5.7	108.0	−8.0	−4.6	−35.5

Source: Central Bank of Guyana, Annual Reports: 1960–1986.

A system of interlocking directorates emerged as the scarcity of managerial personnel, combined with the growing centralization of the public sector administrative machinery, led in many instances to the same officials holding key positions in several institutions. The Guyana State Corporation, for example, was responsible for appointing the Board of Directors of corporations which then selected the general managers of the corporations. These general managers in turn functioned as members of the Board of Guystac. The relationship between Guystac and corporations was undermined as conflicts arose over the involvement of Guystac personnel in the operational aspects of corporations' activities. Ministerial control over certain decisions was an additional consideration that had to be faced by the management of corporations. Thus, in order to obtain imported inputs, approval for the foreign exchange was needed from the Ministry of Finance, and import licenses had to be issued by the Ministry of Trade. In addition, the Ministry of Economic Development could engage in separate negotiations of foreign loans and trade arrangements on behalf of corporations.

The expanded public sector had a number of implications for fiscal activity, particularly the budgetary process. Because the government budget became the principal indicator of policy formulation and measures to be implemented it is useful to examine the budgetary process in some detail. Up to 1964, budget preparation was the responsibility of the Treasury (Ministry of Finance). In practice the estimates of each government department were prepared jointly by officials from the Treasury and the relevant government department. Since 1964 direct responsibility for the preparation of budget proposals for each department was transferred to the officials of these departments. Up to 1979 overall responsibility for the formulation of guidelines, adherence to government priorities, and the final stages of preparation, however, rested with the Ministry of Economic Development and the Ministry of Finance. Since then the State Planning Commission has taken charge of the preparation of the capital component of the budget while the Ministry of Finance has retained responsibility for the current component.

Typically, budget preparation has been supervised by a specially created budget committee comprised of representatives from certain public sector agencies. By 1979 a committee chaired by the Governor of the Central Bank was established to deal with the budget proposals from state corporations. A specific pattern is followed in the preparation of the annual budget. A budget circular is sent to ministries and corporations in September each year outlining government policies and general guidelines to be followed in preparing proposals for the next year's budget. With regard to current expenditures special formats have evolved to take account of every authorized position on the payroll, proposals for new positions, salaries and other direct labor costs, and other current expenditures. Similar formats are prepared for capital projects and for public corporations. Separate formats are sent to the principal sources of revenue such as the Commissioner of Inland Revenue, the Controller of Customs and Excise and the relevant public corporations. In general, all these estimates are based on past trends, while adjustments for changed policies are made centrally.

Proposals submitted to the budget committees are reviewed, and then an overall view of the budgetary position is formed. At this stage the Cabinet is involved in the deliberations to agree upon a general framework. Budget implementation in terms of revenue collection and release of funds lie principally with the Ministry of Finance. Financial responsibility is designated to specific officials to act as receivers of revenue and disbursement of appropriations; the overall spending plan is determined on the basis of spending plans submitted by the various agencies to the Ministry of Finance. Requests for capital expenditure are dealt with by a special committee, the capital releases committee, with representatives from the Ministry of Finance and the State Planning Commission.

Allowance is made for the need to finance expenditure in excess of provisions in the Appropriation Act due to unforeseen circumstances. These requests for supplementary expenditure have included, for example, salary increases which were not estimated in the budget. A transfer of appropriations is also allowed between divisions provided these transfers do not exceed budgetary provisions.

The Budget Office in the Ministry of Finance is in charge of monitoring expenditure and revenue within the fiscal year which coincides with the calendar year. Monthly returns submitted are compared with the record of releases and the monthly plan of expenditures. These returns are also checked against monthly reports from the Central Bank about the Consolidated Fund account kept by the Ministry of Finance. In order to provide a more comprehensive monitoring of public finances quarterly reviews are prepared by the Ministry of Finance. However, these are largely confined to current revenue and expenditure and repayments of both internal and external public debt. A comparison is made between estimates and actual outturns with some analysis of deviations and their likely causes. The limited consideration that is given to the likely developments for the rest of the year is largely confined to the revenue side. While these quarterly reviews are informative they lack comprehensiveness as capital expenditure and financing items are not included.

An important feature of the budgeting process was the involvement of the central bank and the ease with which an accommodative stance of the monetary authority towards fiscal policies was adopted. The build-up of international reserves which occurred during 1974–75, for example, was run down principally through central bank credit to the government which was used to acquire ownership of existing enterprises in the agricultural and distribution sectors. Since these were already existing enterprises, production capacity was not automatically altered, rather this step constituted a transfer in ownership of the economy's productive assets. This did constitute a loss to society, however, since the borrowed funds could have been otherwise used to generate other productive assets in the economy.

The lack of efficient fiscal control was evident in considerable variances between budget estimates and actual outturns. Deviations from the estimates are especially marked in the case of capital expenditure and external financing. A highpoint was reached in 1982 when capital expenditure outturns exceeded estimates by over 100 percent. External financing except for 1974 was substantially below the estimates, and domestic financing correspondingly exceeded the estimates.[8]

Accompanying the absence of formal development plans since 1978 was an increased emphasis on stabilization policies. Unlike the concerns of the development plans of transforming the economy through structural changes, these policies were principally geared towards resolving internal and external disequilibrium. The direct relationship between internal and external disequilibrium was dictated by aspects of the economic structure as well as the conduct and nature of economic policy. As the external imbalance worsened and

Guyana sought increased external support from the IMF and World Bank, these policies became tied in to the performance criteria upon which increased financial assistance was conditioned.

In an attempt to reverse the balance of payments situation a stabilization program was initiated with financial support from the IMF in 1978. The one-year stand-by agreement made the equivalent of SDR 15 million available in loans together with credits from the International Development Association and required constraint on demand in the private and public sectors. This was to be effected through a reduction in subsidies for consumers, upward price adjustments for a wide range of goods and services provided by public sector corporations, ceilings on central government expenditures, and introduction of new tax revenue and collection measures. Some of the specific measures introduced were a 10 percent sales tax, a 10 percent cut in the government's capital works, and a wage freeze for government workers extending to 1980.

These measures had an immediate effect on the public sector accounts. Public sector savings moved from a negative 3 percent of GNP in 1977 to a positive 4.5 percent in 1978, and the overall public sector deficit declined from 29 percent of GNP in 1977 to 14 percent in 1978. The current account deficit of the balance of payments also improved dropping from 23 percent of GNP in 1977 to 6 percent in 1978. Despite these improvements, there was cause for concern since aggregate output fell by 3 percent in 1978 and the inflation rate rose from 9 percent in 1977 to 21 percent in 1978. Gross international reserves represented the capacity to finance only 2.2 months of imports and the external debt/GNP ratio had risen to 0.96 by the end of 1978. Meanwhile payments arrears on external transactions which had grown to G$56.6 million at the end of 1978 and external debt commitments were becoming sources of significant claims on available foreign exchange earnings.

In this context, a three year extended fund facility (EFF) was negotiated with the IMF by mid 1979 giving access to financial resources amounting to SDR 76.2 million. The main objectives of this program were to promote economic growth and sustain the previous year's improvement in the balance of payments. In order to achieve these objectives, the program targets agreed upon an increase in investment spending from 20 percent of GNP in 1978 to 27 percent in 1979, an increase in domestic savings from 14 percent to 17 percent of

GNP, and an increase in interest rates. Also a 3-year wage agreement was reached between the government and the trade union council resulting in a cancellation of a 27 percent increase in minimum wage scheduled to take effect in 1979.

In contrast to the experience of 1978, the fiscal accounts did not show any improvement in 1979. Public sector savings only reached 4 percent of GNP compared with a planned level of 9 percent and the overall public sector deficit rose to 19 percent of GNP. The current account deficit on the balance of payments widened to 17 percent of GNP and real GDP fell by about 1.5 percent largely due to declines in agricultural and bauxite production.

The failure to achieve the fiscal and balance of payments targets led to the cancellation of the 1979 EFF arrangement with the IMF and the negotiation of an alternative program in mid 1980. While the objectives were similar to those of the previous arrangement, there was a difference in approach in the new program. Some concern was shown for the declining consumption standards since these were believed to have "created social and political tensions that affected output growth." This was reflected in the decision to introduce a wage increase of 5 to 7 percent in basic wages, a 5 percent premium for workers with specialized skills, and an incentive scheme involving tax free bonuses based on the achievement of production targets. An additional feature was the decision to establish maintenance and technical assistance contracts with specialized foreign firms, especially for the bauxite industry.

Access to a greater amount of financial resources improved in 1981 with the negotiation of a three-year structural adjustment program between Guyana and the World Bank for US$22 million. This program emphasized the completion of major ongoing projects in irrigation and mining. Measures were also to be taken to increase the efficiency and profitability of public sector enterprises. These included restructuring the public sector administrative machinery, providing for efficient operations, incentives, and World Bank involvement in monitoring the execution of the investment program.

In 1982, after fiscal deficits continued to exceed the targets agreed upon with the international lending agencies, deficit reduction was attempted through tight expenditure policies. Wages were frozen, and, between 1981 and 1984, about 25,000 employees were laid off by the government. This occurred after a three year freeze on nominal wages even though prices had risen by 16 percent per annum (much more on the unofficial market) and new taxes and surcharges had already reduced disposable income. As the economy continued its poor performance and the informal economy grew, circumventing official channels of taxation, the tax base of the government was eroded. With the emigration of skilled personnel and the shortage of foreign exchange, the production units in the public sector suffered continued losses.

As the evidence indicates, the nationalization program was associated with the serious decline in output. The implementation of the strategy was plagued by limitations in terms of the skilled labor supply as some leading decision makers in the public service were transferred to staff public corporations. A rudimentary information system was also not adequately developed to cope with the demands of central planning and monitoring of economic performance. The statistical information and analytical skills were strongest in the very large firms that were nationalized, but with the replacement of management and changes in policies there was no corresponding improvement in the information systems.

These results indicate that state ownership did not automatically improve the government's ability to direct a firm in the most economically productive direction. The way the public sector administrative machinery evolved, for instance, indicated the conflicts of interests that emerged among those responsible for directing economic policy. One common source of this conflict was the need to choose between more employment and greater worker productivity as political factors played an important role in public sector management. The capability of management was another determinant of how adequately the intentions were carried out, and since managerial resources in the government service were in short supply, running the operational entities became a formidable task.

Implications for Policy Analysis and Model Building

A number of characteristics of the economy defined the path of economic policy-making by the mid 1980s. One, the presence of serious distortions reflected in the spread and significance of parallel market activities. Two, the dilapidated state of the capital stock, in particular for the three critical sectors—bauxite, sugar, and rice. According to the World Bank estimates, this requires rehabilitation expenditures that total nearly US$200 million which can only come from external sources in the context of depleted foreign reserves, payments arrears and indications of insolvency.[9] Three, the lack of efficient production technology which adversely affects the economy even if the price distortions were removed and liberalization policies were implemented to enhance a competitive position for the main export sectors.

One immediate step would be to undertake strenuous efforts to encourage foreign investors. Since uncertainty surrounding political stability, rising labor costs, and inadequacy of support services have become severe obstacles, investors would require more than a short term promise of fiscal and other incentives.

Several other issues need to be considered in the design and analysis of economic policies. One of them is the implication of foreign trade on economic performance, particularly a situation in which a few exports constitute a significant share of total income and output. This entails that a reduction in the value of exports is analytically similar to a reduction in domestic investment. At the same time the contractionary influence in the domestic economy presents a balance of payments problem. Whereas in an adaptive economy it may be possible to use expansionary fiscal policy to counteract the domestic contraction, and restrictive monetary policy to counteract the adverse international payments effect, in the case of Guyana as well as other LDCs the experience has shown that this is only a remote possibility.

The reduced degree of freedom in relation to available policy instruments has to do with the existence of certain structural and institutional aspects in the economy. The absence of a developed domestic capital market and limited amounts of private financial capital supplied, for instance, meant that fiscal deficits could only be financed through official external borrowing or expansionary monetary policy. External borrowing, however, was basically linked to repayment of previous debt or for projects with long gestation periods. Consequently, there was great reliance on monetary accommodation which was facilitated by the role and involvement of the central bank in policy making. Under these conditions monetary and fiscal policy effectively collapsed into a single policy instrument that could not be used to pursue simultaneously two independent policy targets. Rather the pursuit of such an expansionary policy did not resolve the problem of international payments deficits, but aggravated it.

Another issue has to do with the growth and significance of the informal economy. The informal markets which developed were inefficient because of the high transactions costs involved. The illegal nature of these activities resulted in incomplete information about prices and availabilities which raised the costs of communication within these markets and led to difficulties in enforcing agreements entered. Thus, there were search costs in terms of time and effort involved in identifying buyers and sellers as well as the cost of persuading them to make or accept offers and reach an agreement.

Further, as these activities spread there was an increase in geographical dispersion as well as in the number of economic agents involved, both of which increased transactions costs associated with parallel market activities. Segmented markets for goods and services, an increase in smuggling as well as bartering represented additional forms of inefficient institutional arrangements. This was compounded by the time lost as the transportation system deteriorated and activities such as queuing and bureaucratic bottlenecks multiplied.

With these developments a number of problems considered below emerged for policy making. One, the expansion of black market activities which led to a relative and absolute decline in governmental revenue. The reaction was a greater use of administrative methods such as stricter tax controls to increase revenues as well as the introduction of austerity measures to match lower revenue growth. This imposed a greater cost to society and ultimately led to other activities being driven into the informal economy in order to avoid the higher taxation.

Two, a deterioration in the ability of the government to manage the economy in terms of its ability to assess the state of the economy and forecast the results of measures taken. To a large extent the government was not able to define the actual increase in GNP, or precisely estimate the pace of inflation, or obtain authentic information about employment of the population as the informal sector increasingly overshadowed the formal sector.

Three, a weakening of the government's social policy. Subsidies, expenditures on health, education, and infrastructure were the first areas to feel the fiscal pressures. Four, a modification of the distribution of income as those partaking in the informal sector were able to put themselves in a position to maintain their consumption levels and standard of living while those excluded suffered from their unfavorable position in the official economy.

Five, the modification of expenses of enterprises and hence, their relative market position as some were able to avoid taxation while others were not. Further, as employees in the official sector shifted to the informal sector, the official sector's performance was often held back and led to greater inefficiency.

Six, an increased inclination to break the rules in organizations and within the population. The norm of breaking rules reduced the risk of exposure of those avoiding the rules as complicity of a larger segment of the population occurred. The establishment of such a norm also solidified patron-client relationships and increased the value of informal relationships. Under these circumstances the policy of maintaining unchanged institutional conditions would mean that the symptoms of economic crises would be coupled with the inability of the economy to renew itself.

Another set of inadequacies in relation to the formulation and implementation of economic policy exists because of the nature of the budgetary process. While the framework for budgeting is comprehensive in relation to the administration and audit of public finances, there is a very weak link between annual budgeting and macroeconomic forecasting. As the procedures examined earlier indicate, there is an absence of specific mechanisms for testing the consistency of budgetary aggregates with available resources and targets of economic policy, whether aimed at promoting structural changes or domestic and external economic adjustments. There has been for instance limited effort to reconcile proposed fiscal aggregates with a projection of the balance of payments and domestic monetary developments.

Further, the relevant data that would provide insights and implications of major budgetary decisions in most instances are not prepared and presented to decision makers because of the way the budgetary projections are made. The initial projection of public sector revenues is the sum of revenues projected by individual ministries and corporations that make these estimates mainly by extrapolating recent trends. While guidelines about policy actions such as anticipated tax rate or price changes are considered, there is limited input with regard to the impact of overall economic conditions on revenue sources. Similarly, expenditure requests are prepared by economic entities under guidelines of priorities rather than under constraints that would make the total consistent with sustainable sources of finance.

The budgetary process also faces the difficult task of reconciling fiscal policies that have diverse origins and objectives. In relation to the attainment of planned investment expenditures, the budget has been an important vehicle for making the objectives of the development plans operational. The budget has also been the centerpiece for the attainment of the adjustment programs agreed upon between the government of Guyana and the IMF and World Bank. Finally, the budget provides the avenue for short term responses to conditions within the economy which have been both causes and consequences of severe internal and external imbalances. As a result of these divergent goals, budget policies are basically uncoordinated, seeking to attain different objectives simultaneously, and often fail to consider short term policies within a longer term perspective.

With regard to the process of model building the description of Guyana's economy provide the following answers to the four basic questions mentioned at the end of Chapter 3. First, interdependence in the economy is exhibited among input and output markets, between the aggregate demand and aggregate supply sides of the economy, between the expenditure and financial sectors, particularly in relation to public sector transactions and interrelationships between the official and unofficial economy. Second, with reference to the structure and performance of the economy the critical sectors are the external and domestic production sectors with resource allocation decisions within the public sector having considerable impact on developments in the economy. The mechanisms which form the links between the critical markets and sectors are associated with excess demands or supplies and associated feedback effects. In general, the multiplier feedback and accelerator feedback mechanisms are not as pronounced largely because of leakages in the form of imports in the case of the former, and low responsiveness of output to investment spending in the case of the latter. Capacity response which relates how factor demands respond to changes in demand in the goods market is sluggish, particularly when the availability of imported inputs is constrained. Liquidity feedback exists because of the transmission of real and monetary impulses through the financial sector and back to other markets through changes in the availability of domestic credit. Finally, there are international linkages which indicate that imports, exports and domestic prices are externally influenced.

With the above considerations in mind an important objective in model construction is to provide a framework that can address the most critical aspects of the poor performance of the economy. In particular, this requires a focus on the behavior of aggregate output and the balance of payments position while taking into account the institutional aspects such as the open nature of the economy and the pervasive influence of the public sector.

Notes

1. F. Long, "Patents In Guyana: The Case for Legal Reform–A Note," *Transition* 5 (1982):71–77.
2. B. Watson, *Supplementary Notes on Foreign Investment in the Commonwealth Caribbean* (Kingston: Institute of Social and Economic Research, University of the West Indies, 1974), 84–88.
3. International Bank for Reconstruction and Development, *World Tables* 3rd ed. (Baltimore: The John Hopkins University Press, 1983).
4. K. R. Hope, *Economic Development in the Caribbean* (New York: Praeger, 1986), 80.
5. Government of Guyana, Ministry of Agriculture.
6. Government of Guyana, Statistical Bureau.
7. Government of Guyana, Statistical Bureau.
8. Government of Guyana, Ministry of Finance, Budget Estimates for various years.
9. IBRD Mission estimates, 1987.

5

A Theoretical Model

This chapter discusses the theoretical model that has guided the empirical work in this study. The first section describes the rationale for the equations that represent the critical relationships in the expenditure, monetary, production, and external sectors. In section 2 a model is proposed consisting of an aggregate demand equation, an aggregate supply equation, and a balance of payments equation which are derived from the equations pertaining to the sectors identified above. The model is then used to analyze the behavior of output, inflation, and the balance of payments. The comparative static results of the basic model are also considered to provide insights about the impact of different policy parameters on the endogenous variables in the system of equations. In order to minimize problems of reference the notation for the variables in the model are listed in alphabetical order in Table 5.1.

Nature of the Model

The model is an attempt to integrate three main ideas. The first is that the economy is open in terms of aggregate demand and aggregate supply with some common factors influencing both the demand and supply sides. This raises the possibility of ambiguous outcomes for the price level and output given shifts in aggregate demand and aggregate supply which result from disturbances in factors that are common to both of these schedules. An assessment of the relative magnitudes of shifts and the slopes of these functions therefore, becomes an important consideration in the analysis. The second idea is that the model should account explicitly for the role played by institutional circumstances and structural factors either as constraints

TABLE 5.1
Variables in the Theoretical Model

Symbols:	
C	personal consumption expenditure
CI	capital inflows
CIM^d	demand for imports of intermediate and capital goods
CIM^s	supply of imports of intermediate and capital goods
CIM	imports of intermediate and capital goods
DC	domestic credit creation
DE	government deficit
e	exchange rate(units of G$ per unit of US$)
e^*	expected exchange rate
EN	energy supply
EP	expected price level
EX	exports of goods and services
G	government consumption expenditure
i	interest rate
I	total investment expenditure
IC	import capacity (foreign exchange receipts)
IM	imports of goods and services
INV	inventory investment
K	capital stock
L	labor employed
L^d	labor demand
L^s	labor supply
M^d	money demand
M^s	money supply
NDC	net domestic credit
NFA	net foreign assets
P	price level
P_e	export price index
P_i	import price index
PRI	private sector investment
PSI	public sector investment
W	wage rate
WH	wealth
Y	total domestic production
ΔY	change in total domestic production
Y^*	productive capacity
π	expected inflation rate

on decision-making or as influences over adjustment processes in general. In relation to the latter issue, for example, the possibility that markets do not clear cannot be ignored in the model building process. The third idea is to provide a model general enough to address the issues of adjustment to macroeconomic imbalances and economic growth in an integrated framework for Guyana. An important requirement in this regard is for the model to take into account the most important macroeconomic policy instruments and targets that are suitable under the circumstances and structural characteristics facing Guyana.

Relation to Previous Work

Consideration of the implications of the first idea for the less developed economy is of fairly recent origin. For a long time the general orientation within the macroeconomics literature on open economies was to conduct independent analyses of the demand side and supply side issues.

Beginning with the work by Polak (1957/58) and Polak and Boissoneault (1959) the concern on the demand side was linked to the analysis of external payments imbalances. Here, the emphasis has been on the positive effect of the domestic credit supply on expenditures in the goods market which spillover to the balance of payments though spending on imports. As a result great importance was attached to credit policies in managing aggregate demand and the balance of payments. One practical example of this approach is the financial programming exercises conducted by the International Monetary Fund for countries seeking assistance from this organization. Studies that have followed in this tradition were provided with a stronger theoretical basis in the form of the monetary approach to the balance of payments. In this framework the case for domestic credit as a policy variable was strengthened since it was shown that in an open economy under fixed exchange rates the monetary authority cannot control money supply but can determine net domestic credit (Johnson 1972).

Supply-side analyses share a consistent focus on the degree of openness in terms of the relative importance of imported inputs (capital and intermediate goods) in production processes within LDCs.

In the literature on economic development, there is the two-gap approach—see Bruton (1955)—which extends the closed economy Harrod-Domar growth model to include capital transfers as an additional source of investment. Because of the reliance on imported inputs, this theory argues that domestic savings and foreign capital transfers are not perfect substitutes. Thus, economic growth may be constrained by a foreign exchange gap which would require appropriate external financing policies.

With the persistent current account deficits and growth in external indebtedness which have mirrored capital transfers in a large number of LDCs, alternative models have gained in prominence. A common theme in one of the more popular approaches—macroeconomic stabilization in LDCs—is the adverse supply side responses in these economies to a wide range of economic policies. Adherents to this view include Hirschman (1949), Diaz-Alejandro (1963), Shea (1976), Krugman and Taylor (1978), Dornbusch (1980), Taylor (1983), Hanson (1983), Gylfason and Risager (1984). These studies provide both theoretical and empirical insights on the contractionary output effects of demand management, structural, and exchange rate policies in relation to supply side openness of the LDCs.

The main problem with the studies that have considered either the demand or supply side consequences of openness is that they provide a limited approach to the design and analysis of economic policy for LDCs. One of the potential difficulties of such an approach lies with the interpretation of the results of empirical tests which focus on either demand or supply aspects when both sets of influences are relevant to the analysis. This study avoids this difficulty by taking into consideration both demand and supply aspects of openness. An added advantage of the model built in this study is that it provides a framework for arriving at a synthesis of the partial approaches since it presents an avenue for reconciling contrasting results about the impact of disturbances, such as exchange-rate changes on the path of output and the balance of payments in the case of an open economy. With regard to the idea of accounting for the role played by institutional circumstances and structural factors, the literature on economic development and disequilibrium provides theoretical arguments which make this approach less ad hoc than it might appear to be. However, a potential weakness of the model is that the choice-theoretic explanations of the institutional aspects considered remain beyond the scope of this study, though this is a deficiency shared by the literature that focuses on issues such as non-market clearing and structural bottlenecks.

In relation to the idea of addressing the issues of structural change and adjustment in an integrated framework the motivation lies with the contemporary experience in a significant number of LDCs which forces them to grapple simultaneously with poor growth performance and severe macroeconomic imbalances such as balance of payments deficits and enormous debt obligations. The literature on growth oriented adjustment—see Corbo, Goldstein, and Khan (1987)—which focuses on the design of policy packages that will simultaneously eliminate macroeconomic imbalances and raise the rate of growth, has moved in the direction of building merged models which combine a growth component with the analysis of the demand side of the economy—see Khan and Montiel (1989). The problem with this approach is that the growth process is tied principally to savings and investment constraints when in fact, in a number of those LDCs that are performing poorly, there is no clear indication of a direct relationship between growth in output and an increased flow of investment.[1]

The model formulated has as its building blocks a version of the IS-LM system for the analysis of aggregate demand, an aggregate supply schedule in the neoclassical tradition which provides the basis for the analysis of the supply side of the economy, and the Keynesian approach to the balance of payments for the analysis of the external sector. These components together determine output, the price level, and the current account position of the balance of payments as the main variables of interest. The building blocks are specified separately to identify relevant constraints, balance sheet relationships, and equilibrium conditions and are then combined to yield an analytical model.

The Expenditure Sector

The Equation for Personal Consumption

The equation representing personal consumption expenditure is derived from the assumption that consumers make decisions about their lifetime consumption path with the object of maximizing intertemporal utility. In the context of Guyana, several factors have an adverse effect on long term planning in consumer decisions. Low per capita income, the absence of a capital market, negligible social welfare provisions, and limited unemployment compensation schemes combine to make consumption less systematic, less organized, and more erratic over time.

Since consumers find it difficult to maintain a stable level of consumption expenditures which follow their lifetime consumption plans, it is hypothesized that current income exerts an important influence on consumption. Moreover, under the assumption that consumers seek to stay on their desired consumption path, a positive wealth effect on consumption is posited as consumer wealth serves to moderate the discrepancies between consumption plans and anticipated streams of income. The usual aggregation conditions are assumed to exist which permit the transition from the equation facing an individual consumer to the following aggregate consumption function:[2]

$$C = C(Y, WH), \tag{5.1}$$

where the expected signs of the coefficients are $C_y > 0$, and $C_{wh} > 0$ respectively.

The Investment Equation

Gross investment is assumed to consist of exogenously and endogenously determined components. Inventory investment and private sector fixed investment are treated as exogenously determined variables. The former because of the influence of events such as bad weather and strikes which affect the major productive activities. The latter because of influences such as the determination of investment policies in the foreign dominated production sector, as part of the global strategies of the parent companies prior to the 1970s and the uncertain investment climate facing the private sector since 1970.

Public sector investment is regarded as an endogenously determined variable. The equation for public investment is derived from the developmental role identified for the public sector under the assumption that, to an extent, public investment implements the process of adjustment between actual and desired levels of capital stock and investment. The adjustment of capital to its desired stock is assumed to be influenced by the cost and availability of investible funds as well as the availability of necessary imports of capital and intermediate goods. Accordingly, credit by the banking system, the interest rate on loans, and the level of capital and intermediate goods imports, are hypothesized to be determinants of public investment. Further, the assumption that the economy obeys a production function in the long run suggests that investment conforms to some form of the accelerator principle. The change in output, therefore, is another explanatory variable in the public investment equation. The equation for gross investment is as follows:

$$I = I(I_0, DC, i, CIM, \Delta Y), \tag{5.2}$$

where $I_o = INV + PRI$, and $I_{dc} > 0$; $I_{cim} > 0$; $I_y > 0$; $I_0 > 0$; $I_i < 0$.

The Government Expenditure Equation

The conscious policy of expanding the role of the public sector by the government witnessed the growth of expenditure and employment in the government sector. The basic constraint on the pursuit of this strategy has been the financial resources available to the government in the form of tax revenues, domestic credit, and net foreign capital inflows. Fluctuations in economic growth, in the balance of payments position, and rising external public debt have resulted in variability in access to internal and external sources of revenue. Steady growth in overall public sector expenditure, combined with tax and non-tax revenue losses due to parallel market activities and sustained operating losses in the major public sector enterprises, resulted in a rapidly rising public sector deficit. With interest payments on the public sector debt accounting for a growing share of the public sector deficit there was increased pressure for deficit reduction through cuts in expenditure. However, not all areas of government spending were treated equally, and in many instances government consumption expenditure was the primary target. In this context of deficit-induced fiscal adjustment, it is postulated that government consumption is inversely related to size of the deficit which is shown in the following equation:

$$G = G(DE), \tag{5.3}$$

where $G_{de} < 0$.

The Equation for Exports

The equation for exports is based on the assumption that export performance is determined on the supply side. Traditionally, Guyana's main exports have been based on contractual arrangements with importing countries which guaranteed export quantities and prices. Export quantities exceeding the quotas as well as other exports account for such a small share of total world supply that Guyana acts as a price taker in the relevant international markets. Since export production accounts for a substantial share of domestic output, it is assumed that the supply of exports is determined by domestic productive capacity. The persistence of a relative shortage of foreign exchange to import necessary inputs creates severe bottlenecks in the economy and acts as a major constraint on the supply of exports. The usual direct relationship between export quantities and export prices is posited, though the price elasticity of export supply is assumed to be small in the short run owing to capacity constraints and delays inherent in export production of a primary nature. The export supply equation is specified as follows:

$$EX = EX(P_e, Y^*), \tag{5.4}$$

where $EX_{P_e} > 0$, and $X_{y^*} > 0$.

The Equation for Imports

The equation for imports is derived from the assumption that imports close the gap between domestic demand and domestic supply. It is also assumed that the supply of imports is infinitely elastic since Guyana accounts for a very small share of total world demand for the products that are imported. Demand theory dictates the inclusion of price and income as determinants of import demand. Since imports and domestically produced goods are very poor substitutes, the price elasticity of import demand is likely to be low and the income elasticity of import demand is likely to be high. Import capacity is also included as an explanatory variable. Since the availability of foreign exchange determines the ability to satisfy import demand, the variable of foreign exchange receipts is taken as a proxy for import capacity. A devaluation of the exchange rate, that is, an increase in the units of domestic currency required to obtain a unit of foreign currency is assumed to reduce imports through the substitution effect. A direct relationship is posited between public sector deficits and the level of imports because public sector enterprises had replaced private firms in the major areas of economic activity (the public corporations therefore faced the import requirements that were formerly accounted for by these private firms) and at the same time the poor financial performance of many of these public sector enterprises was an important source of the growth in the public sector deficit. The import equation is shown below as:

$$IM = IM(P_i, IC, Y, e, DE, P), \tag{5.5}$$

where $IM_{P_i} < 0$, $IM_{ic} > 0$, $IM_y > 0$, $IM_p > 0$, $IM_e < 0$, and $IM_{de} > 0$.

The Monetary Sector

The Demand for Money Equation

The equation for money demand is based on the assumption that people hold money because it acts as a means of payment and as a store of value. The demand for money balances depends positively upon the expenditures to be financed and inversely on those factors that raise the costs or lower the returns of holding money. The narrow range of financial assets in Guyana restricts the asset choices of wealth holders to holding domestic currency, foreign currency, or physical assets such as land, houses, and consumer durables. When prices are expected to increase, people are assumed to shift into foreign currencies or physical assets as a result of the depreciation of the domestic currency's function as a store of value. At the same time, however, an expected increase in the rate of inflation may cause greater use of the domestic currency as precautionary expenditures rise to counter the expected future price level increases especially under the circumstances of a scarcity of basic consumer goods. The interest rate, although institutionally pegged for prolonged periods up to the late 1970s is also included as one of the relevant opportunity costs of holding money and is assumed to be inversely related to the amount of money balances demanded. The demand for real money balances function includes as explanatory variables real income, the interest rate, expected inflation, and expected changes in the exchange rate. The general form this function is as follows:

$$M^d = M(Y, i, \pi, e^*), \tag{5.6}$$

where π, and e^* are the expected inflation rate and expected exchange rate respectively and, $M_y > 0$, $M_\pi > 0$, or $M_\pi < 0$, $M_e^* < 0$, and $M_i < 0$.

The Supply of Money Equation

The equation for money supply combines the relevant domestic and external influences. It is based on the idea that, in a small open economy, changes in the money supply result not only from the actions of the central bank and commercial banks but also from foreign exchange flows which reflect the decisions of foreign and domestic economic agents. It is assumed that changes in net foreign assets or liabilities (equivalent to net exports plus net capital inflows) represent exogenous influences on the money supply since the relevant decisions are largely outside the control of policy makers. Similarly, net domestic credit creation which represents the internal source of money supply changes is assumed to be exogenously determined. This is because of the commercial banks practice of liability management under conditions of excess reserves and excess liquidity as well as the accommodative stance taken by the central bank in meeting fiscal expenditures.

The consistent holding of excess reserves by commercial banks in Guyana undermines the validity of a money multiplier model which makes the stock of money some multiple of central bank determined reserve assets. Instead, under the circumstances where the lending patterns of the banks exhibit risk averse behavior,[3] bank reserves have become largely endogenous and bank advances have become exogenous. A more appropriate money multiplier model, therefore, is one where money supply will change as a result of changes in the supply of bank loans and advances which is exogenously determined.

In addition to commercial bank deposits (which are created through bank lending), currency issue by the central bank constitutes the other component of the money supply which in the central bank accounts is matched by a portfolio of domestic and foreign assets. For the banking system as a whole (both the central and commercial banks) the balance sheet relationship is that total liabilities in the form of commercial bank deposits and currency issued by the central bank (*i.e.* broad money supply) must match total assets in the form of net domestic credit and net foreign assets[4] and the supply of money is specified as

$$M^s = NDC + NFA \tag{5.7}$$

where NDC refers to net domestic credit in the consolidated accounts of the banking system, and NFA is the domestic currency value of foreign assets or international reserves.

The Production Sector

The Production Equation

It is assumed that an aggregate production function represents production relationships in Guyana which require the use of labor services, capital and intermediate imports, and energy supply with fixed techniques of production. As usual for a LDC, there is a low degree of substitutability among the inputs, suggesting that sustained output expansion could be blocked by the limited supply of any of them. It is assumed that the capital stock is fixed, that the energy supply is exogenously determined and that the amounts of labor and imported inputs used are determined by demand and supply conditions facing these inputs. The general equation for the aggregate production function is shown as:

$$Y = Y(L, CIM, EN), \tag{5.8}$$

where $Y_l > 0$, $Y_{cim} > 0$, and $Y_{en} > 0$.

The Equation for Labor Employed

It is assumed that the amount of labor supplied is positively related to the real wage rate and the amount of labor demanded is inversely related to the real wage rate. Because of the existence of high unemployment, the demographic constraint on the supply of labor does not play any role. The money wage rate is assumed to be determined by wage legislation and negotiation. Further, in the context of high unemployment in Guyana, it is postulated that the real wage rate paid is above the market clearing wage rate. The amount of labor employed, therefore, is determined by the demand for labor and the real wage rate paid. Enterprises are assumed to employ workers up to the point where their marginal product equals the real wage, regardless of whether there is an excess supply of labor. With the level of unemployment not fixed, the demand side of the labor market equilibrium condition is only met. The total demand for labor L^d, the labor supplied L^s, and labor employed, L, are shown respectively as:

$$L^d = L(W/P), \tag{5.9}$$

where $L^d_{w/p} < 0$,

$$L^s = L(W/P), \tag{5.10}$$

$$L = L^d \leq L^s. \tag{5.11}$$

The Amount of Imported Inputs Employed

In the market for imported inputs, enterprises are assumed to maximize profits by equating the real import price in domestic currency to the marginal product of these imports. Here the marginal revenue product of imported inputs represents the demand for inputs. The real import price is taken as given since Guyana acts as a price taker in the international markets. Overall, imported input demand is not a significant factor in domestic demand since these inputs are rationed because of the limited foreign exchange. The amount used is then determined on the supply side constrained by the capacity to import. The supply of these inputs, therefore, is assumed to depend on import prices, the import cost in terms of domestic currency, and the capacity to import. The demand, supply, and factor use relationships are shown as follows:

$$CIM^d = CIM(eP_i, P), \tag{5.12}$$

$$CIM^s = CIM(e, P_i, P, IC), \tag{5.13}$$

where $CIM^s_e < 0$; $CIM^s_{P_i} < 0$; $CIM^s_p > 0$; $CIM^s_{ic} > 0$.

$$CIM = CIM^s \leq CIM^d. \tag{5.14}$$

Model Structure

The system of equations representing the expenditure, monetary, production, and external sectors provide the basis for a relatively general but, at the same time, condensed model. To focus the analysis on output, the price level, and the balance of payments, the basic structure of the model is reduced to three equations, an aggregate demand (AD) equation, an aggregate supply (AS) equation, and a balance of payments (BP) equation from the equilibrium conditions in the expenditure, monetary, production, and external sectors as shown below:

$$
\left.
\begin{array}{ll}
Y - [C + I + G + EX - IM] = 0 & \xrightarrow{IS} \\
M^d - M^s = 0 & \xrightarrow{LM}
\end{array}
\right\} AD
$$

$$
\left.
\begin{array}{ll}
Y - Y(L, CIM, EN) = 0 & \longrightarrow \\
L - L^d(W/P) = 0 & \longrightarrow \\
CIM - CIM^s(e, P_i, P, IC) = 0 & \longrightarrow
\end{array}
\right\} AS
$$

$$
EX - IM + CI = 0 \quad \longrightarrow \quad BP
$$

where the three functions of the reduced basic model and their determinants in general form are as follows:

$$
AD: \quad Y = \phi_1(P, WH, I_0, \Delta Y, CIM, DC, DE, Y^*, P_e, IC, e, DE, P_i, M^s) \tag{5.15}
$$

$$
AS: \quad Y = \phi_2(P, w, IC, P_i, e, EN) \tag{5.16}
$$

$$
BP: \quad BP = \phi_3(Y, P, Y^*, e, P_i, IC, P_e, DE, CI) \tag{5.17}
$$

Using the specifications in equations (1) to (14) and the equilibrium conditions above,[5] are assumed to be these functions can be derived in differential form to allow comparative static exercises in the following manner. Equations (1) to (5) which represent the components of total demand for domestic output are equated with the flow of domestic output to determine goods market equilibrium in the form of an IS curve. Monetary equilibrium is derived by equating equations (6) and (7) to yield the LM curve. The solution to the IS-LM construct which combines goods market and monetary equilibria generates the AD equation as a functional relationship between the domestic price level and domestic output given the exchange rate, foreign prices, other exogenous influences, and some fiscal and monetary parameters. Equilibrium in the market for domestic goods occurs when the flow of output equals the demand for it as represented in the identity below:

$$Y \equiv C + I + G + EX - IM \tag{5.18}$$

Incorporating the specifications for C, I, G, EX, and IM into the expenditure identity yields the following condition for goods market equilibrium (that is, the IS function).

$$\begin{aligned} Y = \; & C(Y, WH) + I(I_o, \Delta Y, i, CIM, DC) \\ & + G(DE) + X(Y^*, P_e) - IM(Y, IC, DE, e, P_i, P) \end{aligned} \tag{5.19}$$

Differentiating totally this becomes

$$\begin{aligned} dY = \; & C_y dY + C_{wh} dWH + I_{I_0} dI_0 + I_{y_{t-1}} dY_{t-1} \\ & + I_y dY + I_i di + I_{cim} dCIM + I_{dc} dDC \\ & + G_{de} DE + X_{y^*} dY^* + X_{P_e} dP_e - IM_y dY \\ & - IM_{ic} dIC - IM_e de - IM_{de} dDE \\ & - IM_{P_i} dP_i - IM_p dP, \end{aligned} \tag{5.20}$$

and after rearranging terms we obtain

$$dY = \frac{\Delta_0}{(1 - C_y - I_y + M_y)} + \frac{I_i}{(1 - C_y - I_y + M_y)} di \tag{5.21}$$

where

$$\begin{aligned} \Delta_0 = \; & C_{wh} dWH + I_{I_0} dI_0 + I_{y_{t-1}} dY_{t-1} + I_{cim} dCIM \\ & + I_{dc} dDC + G_{de} dDE + X_{y^*} dY^* + X_{P_e} dP_e \\ & - IM_{ic} dIC - IM_e de - IM_{de} dDE \\ & - IM_{P_i} dP_i - IM_p dP \end{aligned}$$

The IS function is downward sloping in (Y, i) space and the slope is likely to be greater if there is a low interest elasticity of investment demand and a high income elasticity of import demand. Policy variables that have an impact on this function include the government deficit, the exchange rate, domestic credit creation, and the availability of imported inputs. An examination of the signs of the appropriate partial derivatives indicate that an increase in domestic credit or in the exchange rate (that is, a devaluation in the domestic currency price of foreign currency) cause the IS function to shift up to the right. The credit increase encourages greater expenditure while the higher exchange rate has a negative effect on import demand. An increase in the government deficit is assumed to result in a leftward shift of the IS curve because of reduced government consumption expenditures.

Monetary equilibrium exists when money demand equals the stock of money. In the context of open economy accounting relationships, the money supply is equivalent to domestic credit plus net foreign assets and this equilibrium is shown in terms of equations (5.6) and (5.7):

$$M^d(i, Y, P, e) = NFA + NDC \tag{5.22}$$

Totally differentiating this equilibrium condition and rearranging we have

$$dY = -\frac{M_i}{M_y}di + \frac{(dNFA + dNDC - IM_p dP - M_e de)}{M_y} \tag{5.23}$$

which is the monetary equilibrium function (the LM curve) in differential form (The superscript d is dropped in (5.23) since in equilibrium $M = M^d$).

The LM curve is upward sloping in (Y, i) space with the slope $\frac{di}{dY}$ depending on the form of the money demand function. Interest insensitivity of money demand, largely because of a policy of administered interest rates which witnessed infrequent changes in interest rates during the period under of this study, and a high income elasticity of demand for money would make for a steep LM curve. Shifts in this curve occur with changes in the price level, the exchange rate, domestic credit, and foreign reserves. The LM curve will shift to the right with an increase in the exchange rate (domestic currency per unit of foreign currency), increase in foreign reserves, and domestic credit while an increase in the price level (assuming a fixed nominal money supply) causes the curve to shift upward to the left. In the case of the movement to the right this indicates the need for income to increase so as to maintain monetary equilibrium as the money supply increases or as in the case of the exchange rate increase to offset the reduced money holdings which occur with the devaluation. In the case of a price level increase, at a given interest rate, income must fall so as to restore monetary equilibrium as an excess demand for money arises in order to undertake expenditures at the higher price level.

Rewriting the differential equations for the IS and LM curves in matrix notation with dY and di as the endogenous variables we have

$$\begin{bmatrix} (1 - C_y - I_y + M_y) & -I_i \\ M_y & M_i \end{bmatrix} \begin{bmatrix} dY \\ di \end{bmatrix} = \begin{bmatrix} \Delta_0 \\ \Gamma_0 \end{bmatrix}$$

where $\Gamma_0 = dNFA + dNDC - IM_p dP - M_e de$ and Δ_0 as defined above.

Using Cramer's rule to solve the above for dY, we obtain the AD function as the locus of combined expenditure and monetary equilibrium in (Y, P) space as

$$\begin{aligned} &dY[M_i(1 - C_y - I_y + M_y) + M_y I_i] \\ &\quad + (M_i IM_p + I_i IM_p)dP = \Delta_1 M_i + \Gamma_1 I_i \end{aligned} \tag{5.24}$$

where Δ_1 and Γ_1 are the resulting expressions after the terms with dP are taken out of Δ_0 and Γ_0 respectively.

The AS equation is derived by substituting the factor use equations in the production equation to get an output and price level relationship given the wage rate, the exchange rate, foreign prices, energy supply, and the capacity to import required capital and intermediate goods. In order to derive the AS function from the specified equations, we substitute equations (5.11) and (5.14) into equation (5.8) to get

$$Y = Y(L^d, CIM^s, EN) \tag{5.25}$$

Taking the differentials of Y, L^d, and CIM^s in (5.25), (5.9) and (5.13) we have respectively

$$dY = Y_L dL^d + Y_{cim} dCIM^s + Y_{en} dEN \tag{5.26}$$

$$dL^d = L^d_{w/p} \frac{Pdw - wdP}{P^2} \tag{5.27}$$

where $L^d_{w/p} = \frac{dL^d}{d(w/P)} < 0$.

$$dCIM^s = CIM^s_{ic} dIC + CIM^s_{P_i} + CIM^s_p dP + CIM^s_e de \tag{5.28}$$

Substituting (5.27) and (5.28) for dL^d and $dCIM^s$ in (5.25) and rearranging, we obtain the AS function in differential form as

$$\begin{aligned} dY = {} & \frac{Y_L}{P} L^d_{w/p} dw + (Y_{cim} CIM^s_p - \frac{Y_L}{P^2} L^d_{w/p} w) dP \\ & + Y_{cim}[CIM^s_e de + CIM^s_{ic} dIC + CIM^s_{P_i} dP_i] \\ & + Y_{en} dEN \end{aligned} \tag{5.29}$$

In order to consider how changes in the domestic economy affect the balance of payments, a separate equilibrium condition for the external sector will be included in the model. Because of the practice of exchange controls and an interest rate policy that establishes no relationship between the domestic and foreign interest rates, it is assumed that net capital inflows are exogenously determined. Because of the substantial reduction in capital inflows from the mid-1970s and the overwhelming influence of the current account on the overall balance of payments position, the focus on the external sector in this study will be on the current account position, (B), of the balance of payments.

Equilibrium in the current account of the balance of payments occurs when the value of exports of goods and services including unrequited transfers equals the value of imports of goods and services plus transfers. Export and import functions are included in the expenditure sector equilibrium and play a role in determining the AD equation as well as providing an avenue for disturbances outside of the economy to be incorporated in the model. In order to consider how changes in the economy will have an impact on equilibrium in the external sector, we use the exports and imports equations in (5.4) and (5.5) to derive the B function:

$$B = \quad B_{ex}(Y^*, P_e) \; - \; B_{im}(Y, IC, e, D, P_i, P) \qquad (5.30)$$

Totally differentiating this equation, replacing B_{ex} and B_{im} by B and rearranging we obtain

$$\begin{aligned} dB = \quad & B_{y^*} dY^* + B_{P_e} dP_e - B_y dY - B_{ic} dIC - B_e de \\ & - B_{de} dDE - B_p dP - B_{P_i} dP_i \end{aligned} \qquad (5.31)$$

In equilibrium $dB = 0$, and the B function is seen to be downward sloping in (Y, P) space.

These equations capture the main interactions identified as critical in explaining the behavior of output, the price level, and the current account balance in Guyana's economy. From equations (5.24), (5.29) and (5.31), the slopes of the AD, AS, and B functions are respectively

$$\frac{dP}{dY}\Big|_{AD} \quad = \quad -\frac{[M_i(1 - C_y - I_y + M_y) + M_y I_i]}{M_i IM_p + I_i IM_p} \quad < 0$$

$$\frac{dP}{dY}|_{AS} = -\frac{P^2}{wY_L L^d_{w/p}} + \frac{1}{P^2 Y_{cim} CIM^s_p} > 0$$

$$\frac{dP}{dY}|_B = -\frac{B_y}{B_p} < 0$$

A steep IS curve (goods market equilibrium) which indicates that the interest rate does not have considerable influence over investment demand is assumed to exist. This is due to a low interest elasticity of investment that results from the pessimistic expectations on the part of the private sector and the limited adherence to cost considerations in public sector investment. The implication of the steep IS curve is a steep AD curve. At the same time the policy of administered interest rates which has made money demand insensitive to the interest rate generates a steep LM curve (monetary equilibrium).

Thus, the AD curve is downward sloping in (Y, P) space and is likely to have a greater slope the steeper the IS and LM curves (from which the AD curve is derived) are. An examination of the partial derivatives in the expression for the slope the steepness of the AD curve rests on $(1 - C_y - I_y + M_y) > IM_p$ and $M_y > M_p$. Because of the open nature of the economy not only is the marginal propensity to import likely to be high, but the sensitivity of import demand to changes in the domestic price level is also likely to be low. The income elasticity of money demand is also likely to be greater than the responsiveness of money demand to price changes since the latter is subject to offsetting influences, namely the need to undertake greater levels of expenditures because of price level increases and the tendency to substitute away from money because of the higher opportunity cost of holding money.

Shifts in the AD curve occur as a result of changes in the exogenous variables. Concentrating on changes in the exchange rate (e), domestic credit (DC), the public sector deficit (DE), import capacity (IC), and the import price level (P_i), the AD curve is seen to shift up and to the right when e, DC, and P_i increases. When DE and IC increases, the AD curve shifts left.

The AS curve is upward sloping in (Y, P) space, and, because of the nature of the production determining forces in the economy, it is relatively steep with all other variables given. The presence of nominal wage rigidity, an excess supply of labor, and the existence of unused capacity of capital in the economy would seem to imply a flat AS curve. This results from the argument that a price level increase reduces real wages which induces an increase in employment and output under the assumption that diminishing returns to labor has not set in. However, there are offsetting forces because of the limited domestic technological capability and the low degree of substitutability between imported inputs and domestic resources. The implication of strong complementarity and therefore technical interdependence between imported inputs and domestic resources is that sustained output expansion requires that no factor be constraining. However, the prevalence of constraining factors in the form of available foreign exchange to purchase imported inputs and the delivery lags in trade flows result in slow output response to price level changes. In the short run therefore a low price elasticity of supply is assumed to exist.

Variables that shift the AS curve include those that affect the cost of production. Examples include the domestic currency price of foreign currency (e), the foreign price level (P_i), and the wage rate (w). Any increase in costs implies an increase in the price level for the initial level of output to be maintained. Thus, an increase in w, e, or P_i, shifts the AS curve up and to the left in (Y, P) space, while an increase in IC or EN will shift the AS curve to the right.

The B curve is downward sloping in (Y, P) space. The negative slope indicates that an increase in income which worsens the trade balance can be offset by a fall in the domestic price level. Points to the right of the B curve represent combinations of Y and P which generate current account deficits, while points to the left of the B curve are associated with deficits. The slope of the B curve is determined by the magnitudes of the partial derivatives B_y and B_p with the former's magnitudes likely to be greater. Variables that shift the B curve are the export price level (P_e), import capacity (IC), the exchange rate (e), the import price level (P_i), the public sector deficit (DE), and domestic productive capacity (Y^*). An examination of the signs of the partial derivatives indicate that an increase in DE,

e, and P_I cause the B curve to shift to the left while an increase in Y^*, IC, P_e shift the B curve to the right.

Assuming linear forms for the AD, AS, and B functions, the model can be set out in the context of a diagram as in Figure 5.1 to illustrate some of these results. Starting from a position such as E in Figure 5.1, where the aggregate economy clears with the current account of the balance of payments in equilibrium, we will consider the impact of shocks in the system originating in the external sector, the domestic monetary and expenditure sectors, and through changes in the exchange rate.

External Shocks

Changes in the import price level assuming all other things constant have a terms of trade effect on the balance of payments. An increase in the foreign price level of imports, for example, deteriorates the terms of trade which means a given level of exports cannot maintain current levels of imports, and output must fall for the balance on current account to remain unchanged. The increase in import prices also raises production costs and shifts the AS line to the left. At the same time, however, the effect is to shift the AD line to the right with the shift being stronger the higher the price elasticities of demand for exports and for import substitutes. Both of these possibilities are unlikely because of the contractual arrangements that exist for the major exports as well as the weak degree of substitution between domestic and foreign goods.

While the short run equilibrium point for output depends on whether the AD shift is greater than the AS shift, there is an upward pressure on the domestic price level. At the same time, depending on the new output level in relation to the shift leftwards of the B line, the current account situation can lead to a deficit or a surplus. In the case of production declining faster than domestic spending the current account deficit automatically increases and, if this continues, an unstable situation can arise whereby the external imbalance cannot be eliminated.

Another type of external disturbance could be a decrease in foreign demand for the domestic output which will shift both the

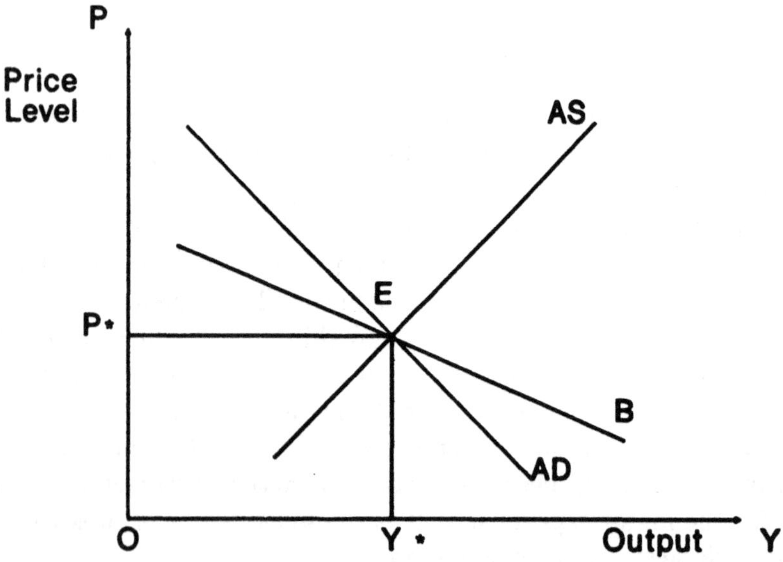

Figure 5.1 Overall equilibrium

AD and B lines to the left, but with the latter experiencing a greater shift, thus causing a current account deficit and reduced output.

A Domestic Monetary Expansion

The effect of an exogenous increase in the domestic money supply is to shift the AD line to the right. Starting from the initial equilibrium point E, in Figure 5.2, the new short term equilibrium point is at T. With a steep AS line, the rightward movement of the AD line will produce a relatively large increase in the price level and a relatively small increase in output. This in turn will likely result in a current account deficit.

An Increase in the Public Sector Deficit

An increase in the public sector deficit causes the AD line to shift right. At the same time higher deficits are associated with higher levels of imports which causes a leftward shift in the B line. The combined effect of these shifts with a relatively steep AS line will produce a relatively small increase in output, substantial price level change and a current account deficit.

An Increase in the Exchange Rate (Devaluation)

A devaluation of the exchange rate increases the cost of production and causes the AS line to shift to the left. The B line can shift to the left or right depending on the responsiveness of exports and imports to the change in the domestic currency price of foreign currency. With a devaluation, the domestic currency value of given levels of exports and imports would both rise but the final outcome depends on how large is the substitution effect on import demand as the relative price of imports increase. The AD line will shift to the right if there is a reduction in the level of imports and domestic goods are substituted for imported commodities, particularly in the areas of private and government consumption.

The preceding discussion indicates that disturbances in a number of the exogenous variables cause two or all three of the functions to shift at the same time. In particular the analysis implies that

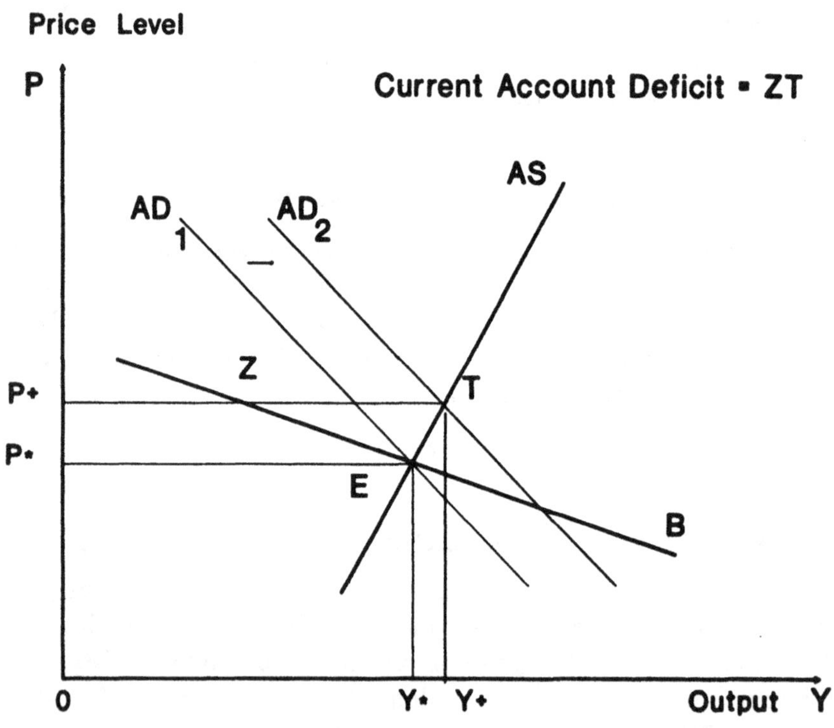

Figure 5.2 The Effect of an Increase in the Money Supply

when the public sector deficit increases, the B and AD curves shift, so that Y and P move in the same direction and, depending upon the slopes of both functions and the relative magnitude of the shifts, a possibility exists for a current account deficit or surplus to occur. Also, when the exchange rate is devalued, the B and AS functions shift to the left while the AD function shifts to the right. Thus, Y and P may move in the same or in opposite directions, and the possibility of a current account deficit exists. In the case of an increase in import capacity, the AS and B functions shift to the right while the AD function shifts left. While the current account position can improve or worsen, Y and P can move in opposite directions.

A more rigorous treatment of the effects of changes in exogenous variables, in particular the policy instruments that have been utilized in recent years by the policy makers in Guyana is possible through algebraic analysis. In order to conduct this type of comparative static exercise, the solutions for dY, dP, and dB will first be derived, incorporating the various kinds of interactions that have been identified earlier. In conducting this exercise, we take as given the skill and quantity of available labor and capital, techniques of production, consumer tastes, and institutional arrangements.

Rewriting the differential forms of AD, AS, and B in matrix notation we get

$$\begin{bmatrix} M_i(1-C_y-I_y+M_y)+M_yI_i & (M_iIM_p+I_iIM_p) & 0 \\ P^2 & (wY_LL^d_{w/p}-Y_{cim}CIM^s_p) & 0 \\ +B_y & +B_p & 1 \end{bmatrix} \begin{bmatrix} dY \\ dP \\ dB \end{bmatrix} = \begin{bmatrix} \Delta \\ \Gamma \\ \Theta \end{bmatrix}$$

where

$$\Delta = M_i\left[C_{wh}dWH + I_{I_0}dI_0 + I_{y_{t-1}}dY_{t-1} + I_{cim}dCIM + I_{dc}dDC + G_{de}dDE + X_{y^*}dY^* + X_{P_e}dPe - IM_{ic}dIC - IM_ede - IM_{de}dDE - IM_{P_i}dP_i\right] + I_i[dNFA + dNDC - M_ede]$$

$$\Gamma = PY_LL^d_{w/p}dw + P^2Y_{cim}[CIM^s_{ic}dIC + CIM^s_{Pi} + CIM^s_ede) + P^2Y_{en}dEN$$

$$\Theta = B_{y^*}dY^* + B_{P_e}dPe - B_{P_i}dPi - B_{ic}dIC - B_e de + B_{de}dDE$$

and using Cramer's rule the solution of the model for the three endogenous variables are:

$$dY = \frac{\Delta[wY_L L^d_{w/p} - Y_{cim}CIM^s_p] - \Gamma(M_i IM_p + I_i IM_p)}{G} \quad (5.32)$$

$$dP = \frac{\Gamma[M_i(1 - C_y - I_y + M_y) + M_y I_i] - \Delta(P^2)}{G} \quad (5.33)$$

$$dB = \frac{\begin{array}{l}\{\Delta[P^2 B_p - B_y(wY_L L^d_{w/p} - Y_{cim}CIM^s_p)] \\ - \Gamma[B_p\{M_i(1 - C_y - I_y + M_y) + M_y I_i\} \\ - B_y(M_i IM_p + I_i IM_p)] + \Theta[(M_i(1 - C_y \\ - I_y + M_y) + M_y I_y))[wY_L L^d_{w/p} - Y_{cim}CIM^s_p] \\ - P^2(M_i IM_p + I_i IM_p)]\}\end{array}}{G} \quad (5.34)$$

where

$$G = (wY_L L^d_{w/p} - Y_{cim}CIM^s_p)[M_i(1 - C_y - I_y) + M_y I_i] - P^2(M_i IM_p + I_i IM_p) > 0$$

Considering the exogenous variables in terms of exchange-rate policy (e), fiscal policy (DE), monetary policy (M), import capacity (IC), and the import price level (P_i), and taking the derivatives of the endogenous variables dY, dP, and dB with respect to these exogenous variables gives the short run comparative static results of the model as shown in Table 5.2.

TABLE 5.2

Effects of Changes in DE, e, IC, dM, dP_i on Y, P, and B

	dDE	de	dIC	dM	dP_i
dY	+	?	?	+	?
dP	+	+	–	+	+
dB	–	?	?	–	?

An increase in Y, P, or B which is denoted by (+), a decrease shown by (–) while the ambiguous cases designated by (?) depend on the magnitude of the shifts and the respective slopes of the AD, AS, and B functions.

These results indicate that there is a diagnostic problem with regards to policy suggestions. The list of unconditional proposals for policy makers is generally limited. This idea is reinforced when the policies that have been tried in recent years in Guyana are examined within the framework of the model. Thus, in the previous chapter it was indicated that the more recent approach involved the use of policy instruments such as the exchange rate and reduction in the public sector deficit. This approach was not very successful. Through an inversion of the procedure that was adopted to conduct the comparative static exercise, the required changes in policy instruments that can lead to desired changes in target variables can be investigated to provide insights into the lack of success. In this case the changes in the target variables (previously the endogenous variables, dY and dB) become the knowns and the system is solved to obtain the required changes in instruments which are now the unknowns.

The model is the same as before, consisting of the AD, AS, and B equations, but for the present analysis the variables dY and dB are treated as exogenously determined targets (with dP as an unknown determined by the system) and the instruments being de, dDE and dIC. Assuming that changes in the remaining exogenous variables would be zero, the matrix representation obtained through this inversion of variables process is:

$$\begin{bmatrix} -M_iIM_e & M_iG_{de}-M_iIM_{de} & -M_iIM_{ic} \\ P^2Y_{cim}CIM_e^s & 0 & P^2Y_{cim}CIM_{ic}^s \\ B_e & B_{de} & B_{ic} \end{bmatrix} \begin{bmatrix} de \\ dDE \\ dIC \end{bmatrix} = \begin{bmatrix} \delta \\ \gamma \\ \theta \end{bmatrix}$$

where

$$\begin{aligned} \delta &= [M_i(1 - C_y - I_y + M_y) + M_yI_i]dY + (M_iIM_p + I_iIM_p)dP \\ \gamma &= \quad P^2dY + Y_LL^d_{w/p}wdP \\ \theta &= \quad -B_ydY - B_pdP - dB + B_{y^*}dY^* + B_{P_e}dP_e - B_{P_i}dP_i \end{aligned}$$

Using Cramer's rule and solving for de, dDE, and dIC we have

$$de = \frac{\begin{aligned}&\{\delta[-B_d(P^2Y_{cim}CIM_{ic}^s]\\ &-\gamma[B_{ic}(M_iG_{de} - M_iIM_d) - B_{de}(M_iIM_{ic})]\\ &+\theta(M_iG_{de} - M_iIM_{de})P^2Y_{cim}CIM_{ic}^s\}\end{aligned}}{G}$$

$$dDE = \frac{\begin{aligned}&\{-\delta[B_eP^2Y_{cim}CIM_{ic}^s\\ &- B_{ic}(P^2Y_{cim}CIM_e^s)] + \gamma[B_{ic}(-M_iIM_e)\\ &+ B_e(-M_iIM_{ic})] - \theta[P^2Y_{cim}CIM_{ic}^s\\ &(-M_iIM_e) + M_iIM_{ic}(P^2Y_{cim}CIM_e^s)]\}\end{aligned}}{G}$$

$$dIC = \frac{\begin{aligned}&\{\delta[B_dP^2Y_{cim}CIM_e^s]\\ &-\gamma[B_d(-M_iIM_e) - B_e(M_iG_{de} - M_iIM_{de})]\\ &+\theta[(-M_iG_{de} + M_iIM_{de})P^2Y_{cim}CIM_e^s]\}\end{aligned}}{G}$$

where G is the determinant of the 3×3 matrix above. The sign of the partial derivatives of an instrument with respect to a target will indicate the direction in which the instrument must change if one of the target variables is to be moved in a desired direction while the other target variable remains unchanged. An inspection of the partial derivatives of each of the instruments e, DE, and IC with respect to changes in targets Y and B indicates ambiguous outcomes in all cases.

The implication of these results is that policy proposals must be viewed as being conditional upon the extent and direction of influences over the behavior of the AD, AS, and B functions. It is in this context that a strong case exists for greater reliance on empirical analysis as a means of determining which outcomes are more likely than others. This requires an investigation of a number of hypotheses and issues that have been suggested in the present analysis. These include the notion of a low interest sensitivity of money demand and investment demand and the hypothesis that the responsiveness of the AD and AS functions to domestic price level changes is low. In addition, the relative impact of various shocks on the three endogenous variables of the model needs to be ascertained before any firm statements can be made about the consequences of introducing the policy measures that are available to policy makers.

Notes

1. In the case of Guyana, for example, the incremental output capital ratio has been extremely low and even negative in some years during the period 1960–1984.

2. These conditions are discussed in D. Fisher, *Macroeconomic Theory: A Survey* (London: Macmillan, 1983).

3. The indications of this are in the unwillingness of banks (especially the branches of foreign banks) to make loans for projects which may either have long gestation periods or viewed as inherently risky (e.g. small scale agricultural projects) in spite of government support for these kinds of activities. Working capital loans primarily to firms involved in import trade or the large export firms, and holding of treasury bills accounted for the major portion of bank lending.

4. The central bank does not lend to the private sector, and other liabilities and equity are assumed to be absorbed in these figures.

5. For purposes of simplicity expected variables have been replaced by the actual variables.

6

An Econometric Model for Guyana: Estimation, Simulation, and Implications

Introduction

A macroeconometric model for Guyana's economy constructed in this chapter is based on the theoretical model in Chapter 5 and allows causal interpretation of the equations in the system. The discussion also illustrates the transition from a theoretical model to an econometric model. As Haavelmo (1944) pointed out,

in general observed economic data are not generated from experiments that would allow the economic phenomena to be artificially isolated from "other influences" which is ideally what is required for the verification of economic hypotheses. Under these circumstances, according to Haavelmo, the task is to "try to adjust our theories to reality as it appears before us ... try to choose a theory and a design of experiments to go with it, in such a way that the resulting data would be those which we get by passive observation of reality."[1]

It is in the sense of incorporating a proper design of experiments that Spanos (1986) contends that, in addition to economic theory, the nature of the sampling distribution and probabilistic structure of the underlying data must be considered when specifying an econometric model. In particular, this takes the form of assumptions about the probability and sampling model in terms of the observable random variables rather than the more conventional assumptions about the error term. From the standpoint of empirical econometric work, the main implication of the emphasis on data related assumptions is that there is greater need for statistical misspecification testing. In the context of the linear regression model, for instance, (the most widely used statistical model in econometric modeling), this means examining whether the underlying assumptions of normality, linearity, homoscedasticity, parameter time invariance, and independent sampling are valid for the data at hand. In this regard the design of an econometric model and the assessment of the properties of the resulting empirical estimates are discussed together with the implications of data related issues for modeling.

Against this background this chapter in the following section provides a description of the data collection procedures used to obtain the published data on Guyana and considers the implications for the formulation of the model. The next section considers the stochastic equations for the aggregate demand, aggregate supply, and balance of payments function respectively and discusses the issues pertaining to statistical inference (estimation, specification testing, and prediction in the context of a simultaneous equation model). The ordinary least squares (OLS) and two-stage least squares (TSLS) techniques are then used to derive coefficient estimates for the structural equations as well as to conduct diagnostic tests of the assumptions. The latter exercise involves testing for departures from multivariate normality, linearity, homoscedasticity, parameter time invariance, and independence of the sampling model. A discussion of the results will then follow in relation to the main hypotheses specified in Chapter 5, with an emphasis on the multiplier properties of the model. A third section will then focus on forecasting issues and simulation exercises as a check to the econometric results. A final section discusses the implications for policy.

Data Collection and Measurement

The procedures for data collection take into account the unavailability of information for some of the variables under consideration either before 1960 or after 1984. The principal data sources are the publications and estimates provided by the Central Bank, the Statistical Bureau within the Ministry of Economic Development, the Ministry of Finance, and the State Planning Secretariat of Guyana. Additional sources are the publications of international agencies including the United Nations Yearbook of National Income Statistics, the World Debt Tables published by the World Bank, and the

Balance of Payments Yearbook, International Financial Statistics and Government Financial Statistics published by the International Monetary Fund.

Two broad accounting frameworks are used to generate the published estimates for most of the aggregate variables used in this study—the national income accounts and the asset-liability accounts of the financial system. The provision of estimates within these frameworks generally follows the guidelines established by the United Nations System of National Accounts (SNA). Some institutional features, sampling impurities, and observational errors, however, have given rise to great variability in coverage and accuracy in the published data. One important contributory factor in this regard has been the absence of comprehensive coverage of the existing variables in a common source or set of sources which has resulted in significant discontinuities and definitional inconsistencies in some of the data.

Identifying the precise nature of data limitations and the variables which are most highly subject to measurement error becomes an important consideration in the empirical analysis. While, this in itself is an enormous task, for purposes of this study some insight is provided from a discussion of the procedures utilized and the reliability of the available estimates in relation to (1) National Accounts Statistics (2) Balance of Payments Statistics (3) Financial and Monetary Statistics (4) Fiscal Accounts and (5) Price Data.

Within national income accounting, the use of income, expenditure, and product statistics is the standard way of deriving aggregate estimates of these variables. Each of these approaches provides an alternative way of measuring total output, and in theory, as long as a consistent set of prices is used for valuation throughout, these estimates are expected to be consistent. It is their combined use, however, that has proved to be most useful in practice.

While the procedure adopted in Guyana is indeed one of combining elements of the three approaches, the product (value added) approach forms the basis for deriving the gross domestic product (GDP) with a limited role affixed to the income and to a lesser extent the expenditure approaches. In the case of export activities the value added estimates are relatively easy to obtain from the organized accounting systems of exporting firms. Estimates for non-exports tend to be a problem, however, since these depend on output projections, reporting, or survey responses, which have become increasingly deficient in coverage over the past two decades. The value added estimates for non-agricultural activities with domestic end uses, for instance, are based on sample surveys and periodic reports provided by the established firms. But the closure of some of these established private businesses combined with non-reporting by some firms and limited monitoring by the statistical gathering agencies due to personnel problems have resulted in a highly suspect data base.

In the case of non-export agriculture, value added for a given year is based on output projections that are extrapolations of figures of the preceding years. In the context of sharp swings in the output levels in the farming sector, the observed data either underestimate or overestimate the actual levels of production. Service sector activities also pose problems for data gathering of a conceptual and practical nature. Because of difficulties pertaining to measurement, the estimates of value added in the service sector are based on the income approach with imputations of value added employed where factor payments are not clearly defined. Under the assumption that the payment received by factors reflects their contribution to output and because labor is the primary factor used in the services sector, value added is measured in terms of compensation to labor.

In addition to the limited scope for checking the consistency of the published GDP figures, the heavy reliance on the value added approach poses a peculiar problem for national income accounting as could be illustrated in the case of the bauxite industry. This is the possibility of non-positive value added. In 1983, for example, the value added of the bauxite industry was reported to be zero because the intermediate production costs turned out to be greater than the value of output sold. This resulted from negligible export sales due to a collapse in the external demand for Guyana's bauxite. At the same time, even though work continued in the removal of the overburden which then allows bauxite mining, there was little mining because of the limited storage capacity. If the income approach were used in reconciling the national income accounts, then there would have been a more accurate way of valuing the factor services utilized in the bauxite industry in that period. This problem becomes an important consideration when output levels are very much below capacity and when export sales are low due to unforeseen external market conditions as has been the experience for Guyana since the early 1980s.

Apart from these problems in measurement of recorded activities, there is the consideration that observed GDP does not cover total economic activity, for instance, work within households and voluntary work, because of the difficulty in obtaining such information. The magnitude of the excluded activities is compounded when it is considered that some activities which in principle can and should be included in the GDP estimate are not, because of deliberate efforts to conceal them from data gathering agencies. This latter type encompasses marketed and non-marketed activities in the parallel economy as well as those arising from tax evasion. As the extent of these unrecorded activities has grown, there has been some attempt to make adjustments to the official data, for example, in determining the value of certain balance of payments transactions, though this has not been systematically attempted. Together with the problems that characterize the derivation of total value added, there are questions about the decomposition of total output in terms of the standard categories of final expenditure. Aggregation of the value added obtained from the estimates of the commodity and services sector yield a figure for total domestic product which is then combined with the fiscal accounts, balance of payments statistics, and a commodity flow estimate of private investment to generate private consumption as a residual. However, the observed data on personal consumption are unsatisfactory since they are obtained as a residual and will tend to reflect all the errors that may have occurred in the other components. In addition, the residual method of derivation does not permit the breakdown of household spending by object of expenditure.

The balance of payments statistics provide data on the current account and capital account transactions but, because of the growth of smuggling, the figures on exports and imports do not correctly reflect the magnitude of current account transactions. In the case of non-factor services, for example, foreign exchange for travel when obtained from the parallel market inflates the magnitude of travel expenditures, though this is not adequately represented in the official statistics. Similarly, with the uncertainty of the investment climate and the resulting increase in capital flight through unofficial channels, the existing capital account data do not capture all the relevant transactions.

Among the macroeconomic accounts, the monetary survey provides the most reliable and complete statistics. The balance sheets of the central bank, commercial banks, and other financial institutions provide information on critical variables such as the money supply, domestic credit, and foreign assets and liabilities. Because of the relatively detailed coverage, it is possible to conducted financial programming exercises which seek to ensure consistency among various policy targets subject to existing financial constraints.

The fiscal accounts are based on data obtained from central government accounts, the accounts of local authorities and the financial statements of public corporations. The main problem with these data is the difficulty faced in classifying some expenditure items under current or capital expenditures which would allow for a proper separation of public sector consumption and investment expenditures. For example, interest payments and loan repayments are actually combined instead of the former being treated as current expenditure and the latter as capital expenditure. For the past years as well, expenditures on the national service were treated as capital expenditures whereas the bulk of those was in the form of current transactions, the fact which tended to exaggerate the level of public investment. (Since 1979, however, this particular problem was corrected.)

In relation to price level data, the most consistently published indicator of price movements in Guyana is the Consumer Price Index (CPI). These data are available monthly, quarterly, and yearly from 1960 onwards in the form of an urban price index, a rural price index and an overall consumer price index which is a weighted average of the rural and urban indices. The base year for the annual indices is 1970, and this poses a number of problems for the use of the existing series as measures of price behavior since the late 1970s. Many of the items covered in the standard 1970 bundle have become unavailable to the average consumer, with the import and price controls that resulted in the disappearance of some items and, in most instances, the existence of severe shortages.

The approach that was adopted by the agency responsible for constructing these indices was to look at the prices of substitute commodities for those commodities that were prohibited and to use the official price for other items even though they may be carrying much higher prices in the blackmarkets. The effect of such an approach was to maintain the overall price index at artificially low levels. Thus, while the housing component of the CPI showed the slowest increase in the CPI between 1970 and 1977 because of the existence of a Rent Control Act, this highly understated the actual rents paid by tenants. To the extent that the CPI is used to deflate nominal aggregates in order to generate real values for these variables, then these real magnitudes may be overstated as well. There are no other price indices which are published in Guyana, though it is possible to obtain estimates of the implicit GDP deflator in the UN Yearbook and the International Financial Statistics which is an average of the indices of various components of total output. However, since the CPI is the only series that provides the longest period of coverage, in this study it has been used as the deflator in converting nominal values into real values.

On the basis of the analysis of the published data, there are some implications for better ways of collecting and processing information. In the case of personal consumption, for example, the generated data can be obtained either by the direct method which involves inflating the data collected by sample surveys or by the commodity flow method which is based on information on the supply of goods and services from domestic and foreign sources and its allocation to household consumption purposes. In general, there is greater need for a more integrated approach toward data collection which not only optimizes the use of limited qualified personnel but requires the adoption of alternative ways of collecting data aimed at ensuring greater consistency, accuracy, and coverage.

The varied sources of measurement problems and their pervasiveness for most variables inherent in the published aggregates make it difficult to ascertain whether the direction of bias is upward or downward for the generated data on individual variables. The implications for corrective procedures, therefore, are not straightforward, and serious questions are raised about the statistical significance and economic plausibility of parameter estimates. Under these circumstances, an examination of the statistical adequacy of the model which uses the observed data becomes a much more important consideration if exercises in structural modeling and theory testing are to be conducted. In particular, for the linear regression model this entails testing the validity of assumptions such as normality, linearity, homoscedasticity, parameter time invariance, and independent sampling for the data at hand. Some specific tests exist in the econometric literature for examining the validity of these assumptions, and the usual procedure is for the null hypothesis to refer to the particular assumption that is being tested while the alternative hypothesis refers to departures from the null. Since the null is uniquely defined but the alternative can take numerous and therefore non-unique forms, the choice in a test is between rejecting or not rejecting the null rather than accepting the alternative.

Testing for Departures from Sampling and Probability Model Assumptions

(i) The Independent Sample Assumption

The independent sample assumption implies that the ordering of the observations for endogenous and predetermined variables plays no role in the statistical analysis and results of an econometric model. Two broad approaches exist in the econometric literature with regard to modeling the source of a non-independent sample. There is the autocorrelation approach which interprets the dependence in the sample as due to error temporal correlation. The alternative is that non-independence is due to temporal dependence among the observable random variables with the error term treated as the non-systematic component of the model. Because the data used in this study is in time series form the latter modeling strategy is assumed to a plausible one.[2] As Spanos (1986) argues testing for independence may be organized around the significance of the parameters in the following forms of a linear regression model.

$$y_t = \beta' x_t + u_t, \qquad t = 1, 2, \ldots, T \tag{6.1}$$

and

$$y_t = \beta_0' x_t + \sum_{i=1}^{m} (\alpha_i y_{t-i} + \beta_i' x_{t-i}) + u_t, \qquad t > m \quad t = 1, 2, \ldots, T \tag{6.2}$$

where T refers to the sample size, k is the number of unknown parameters in (6.1), m refers to the maximum lag for the lagged variables in (6.2), $\beta'(=\beta_0') \equiv (\beta_1, \beta_2, \ldots, \beta_k)$, $\beta_i' \equiv (\beta_1', \ldots, \beta_m')$, and α_i represent unknown parameters, x_t is a matrix of observable variables, and y_t represents observations on the dependent variable.Within the framework of (6.1) and (6.2) the assumption of independence among the observable random variables implies testing the hypotheses

$$H_0 : \alpha = 0 \qquad \text{and } \beta^* = 0$$

against

$$H_1 : \alpha \neq 0 \qquad \text{or } \beta^* \neq 0.$$

where $\alpha \equiv (\alpha_1, \ldots, \alpha_m)'$, $\beta^* \equiv (\beta_1', \ldots, \beta_m')'$.

In view of the linearity of the restrictions an F-test type procedure is appropriate and for small samples Spanos (1986) suggests the following test statistic

$$\Gamma(y) = \frac{RRSS - URSS}{URSS} \left(\frac{T - K(m+1)}{mK} \right)$$

where $RRSS$ refers to the residual sum of squares for the restricted form of the model as in (6.1) and $URSS$ the residual sum of squares of the unrestricted model in the form of (6.2). T is the sample size, K is the number of regressors including the constant term in the restricted model, and m is the number of lags in the unrestricted model.

Considering this test for the output (AS), price level (AD), and the current account balance (B) equations used in this study—these specifications are explained later in the chapter—the restricted model equations take the forms:

$$\begin{aligned} AS: \quad \hat{Y}_t &= \alpha_0 + \alpha_1 P_t - \alpha_2 RE_t + \alpha_3 EN_t \\ &\quad - \alpha_4 DL_t - \alpha_5 P_{i_t} + \alpha_6 IC_t + u_t \end{aligned} \tag{6.3}$$

$$\begin{aligned} AD: \ \hat{P}_t &= \beta_0 - \beta_1 Y_t + \beta_2 Y_{t-1} + \beta_3 M_t + \beta_4 DE_t \\ &\quad - \beta_5 IC_t - \beta_6 RE_t + \beta_7 TT_t + \beta_8 CIM_t + u_t \end{aligned} \tag{6.4}$$

$$B: \quad \hat{B}_t = \theta_0 + \theta_1 RE_t - \theta_2 Y_t + \theta_3 Y_{t-1} \\ - \theta_4 IC_t - \theta_5 P_t + \theta_6 XD_t + u_t \tag{6.5}$$

where Y is real output (GNP), P is the aggregate price level, B is the current account position of the balance of payments, RE is the exchange rate deflated by the domestic price level, EN is the amount of electricity used by businesses, DL is the amount of mandays lost due to strikes, P_i is the import price index, IC is import capacity which is measured by foreign exchange receipts, M is broad money supply (currency in circulation plus demand, savings, and time deposits), DE is the public sector deficit, TT is the ratio of the import price level to the export price level, CIM is imports of capital and intermediate goods, and XD is external debt denominated in Guyana dollars.

Choosing a maximum lag of 1, because of a degrees of freedom problem, the unrestricted model equations for AS, AD, and B include the variables in (6.3), (6.4), and (6.5) respectively and these variables lagged up to 1 period.[3] Using the estimation period 1961 to 1984 the $RRSS$ and $URSS$ for each of the equations were as follows[4]

$$AS: RRSS = 46657.9 \qquad URSS = 19281.3$$

$$AD: RRSS = 938.1 \qquad URSS = 445.5$$

$$B: RRSS = 65940.8 \qquad URSS = 44802$$

Given these values for each equation with $T = 24$, $m = 1$, and using the appropriate number of regressors (K), from (6.1), (6.2) and (6.3) the test statistic yield the values

$$\Gamma(AS) = 2.02, \quad \Gamma(AD) = 0.73, \quad \Gamma(B) = 0.67$$

and with critical values at the 5 percent level and degrees of freedom (10,7), (6,9) and (10,7) being 3.64, 3.37, and 3.64 respectively, the null hypothesis is not rejected. That is, the independence assumption is not found to be invalid.

(ii) The Assumption of Normality

Multivariate normality is an important assumption that is often made about the probability model underlying the samples used in econometric modeling. The main consequences of non-normality lie with those tests which depend on the distribution of the sample variance such as some heteroscedasticity and structural change tests. The available tests for departures from normality include parametric and non-parametric tests with the latter type in general being asymptotic tests. In the context of the relatively small sample that is being used in this study, greater reliance is placed on an appropriate non-parametric test. In particular, Shapiro and Wilk (1965) developed the following analysis of variance test for normality for small sample situations.

$$W(y) = \left[\sum_{t=1}^{n} a_{tT}(\hat{u}_{(T-t+1)} - \hat{u}_{(t)})\right]^2 / \sum_{t=1}^{T} \hat{u}_t^2$$

where T is the sample size, $\hat{u}_{(1)} \leq \hat{u}_{(2)} \leq \cdots \leq \hat{u}_{(T)}$ are the ordered (from small to large values) residuals derived from the estimation of a regression model (y) using the sample that is being tested for normality, and a_{tT} is a weight coefficient tabulated by Shapiro and Wilk for sample sizes $2 < T \leq 50$. The weight coefficient is derived from the mean and covariance generated from an underlying normal distribution for different sample sizes. Performing the regressions for equations (6.3), (6.4), and (6.5), ordering the residuals for each equation in ascending order, and then applying the test statistic, the following values were deduced for the aggregate supply (AS), aggregate demand (AD), and the current account balance (B) equations respectively.

$$W(AS) = 0.956, \quad W(AD) = 0.970 \quad W(B) = 1.00$$

Using the rejection region $C_1 = \{y : W < c_\alpha\}$ where c_α is tabulated by Shapiro and Wilk for different levels of significance it is seen that the computed W for each equation is greater than the critical value (c) of 0.95 at the 50 percent point of the null distribution which is taken to be an acceptable indication by Shapiro and Wilk (1965:606) that the null hypothesis of normality is not rejected.

(iii) The Assumption of Linearity

The implications of non-linearity are serious with regard to the properties of parameter estimates and the sample variance since these would tend to be biased and inconsistent estimators of the true coefficients and the population variance. There is also the added consideration that the testing and prediction results have been shown to be generally invalid when there is non-linearity. In testing for non-linearity, the null hypothesis is that the dependent variable is linearly related to the predetermined variables. Analogous to tests for linear restrictions, an F-type test is used to test for linearity using the residual sums of squares of the specified model and an auxiliary regression which includes the original variables and their cross products. These cross products may be second order or even third order terms, for example if there are k regressors (x_{kt}) where $t \in T$ and T is the sample size in the original model second order terms would be $x_{it}x_{jt} \quad i \geq j, \quad i,j,= 2,3,\ldots,k$. Testing for linearity involves testing the significance of the parameters of the cross product terms. The F-test takes the form

$$FT(Y) = \frac{RRSS - URSS}{URSS}\left(\frac{T - K^*}{m}\right),$$

where $RRSS$ and $URSS$ refer to the residual sum of squares for a restricted and unrestricted model respectively; T is the sample size, K^* is the number of parameters in the unrestricted model, and m refers to the number of restrictions equal to the difference between the number of parameters in the restricted and unrestricted models.

The restricted model refers to equations (6.3), (6.4), and (6.5) while each equation for the unrestricted model has the variables in the restricted equations and some cross products of these variables. Because of collinearity among some variables and a degrees of freedom problem not all possible second order cross products were included in deriving the $URSS$ for each endogenous variable. In particular, the following forms were taken for the unrestricted equations:

$$AS : \hat{y}_t = \beta_0' x_t + \alpha_1 REEN_t + \alpha_2 REIC_t + \alpha_3 ENP_{it} + u_t \tag{6.6}$$

$$AD : \hat{P}_t = \beta_1' z_t + \theta_1 YM_t + \theta_2 YDE_t + \theta_3 ICDE_t + \theta_4 DERE_t + u_t \tag{6.7}$$

$$B : \hat{B}_t = \beta_2' h_t + \beta_1 YRE_t + \beta_2 REIC_t + \beta_3 DERE_t + u_t \tag{6.8}$$

where $\beta_0' x_t$, $\beta_1' z_t$, and $\beta_2' h_t$ refer to the right hand side terms in equations (6.3), (6.4), and (6.5) respectively with the β's representing vectors of unknown parameters and x_t, z_t, and h_t matrices of the regressors. The residual sum of squares for each of the estimated unrestricted equations are $URSS(AS) = 25132.7$, $URSS(AD) = 915.7$, $URSS(B) = 48372.8$, which, when taken with the $RRSS$ obtained earlier for the aggregate supply (AS), aggregate demand (AD), and current account balance (B) equations, with $T = 23$, and the appropriate values for K^* and m yield the following

$FT(AS) = 2.56$, $FT(AD) = 0.06$, $FT(B) = 1.08$.

At the 5 percent level, with degrees of freedom of (13,3), (10,4), and (13,3) the critical values for rejection of the null hypothesis for the AS, AD, and B equations respectively are 8.73, 5.96, and 8.73 which indicates that the assumption of linearity is not rejected in each of these equations.

(iv) The Assumption of Homoscedasticity

The assumption of homoscedasticity is that the population variance is free from influence by the predetermined variables. This assumption is closely related to the assumption that the sample distribution is multivariate normal. The implication of heteroscedasticity is that the parameter estimates might be inefficient even if they are unbiased and consistent. A variety of measures exist for testing for departures from homoscedasticity. One of the commonly used tests for homoscedasticity is that proposed by White[5] (1980) which is derived in the following manner. First, perform regressions for the model at hand using the sample that is being tested for homoscedasticity. Second, obtain the residuals, $\hat{u}_t$, using the regression results and square them to get $\hat{u}_t^2$. Next, regress the squared residuals against all the variables in the first step plus the squares of all the independent variables plus the cross products of every pair of regressors. Finally, compute the following test statistic:

$$TR^2 \sim \chi^2(k-1),$$

where T refers to the sample size, R^2 is the unadjusted coefficient of determination of the auxiliary regression with the squared residuals of the original model against the variables of the original model plus their squares and cross products, and $k-1$ refers to the degrees of freedom equal to the number of regression coefficients (k), in auxiliary regression with $\hat{u}_t^2$ as the dependent variable excluding the constant.

Again, because of the relatively small sample size all of the variables in the auxiliary regressions could not be included (the number of terms become large because of the square and cross product terms, for example with 7 explanatory variables in the original model the number of terms in the auxiliary model becomes 28 (taking into account the squared and cross product terms) which exceeds the sample size. Accordingly the derived values of the test statistic are based on auxiliary regressions which include the original variables, the cross product terms used in the test for linearity plus the square of the *RE* variable to make the estimations possible. Using the resulting R^2 with the sample size the values of the White test statistic obtained for the aggregate supply, aggregate demand, and current account balance equations respectively were 21.3, 11.4, and 15.1. When compared with the critical values of 22.3, 23.6, and 18.3 for each of the three equations respectively, at the 5 percent level it is seen that the null hypothesis of homoscedasticity is not rejected.

(v) Parameter Time Invariance

The main consequence of parameter changes over time is that it undermines the plausibility of policy analyses and prediction based on the parameter estimates. One method for checking whether parameter estimates are stable over time consists of estimating the model recursively.[6] But in a situation with a limited number of observations, the suggested procedures for testing for parameter time invariance are difficult to apply. However, testing for parameter structural change can provide some insight since this can be interpreted as a special case of time dependence where a priori information does suggest changes in the structure of the economy. Based on the discussion in the preceding chapter the Aggregate Supply (AS), Aggregate Demand (AD), and Balance of Payments (B) schedules could be expected to have undergone some kind of parameter changes by 1975. One structural change test is the F-type test proposed by Chow (1960):

$$\Gamma(Y) = \left(\frac{RRSS_T - URSS_1 - URSS_2}{URSS_1 + URSS_2}\right)\left[\frac{T-2K}{K}\right]$$

where $RRSS_T$, $URSS_1$, and $URSS_2$ refer to the restricted and unrestricted residual sums of squares for the whole sample, subperiod 1 ($t = 1,2,\ldots,T_1$) and subperiod 2 ($t = T_1 + 1,\ldots,T$) respectively. The test statistic for the output (AS), and current account balance (B) equations based on the subperiods 1960-1975 and 1976-1984 yielded values of 5.14 and 1.40. Given that the critical values at the 5 percent level were 3.64 and 1.40 respectively, it is seen that in the case of the AS equation the null hypothesis of no structural change is rejected while the same hypothesis for the B equation is not rejected.

Empirical Results

Aggregate Supply

Before examining the system estimation, a useful point of departure is provided by the results of estimating the model by OLS. Though these results are inconsistent they are introduced as a guide to the effect of the system estimation. The aggregate supply equation in linear form was initially estimated from annual time series for

1960–1984, based on the specification in equation (6.3). This equation has as its regressors the variables specified in Chapter 5 for the aggregate supply schedule except for the wage rate variable (w) which was excluded because of a lack of data. It should be pointed out that this omission may not be a cause of great concern in the present instance because of the relative stability of wage rates in Guyana due to the periods of wage freeze imposed by the government.

Using OLS to regress Y_t on RE_t, P_t, EN_t, IC_t and P_{it} yields

$$\begin{aligned} \hat{Y}_t = \; & \underset{(1.61)}{410.9} - \underset{(-0.50)}{29.2\, RE_t} + \underset{(2.50)}{5.3\, P_t} \\ & + \underset{(-2.09)}{0.8\, EN_t} + \underset{(3.94)}{0.3\, IC_t} - \underset{(3.15)}{2.8\, P_{it}} \end{aligned} \tag{6.9}$$

$$R^2 = 0.89, \quad \bar{R}^2 = 0.86, \quad D.W = 1.74, \quad SEE = 55.57$$

where R^2 is the multiple correlation coefficient, $\bar{R}^2$ is the adjusted R^2, and SEE is the standard error of the regression and the t-statistics are shown in parentheses below the parameter estimates.In general, even though these results give a reasonable fit, a plot of the residuals indicate outlier problems since some of the errors fall outside of two standard deviations from the regression line. The problem years were 1962, 1963, and 1977. One likely explanation for the overprediction of the model in these years is the effect of labor disputes and strikes on output performance which was indicated in Chapter 4.

An improvement upon this equation in terms of a lower SEE, a better fit and the elimination of the outlier problem is obtained by taking into account output losses that tended to occur as a result of labor disputes and strikes, particularly in the sugar and bauxite industries. The following equation is an aggregate supply equation which takes into account this impact with the inclusion of the DL variable which represents the annual amount of mandays lost[7] due to labor disruptions in the economy.

$$\hat{Y}_t = \underset{(2.02)}{471.5} - \underset{(-0.68)}{36.0\, RE_t} + \underset{(2.66)}{5.2\, P_t} + \underset{(3.28)}{0.7\, EN_t}$$

$$- 0.07\,DL_t + 0.4\,IC_t - 2.8\,P_{it} \quad (6.10)$$
$$(-2.19) \qquad (3.94) \qquad (-2.35)$$

$$R^2 = 0.91, \quad \bar{R}^2 = 0.89, \quad D.W = 2.10, \quad SEE = 50.47$$

All the variables except RE_t, the deflated exchange rate variable, are significant at the 5 percent level since with $n-k = 25-7 = 18$ d.f., the critical t-value is $t_{0.05} = 1.73$. Moreover, the import price index, import capacity, energy utilization, and the price level variables are significant at the 1 percent level since the critical t-value is 2.25. The R^2 and $\bar{R}^2$ are reasonably high, and the Durbin-Watson statistic of around 2.10 is not a cause of concern. With a SEE of 50.47, the plot of residuals indicate that there is no outlier problem since the residuals fall within two standard deviations of the regression line indicating that at least 95 percent of the residuals fall within an acceptable region.

Aggregate Demand

The aggregate demand equation specified in linear form according to the theoretical model in Chapter 5 resulted in equation (4) after a number of variables were dropped. The Y^*, and WH, variables were excluded because of the unavailability of data, the DC variable was dropped because of its strong collinearity with M and the choice between the two influenced by the notion that M may serve as a proxy for the wealth variable. In an attempt to reduce the number regressors the P_e and P_i variables were combined to form TT, which represents the ratio of P_i to P_e. This equation estimated using OLS for the period 1961–1984 yielded

$$\hat{Y}_t = 161.8 - 0.033\,P_t - 0.01\,Y_{t-1}$$
$$(1.25) \qquad (-2.23) \qquad (-1.20)$$

$$+ 0.12\,M_t - 29.2\,RE_t - 0.04\,IC_t \quad (6.11)$$
$$(2.10) \qquad (-3.25) \qquad (-1.76)$$

$$0.09\,TT_t + 0.02\,D_t + 0.03\,CIM_t$$
$$(0.79) \qquad (2.15) \qquad (1.26)$$

$$R^2 = 0.978, \quad \bar{R}^2 = 0.96, \quad SEE = 60.25$$

Specification testing based on these results for the AD equation indicates that, while most of the variables have the expected signs for the coefficient estimates, in a number of cases the estimates are insignificant at the 5 percent level. Only M, RE, and the constant term have t-ratios greater than 2.0 while with 15 d.f., the critical t-value is $t_{0.05} = 2.13$ which is exceeded by six of the chosen variables. The R^2 and $\bar{R}^2$ are high and the SEE gives a plot of residuals which do not indicate outlier problems. Even though the lagged income variable is not significant with a t-ratio of 0.47, its appearance as a lagged dependent variable in the equation makes the DW test for autocorrelation invalid, therefore it is not reported.

Balance of Payments

As indicated in the previous chapter, the focus of the study is more on the current account position of the balance of payments than in the overall position which takes into account capital inflows. The specification of the current account equilibrium equation based on the reasoning in Chapter 5 led to the following estimated equation. The notable differences with the theoretical specification is the exclusion of the Y^* variable because of a lack of data and the exclusion of the P_e and P_i variables because of their statistical insignificance. Further, collinearity problems led to the replacement of the public sector deficit variable by the external debt which is directly related to the interest payments—the fastest growing component—in public sector expenditure. The lagged output value was included to capture the effects of trade delays which in the context of a highly open economy tend to make current external transactions depend considerably to output performance in the previous period. Using the OLS method for the period 1961 to 1984 yielded

$$\hat{B}_t = \underset{(-0.11)}{-38.4} + \underset{(0.95)}{64.0\,RE_t} - \underset{(-1.40)}{0.3\,Y_t} + \underset{(2.32)}{0.6\,Y_{t-1}}$$

$$- \underset{(-4.98)}{0.9\,IC_t} - \underset{(-1.08)}{1.6\,P_t} + \underset{(1.39)}{0.2\,XD_t} \qquad (6.12)$$

$$R^2 = 0.76, \quad \bar{R}^2 = 0.67, \quad SEE = 61.2$$

While most of the coefficients do have the expected signs, they are generally insignificant at the 5 or even 10 percent levels of significance except for the import capacity variable. The specification of this equation, therefore, would appear to be unsatisfactory as a generating mechanism for the data utilized. The R^2 and $\bar{R}^2$ are relatively low in the context of time series estimation, and the in-sample forecasts generate residuals which indicate the existence of outlier problems. Though these results are disappointing from the standpoint of control and prediction, extenuating circumstances in the form of data-related issues are a likely source of explanation. The discussion of the problems surrounding the accuracy and coverage of the available data serves to indicate that to a large extent the behavior of the balance of payments variable may not be adequately portrayed. The exclusion of external transactions in commodities which pass through unofficial channels, for instance, distorts the behavior of this variable to an extent that may not coincide with the degree of distortion in the explanatory variables. The choice of alternative explanatory variables did not lead to marked improvement in results, though a version of the auxiliary equation used to test for independent sampling improved the fit somewhat.

In addition to assessing the statistical significance, economic plausibility, and robustness of OLS estimates, there is the question of what is the most appropriate estimation method to be utilized. Though current knowledge on estimation processes does not provide a blueprint for the choice of estimation technique, and much is left to the discretion of the model builder when making this decision, one general guideline is that in choosing an estimator to apply to sample data one must utilize the information content in the system of equations.[8] For instance, the "prior information" contained in the three equations (6.3), (6.4), and (6.5) which represent a version of the system outlined in the previous chapter pose two major problems for the application of the OLS technique. One is that there are interrelationships between the endogenous variables which makes the OLS estimates subject to simultaneous equation bias. An examination of the matrix of endogenous variable coefficients shown below indicates this since there are non-zero elements both above and below the diagonal.

$$\begin{bmatrix} 1 & -\alpha_5 & 0 \\ -\beta_1 & 1 & 0 \\ \theta_2 & \theta_5 & 1 \end{bmatrix} \begin{bmatrix} Y \\ P \\ B \end{bmatrix}$$

The second problem is that the equations are overidentified suggesting that there are a number of parameter estimates that can be derived from the reduced form of these equations. In order to cope with these problems the model is re-estimated using the TSLS technique which generates unique parameter estimates while avoiding the problem of simultaneity bias.

Two Stages Least Squares Estimation

Aggregate Supply

The TSLS method of estimation yielded the following aggregate supply equation.

$$\begin{aligned} \hat{Y}_t = \; & \underset{(1.38)}{346.4} + \underset{(3.21)}{7.4\, P_t} - \underset{(-0.34)}{18.8\, RE_t} + \underset{(3.06)}{0.65\, EN_t} \\ & \underset{(-2.06)}{-0.06\, DL_t} - \underset{(-2.90)}{4\, IMPI_t} + \underset{(3.34)}{0.35\, IC_t} \end{aligned} \tag{6.13}$$

$$R^2 = 0.91, \quad \bar{R}^2 = 0.88, \quad SEE = 52.3$$

Again, all the variables except the deflated exchange rate and the constant are significant at the 5 percent level with t-statistics in parentheses being greater than the critical t-value at $t_{0.05} = 1.73$. The R^2 and $\bar{R}^2$ have dropped a little, the signs are those expected on the basis of the arguments in the theoretical model, and the same set of parameter estimates are found to be significant as in the OLS estimation. This is not too surprising since the econometric literature suggests that in cases of relatively small samples there is not much that separates the results of such estimation methods as the OLS and TSLS.

The differences between the magnitudes of the parameter estimates give an indication of the bias that results for the choice of the

OLS method. For example, fixing all the variables in the *AS* schedule but P, the *AS* equation will be projected on the (Y, P) plane where the slope is approximately 0.2 and 0.13 respectively indicating that the slope of the *AS* schedule is relatively greater according to the TSLS estimates. In both instances, however, the derived elasticity results are consistent with the reasoning which suggested that the *AS* schedule is relatively inelastic with respect to price level changes rather than flat as is often assumed for countries with surplus labor. Using the TSLS results, with the means for the price level and aggregate output variables, for example, the price level elasticity of the aggregate supply schedule is seen to be 0.74. The relative impact of the other variables on output are made comparable through the derivation of standardized (beta) coefficients which measures the effect of a unit standard deviation change in the explanatory variable on an endogenous variable. An examination of these results indicate that the variables that would appear to cause the greatest shifts in the *AS* schedule would be P_i, followed by IC, and EN with standardized estimates of − 1.87, 0.37, and 0.32 respectively. Again, these results confirm the analysis embedded in the specification of the theoretical model.

The impact of shocks on aggregate demand can therefore be expected to result in relatively small changes in output but relatively greater changes in the price level assuming a stationary *AS* schedule. The impact of the shocks which cause the *AS* schedule to shift, however, depends on the slope and position of the *AD* schedule which will now be explored.

Aggregate Demand

As in the case of the aggregate supply equation, in order to obtain the aggregate demand equation which is overidentified in the three equation simultaneous system, TSLS is utilized. Using the TSLS procedure we get for the AD equation

$$\begin{aligned} \hat{P}_t = \; & \underset{(3.71)}{161.2} - \underset{(-0.14)}{0.008\, Y_t} - \underset{(-0.83)}{0.03\, Y_{t-1}} \\ & + \underset{(3.51)}{0.12\, M_t} + \underset{(0.73)}{0.02\, D_t} - \underset{(-1.47)}{0.04\, IC_t} \end{aligned} \tag{6.14}$$

$$- 29.3\, RE_t \underset{(-5.41)}{} + 0.08\, TT_t \underset{(0.28)}{} + 0.02\, CIM_t \underset{(0.85)}{}$$

$$R^2 = 0.97, \bar{R}^2 = 0.96, \quad SEE = 7.9$$

The signs are generally consistent with what was expected on the basis of the theoretical model and there was marginal improvement in the t-ratios for some of the coefficient estimates. However, the estimates for P_t, Y_{t-1}, D, RE, TT, and CIM fail to reject the null hypothesis at a 5 percent level of significance. The R^2 and $\bar{R}^2$ are high and with $n - k = 24-9 = 15$ d.f., the critical value is $t_{0.05} = 1.75$. The RMSE (root mean square error) of 7.91 is an improvement over that of the OLS estimation, and an examination of the residual plots indicate no serious outlier problems.

While the estimates of coefficients for Y_{t-1}, Y_t, D_t, IC_t, TT_t, and CIM_t are individually insignificant, the Wald F-test is used to test whether they are jointly significant. From the F-statistic, the null hypothesis that all the regression coefficients except the constant term are zero is rejected, and these variables have been retained in order to avoid the misspecification of omitting important variables.

Fixing all variables in the AD equation but Y, the AD equation will be projected on the (Y, P) plane where the slope is seen to be very low about $-$ 0.008. The derived the elasticity of the aggregate demand schedule with respect to price level changes (using this result and the means of the price level and output) is 11.4 which is indicative of a highly elastic aggregate demand schedule contrary to the conclusion that was reached in Chapter 5. The implication here is that the relative magnitudes for the interest sensitivity of investment and money demand as well as the sensitivity of imports to income do not support the assumptions made in the theoretical model with respect to these effects. At this stage, however, because a more disaggregated analysis is not possible within the framework of this study it remains unclear as to what actual estimates for these effects are.

The elasticity result for the AD schedule indicate that supply side policies have a significant role to play since shifts in the AS schedule would have a relatively greater impact on output as opposed to the price level.In keeping with the theoretical discussion, the impact of a change in the public sector deficit, money supply, and imports of capital and intermediate goods are positive. From an examination of the standardized (beta) coefficients we see that the variable exerting the greatest influence on the position of the AD schedule is RE with a standardized estimate of -0.59. The standardized estimate for other policy variables such as DE and M are 0.06 and 0.49 respectively which suggests relatively greater scope for shifting the AD schedule through changes in the money supply than in the public sector deficit, though the impact would be relatively small. As indicated in the discussion in Chapter 4, however, there are problems facing the use of the conventional instruments of monetary policy such as changing the reserve requirements or discount rate since excess liquidity within the commercial banking system undermines the ability of the central bank to control the money supply.

The Current Account of the Balance of Payments

The TSLS procedure for the B equation yielded

$$\hat{B}_t = \underset{(0.25)}{92.6} + \underset{(0.69)}{50.0\,RE_t} - \underset{(-1.57)}{0.4\,Y_t} + \underset{(2.27)}{0.7\,Y_{t-1}}$$

$$- \underset{(-4.96)}{1.0\,IC_t} - \underset{(-1.47)}{2.4\,P_t} + \underset{(1.7)}{0.3\,XD_t} \qquad (6.15)$$

$$R^2 = 0.76, \quad \bar{R}^2 = 0.67, \quad SEE = 62.2$$

The parameter estimates for lagged income and import capacity are statistically significant at the 5 percent level. The signs of the estimates can be reconciled with the theoretical discussion, though it was anticipated that an increase in external debt would have had an adverse effect on the current account balance. The R^2 is about the same as for the OLS results, which is relatively low for a time series regression. If current account balance is assumed to exist and solving for Y, keeping all variables on the right hand side fixed except the price level then the slope of the B line is -0.19 which yields an inelastic schedule with an elasticity value of 0.52.

Multiplier Analysis

Considering the effect of predetermined variables on the endogenous variables, the reduced form estimates provide information on various multipliers. The matrix below gives the impact multipliers obtained from the TSLS estimates. Given 11 predetermined variables and three endogenous variables, the coefficient matrix is 3 × 11.

$$\begin{pmatrix} \hat{Y} \\ \hat{P} \\ \hat{B} \end{pmatrix} = \begin{bmatrix} 0.155 & 0.612 & -0.064 & 0.592 & -3.785 & 0.206 \\ 0.020 & -0.005 & 0.000 & 0.079 & 0.033 & 0.027 \\ 0.122 & -0.273 & 0.028 & -0.468 & 1.692 & -0.163 \end{bmatrix} \begin{pmatrix} DE \\ EN \\ DL \\ TT \\ P_i \\ CIM \end{pmatrix}$$

$$\begin{pmatrix} \hat{Y} \\ \hat{P} \\ \hat{B} \end{pmatrix} = \begin{bmatrix} 0.894 & -0.017 & -222.818 & 0.000 & -0.273 \\ 0.120 & -0.049 & -27.409 & 0.000 & 0.036 \\ -0.707 & -0.880 & 220.126 & 0.369 & 0.924 \end{bmatrix} \begin{pmatrix} M \\ IC \\ RE \\ XD \\ LRY \end{pmatrix}$$

An examination of the above matrix gives an idea of the magnitude and direction of these impact or short-term multipliers. For example, the $\hat{Y}$ row in the matrix indicates the impact of unit increases in each of the exogenous variables on income (Y), with the columns of the matrix coinciding with the order of the variables in the right side vector. Thus, a unit increase in DE, leads to an income multiplier of 0.15 or just over one- sixth. Among those variables that portray a negative multiplier effect on output, the mildest effects are associated with changes in DL and IC, which yield output multipliers of − 0.06 and − 0.02 respectively, and the greatest multiplier effect arises through changes in RE. For the variables that exert a positive effect on output, the greatest impact is captured through changes in M and EN. The income multipliers that are negative pertain to the loss of man-days, the import price index, the deflated exchange rate, lagged income, and import capacity. The latter two multipliers possess signs that are contrary to expectations, though in the case of IC it is mildly negative. The magnitude is considerable in the case of a change in RE, (reduced output of G$222.8 million if RE increases by one unit) and of some influence in the case of a unit change in P_i (output falls by G$3.78 million if P_i increases by one unit).

In the case of the price multipliers, the variable that exerts the most influence is RE, though the direction is not consistent with expectations. The other multiplier effects on prices are consistent with expectations but are relatively small. Examining the $\hat{B}$ row in the matrix it is seen that the variables that have a positive impact on the current account balance are DE, DL, P_i, RE, XD, and LRY, whereas the variables that have an adverse effect on the current account balance are EN, TT, CIM, M, and IC. Again, however, these effects are mild with the RE variable exerting the greatest effect, an improvement in the current account position in the short term of G$220.1 if RE increases by one unit.

Total or long-term multipliers are shown below. These multipliers give the total effect of a predetermined variable on an endogenous variable. This comprises the direct effect of a predetermined variable on an endogenous variable and the indirect effect which takes into account the ways a predetermined variable influences all other endogenous variables which in turn influence the endogenous variable in question.

$$\begin{matrix} Y \\ P \\ B \end{matrix} \begin{bmatrix} DE & EN & DL & TT & P_i \\ 0.122 & 0.480 & -0.050 & 0.464 & -2.972 \\ 0.016 & -0.022 & 0.002 & 0.062 & 0.142 \\ -0.010 & 0.170 & -0.018 & -0.038 & -1.054 \end{bmatrix}$$

$$\begin{matrix} RY \\ P \\ B \end{matrix} \begin{bmatrix} CIM & M & IC & RE & XD \\ 0.161 & 0.702 & -0.103 & -174.960 & 0.000 \\ 0.021 & 0.094 & -0.048 & -20.977 & 0.000 \\ -0.013 & -0.058 & -0.893 & 54.427 & 0.369 \end{bmatrix}$$

These results allow a comparison of the impact and total multipliers. Again, the three rows are associated with the endogenous variables,

Y_t, P_t and B_t, and the columns indicate the impact that the exogenous variables have on the endogenous variables but over a longer period. Whereas a unit increase in DE that takes effect in the same time period is 0.15—the value located in the first row and first column of the first matrix—in the total multiplier matrix the impact is lower, at 0.12, indicating a multiplier of one-sixth in the immediate period and over one-eight in the five year period. Further comparison of the short term and long term multipliers indicate the following. The RE variable which had the greatest impact immediately also has the greatest impact over a longer period though reduced. There are also some sign reversals between the impact and total multipliers. In particular, the energy use variable has a negative impact on the current account balance immediately, (deterioration of the current account by G$0.27 million) but a positive impact over a longer period—G$0.17 million. The loss of man-days was seen to have a positive impact on the current account balance in the short run, but reversed to a negative impact over a longer period. Also the impact of the P_i variable was a positive one on the current account balance in the short run, but negative over the five year period. The magnitudes involved in these differences are relatively small.

Interim multipliers for periods one through five were also examined. The results showed a fluctuating pattern in the multipliers over a five year period with a dampening of the multiplier effects over time in the case of all exogenous variables. To the extent that this is indicative of a pattern of convergence then the long run multipliers have operational meaning and is preferred to interim multipliers as a guide for policy making beyond the short term period.

Forecasting

In addition to its role for policy, forecasting has evolved as an important component of existing model evaluation procedures. Two broad types of forecasts are emphasized in the econometric literature. These are, conditional forecasts based on instances where the values of the exogenous variables are given, and unconditional forecasts which are based on exogenous variables generated either by the model itself or by an auxiliary model. Three time periods are identified as relevant in a forecasting environment that consists of conditional and unconditional forecasts. First there is the in-sample period which refers to the period over which the model is estimated and fitted values (in-sample forecasts) are obtained. Second, there are ex-post forecasts which use in-sample parameter estimates with the actual values of predetermined variables in the post sample period to generate forecasts. Third, there are ex-ante forecasts which are out-of-sample forecasts based on unknown values of the predetermined variables given the parameter estimates obtained from the in-sample period.

In relation to the different time periods in the forecasting environment, in-sample forecasts are conditional because the values of the predetermined variables are given. Ex-ante forecasts are unconditional because they require the generation of predetermined variables. Ex-post forecasts, however, can be either conditional or unconditional depending on how they are obtained. Of the three main types of forecast periods, emphasis in this study is placed on the ex-post and in-sample forecasts. Each of these periods has certain advantages. The first type gives an indication of the "tracking" performance of the model though the criticism against this approach is that its success depends heavily on the same data which provided the estimates. Ex-post forecasts are more common than ex-ante forecasts primarily because of the uncertainty surrounding the generation of the predetermined variables in the latter approach. Particularly in this study, where there is a host of problems with the observed data, unconditional forecasts are not used because of the errors that are likely to occur.

Figures 6.1, 6.2, and 6.3 illustrate the tracking performance of the model using in-sample forecasts. These forecasts are referred to in the figures as fitted values for the endogenous variables and are obtained by using the TSLS parameter estimates with the actual values of the predetermined variables in each equation. Direct inspection of the figures indicates that the in-sample tracking performance is not perfect, since there is evidence of overprediction and underprediction for each of the endogenous variables and a number of turning points in the historical time paths for endogenous variables were missed by the in-sample forecasts.

Two other evaluation procedures indicate that these errors do not exclude a favorable assessment of the within sample tracking performance of two of the model equations. For instance, the ratio

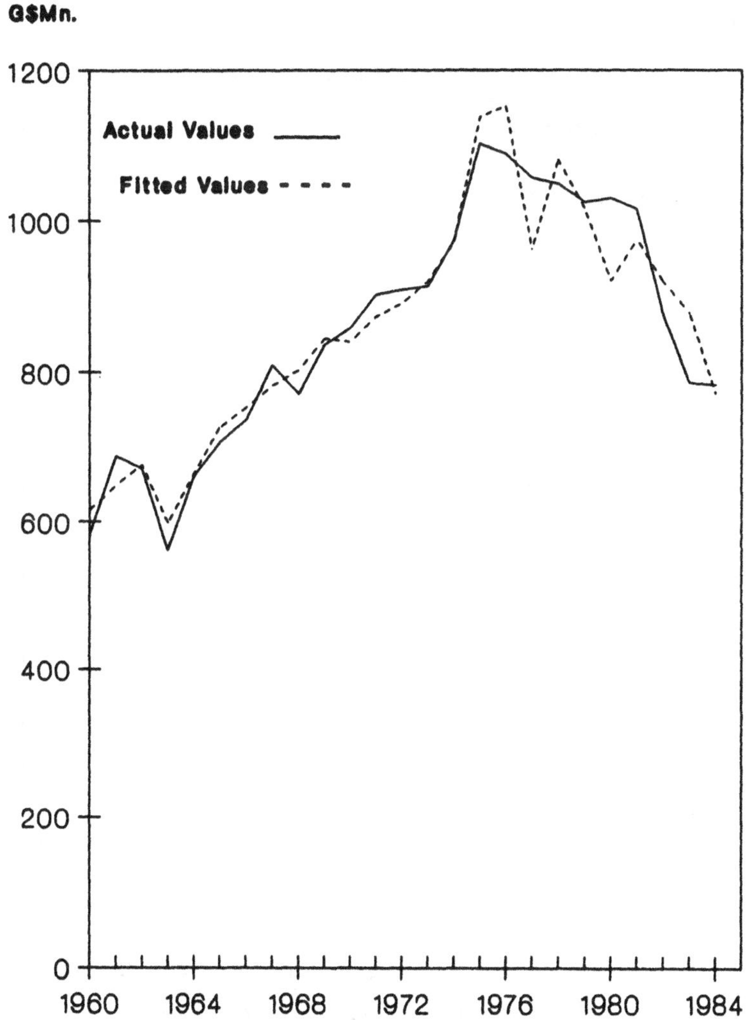

Figure 6.1 In-Sample Forecast for Output

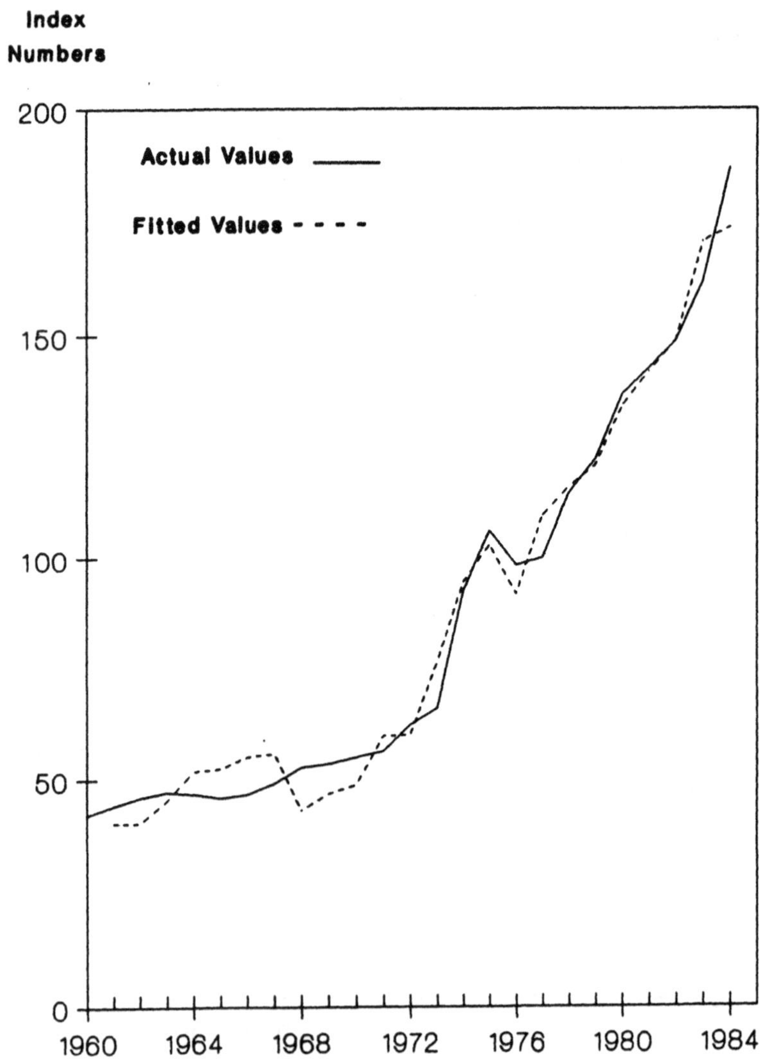

Figure 6.2 In-Sample Forecast for the Price Level

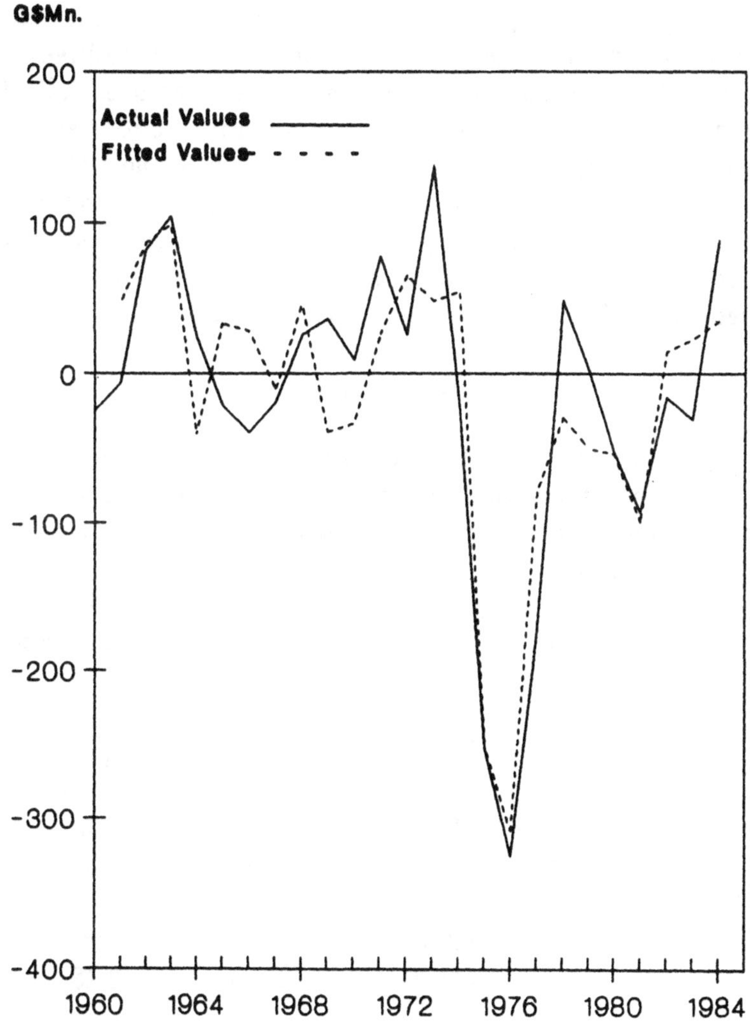

Figure 6.3 In-Sample Forecast for Current Account Balance

of underpredictions to overpredictions, which is usually utilized to indicate whether there is a tendency for the endogenous variables to be systematically over or under predicted, is close to the desired valued of unity in the case of all three endogenous variables. For each year in the period the difference between actual and forecasted values for aggregate output, the price level, and the current account position of the balance of payments are computed with positive differences indicating underprediction and negative differences indicating overprediction. Counting the number of underpredictions and overpredictions and expressing the former as a ratio to the latter yields values of 1.2, 0.8, and 1.08 for the output, price level, and current account balance equations respectively. Another evaluation procedure used is based on OLS regressions of the forecasted values on observed values for each dependent variable as in

$$Y_t^f = \hat{a} + \hat{b}Y_t + e_t,$$

where Y_t^f represents the fitted values for an endogenous variable and Y_t represents the actual values of the endogenous variable, with perfect tracking resulting in $\hat{a} = 0$ and $\hat{b} = 1$, and tested with the appropriate t-tests.

Performing the appropriate regressions for each of the endogenous variables yielded the following results with the t-statistics in parentheses.

	Y_t^f	P_t^f	B_t^f
$\hat{a}$	56.36 (1.05)	1.77 (0.59)	− 3.5 (−0.35)
$\hat{b}$	0.93 (15.3)	0.93 (31.9)	0.74 (8.18)

These results provide a value for $\hat{b}$ of 0.93 that is close to one and statistically significant at the 1 percent level for the aggregate supply (Y) and aggregate demand (P) equations, with a high constant for the former equation. In all cases the constants are not significant at the 1 percent level suggesting that the null hypothesis of $\hat{a} = 0$ is not rejected. The balance of payments (B) equation, however, portrays a $\hat{b}$ value of only 0.74 that is statistically significant at the 1 percent level, reinforcing the earlier indications of poor forecasting performance for this equation.

In order to assess how well the model performs in terms of its out-of-sample tracking performance, ex-post forecasts are generated and examined. Because of the unavailability of data for all the relevant variables beyond the estimation period, this exercise required a re-estimation of the model for a sub-period within the sample and the use of the data on the remaining years for comparison with predicted values. The equations were re-estimated for the period 1960 to 1980 and the parameter estimates generated prediction errors e_i shown below for the years 1981 to 1984 where e_i equals the difference between forecasted values and actual values $(Y_t^f - Y_t)$ for the ith year.

Y-equation:

$$e_1 = 135.1, \quad e_2 = 249, \quad e_3 = 153.6, \quad e_4 = 194.$$

P-equation:

$$e_1 = -4.9, \quad e_2 = -7.0, \quad e_3 = -22.8, \quad e_4 = -56.7.$$

B-equation:

$$e_1 = -31.0, \quad e_2 = 23.0, \quad e_3 = 172.0, \quad e_4 = 100.0.$$

As can be seen, the first equation systematically overpredicts, while the second equation underpredicts, and the third equation does both. Other measures of predictive ability such as the *RMSE* (root mean square error), the *MAE* (mean absolute error) and *U* (Theil's inequality coefficient) were also considered. These results for each of the forecast steps are as follows:

Steps	*RMSE*	*MAE*	*U*
Y Equation			
1	163.5	158.6	2.1
2	213.3	209.3	1.2
3	168.0	166.9	0.7
4	194.0	194.0	0.8

P Equation			
1	32.5	23.7	2.4
2	31.6	23.8	1.3
3	37.6	34.0	1.1
4	56.4	56.4	1.1
B Equation			
1	44.8	36.1	0.6
2	124.2	102.8	0.9
3	198.6	188.0	0.8
4	98.9	98.9	0.7

The closer these measures of predictive ability to zero, the greater the indication that the equations track the observed data well. The relatively high values for MAE and $RMSE$ indicate the weakness in the predictive ability of the equations, though the U statistic does indicate relatively better forecasts for all three equations since it declines as the forecast period is extended to the fourth year.

One likely reason for these results is the possible time dependence of the estimated coefficients which was indicated by the structural change test and reinforced by the changes in the magnitudes of the parameter estimates over the shorter period. It must also be recognized that the limited sample posed a degrees of freedom problem. Additionally, there is the problem with the accuracy of the data which became much more serious since the end of the 1970s. As a result, the values for the years 1981 to 1984 might not be too indicative to test how well the equations perform.

Simulations

In general, simulation of a model comprises two sequences (or "runs") of solutions over the same time period, known as the simulation period. The first of these sequences is usually called the control run and the second the shocked run. The control run provides a solution to the model that can either be a static simulation or a dynamic simulation. The difference between the two is that the former procedure uses historical values of the lagged endogenous variables in every period to obtain the solution whereas for the latter procedure the solution is obtained using the period 1 solution values for the endogenous variables as the period 2 values for these variables and so on for successive periods. Another detail in simulation exercises is that they can be further classified as either deterministic or stochastic depending on whether the residuals are set to zero or are artificially generated. In this study simulations are dynamic and deterministic. Dynamic, because it focuses on the outcomes that would have occurred if the true system had been exactly portrayed by the model equations, and deterministic for reasons of greater reliability and simplicity.

The parameter estimates indicated for the output(Y), the price level(P), and the current account of the balance of payments(B) equations indicated earlier in the chapter, are used with actual values all the explanatory variables except the lagged output variable (Y_{t-1}) in the P and B equations to generate the simulated paths for the three endogenous variables over the period 1960 to 1984. In the case of the lagged output variable the relevant solution values for Y are used. Thus, the lagged output value for 1962 is the solution value for Y in 1961 based on the parameter estimates and the actual values of the explanatory variables in the aggregate supply equation. Figures 6.4, 6.5, and 6.6 depict these control-run (solution) time paths for the dynamic simulation of the endogenous variables with their historical time paths for purposes of comparison.

Direct inspection indicates consistent overprediction of the simulated time paths for all three endogenous variables. It is important in instances of large simulation errors to separate the different sources of the errors into three broad categories, the estimation residual, the simultaneity error, and the dynamic error. The first type of error arises because the equations in question do not provide a perfect explanation, given the observed values of the explanatory variables, to the endogenous variables in every period. The second type arises because the solution values which the system generates, given the observed values of the predetermined variables, do not coincide exactly with the values predicted by each estimated equation for the endogenous variables. The third type arises because the solution values from the earlier periods that are used for the lagged endogenous variables do not coincide exactly with their historical observed values.

While the breakdown of the error sources is important for cor-

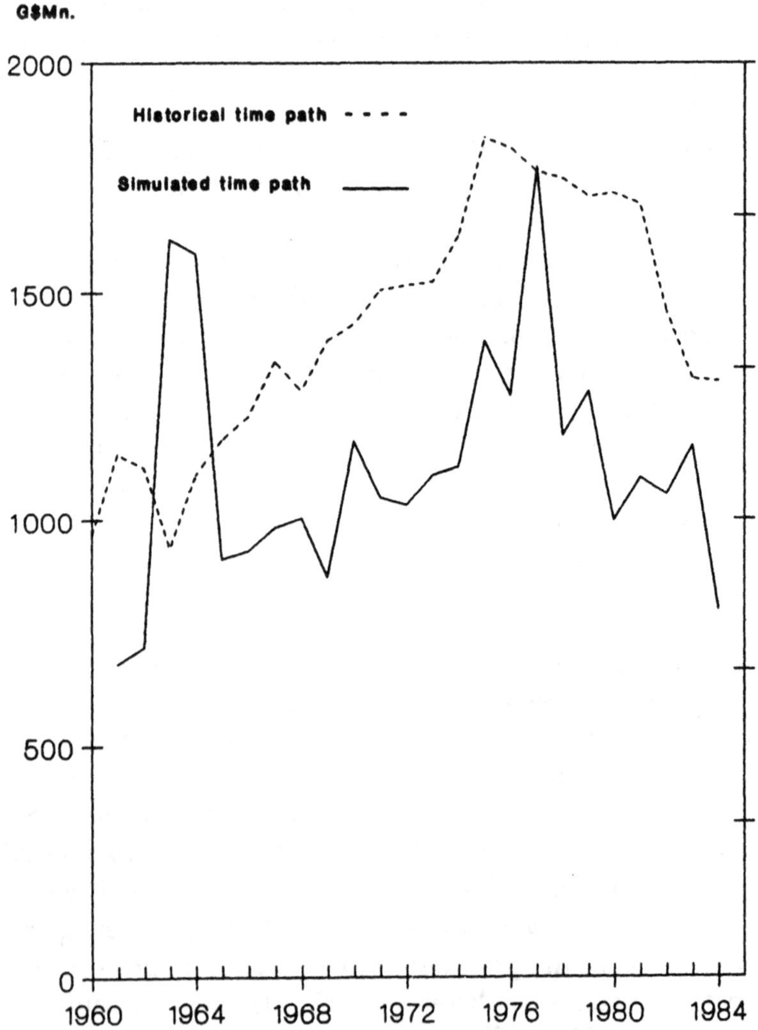

Figure 6.4 Historical and Control Run Time Paths (Output)

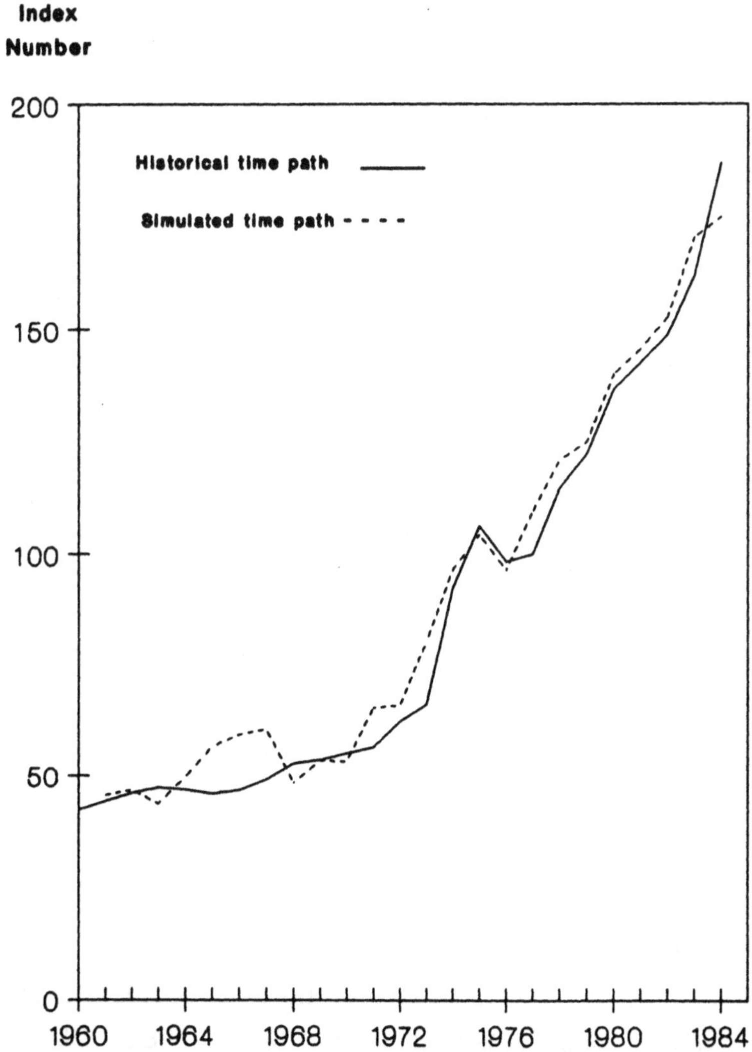

Figure 6.5 Historical and Control Run Time Paths (The Price Level)

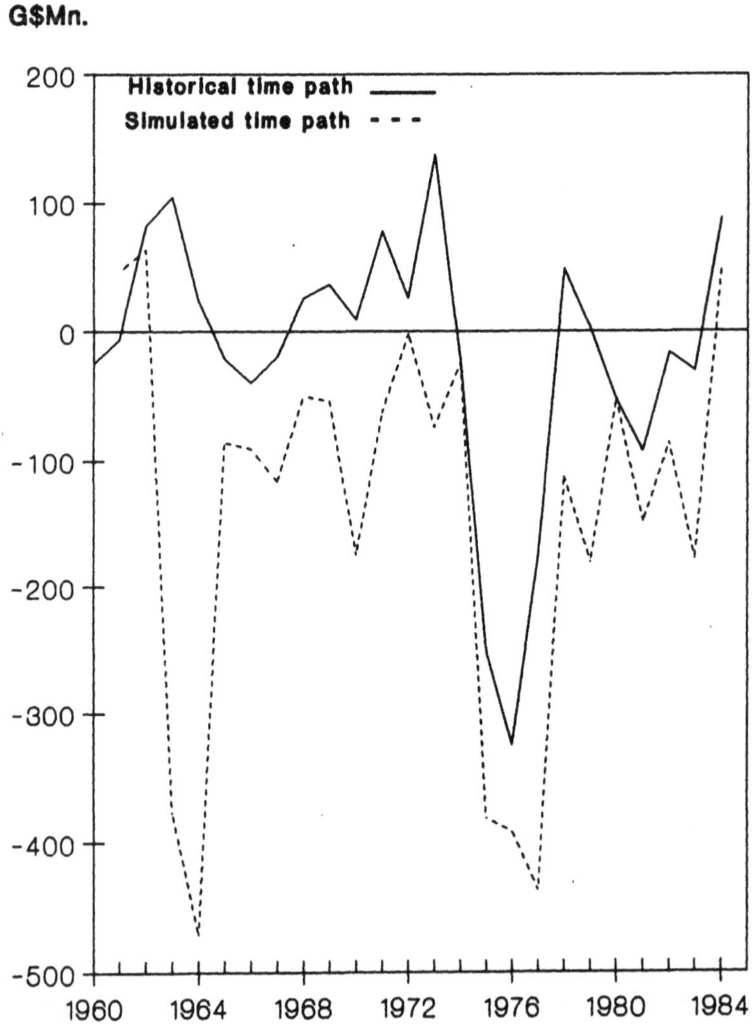

Figure 6.6 Historical and Control Run Time Paths (Current Account Balance)

rective procedures, it is also important to note that the benchmark for comparisons with shocked runs that is often used is the control-run. The reason has to do with the recognition that the model is an attempt to represent the true system and therefore, it is likely to be subject to errors and inadequacies. Accordingly, in measuring the response of the model to shocks it is important to abstract from these inadequacies and use the control-run time paths for the endogenous variables as benchmarks.

One of the more common uses of simulation analysis is to examine the impact of shocks to the system in the form of a one-for-all change in one or more of the exogenous variables or to consider the effect of a certain change that is maintained over a period of time. Such exercises provide an added opportunity to judge the elasticity results that have been derived from the estimates of the structural parameters. For example, the elasticity of the aggregate supply schedule can be derived by considering the output and price level changes between the control run and a shocked run that involves changing the public sector deficit. The theoretical analysis indicated that an increase in the public sector deficit would shift the AD schedule to the right with the AS schedule remaining fixed. Thus the ratio of the percentage change in output to the percentage change in the price level between the results of the control run and a shocked run would provide an indication of the responsiveness of output to the price level since only the AD schedule is assumed to have shifted. A 10 percent increase in the public sector deficit was tried for 1983, and the resulting change in output for that year between the value of output in the control run and the result from the shocked run was 0.38 percent. For the same year the percentage change in the price level was 0.39 percent. This results in an elasticity value of 0.96 which still suggests an inelastic aggregate supply schedule but not as unresponsive to the price level as the result derived from the parameter estimates.

The simulation technique was also used to answer the counterfactual question: what time paths would have been taken by the three endogenous variables if the structure of the economy represented by the parameter estimates based on estimation from 1960 to 1972 had not changed? The results indicate much better performance for the economy in relation to output and the price level though the balance of payments position would have been much worse. In 1984, for example, whereas actual output was G$782 million the projected real output was G$989 million. In the case of the price level the actual price index number was 187 and the projected was 59. In the case of the current account position the actual level was a surplus of G$88 million in 1984, but the projected was a deficit of G$667 million. The changes that occurred in terms of the parameter estimates suggest that as the role of the public sector grew within the economy the ensuing adjustments by economic agents resulted in a significant decline in production performance that may not have occurred even with the path taken by the exogenous variables.

Policy Issues

The empirical results presented in this chapter provide support for the argument that the *AS*, and *B* schedules are relatively inelastic but that the *AD* schedule is relatively elastic. The implications for policy are that output changes are relatively smaller than price level changes for given shifts in the *AD* schedule that may arise from demand management policy initiatives. The elastic *AD* schedule indicates, however, that there is considerable scope for policies that can shift the *AS* schedule to the right as a means of achieving output increases without inflationary problems. The experience over the period under study indicates, however, that it has been difficult to maintain sustained improvement in output because of production bottlenecks and as the empirical estimates of the standardized coefficients for the *AS* equation indicate the variables included in the model do not appear to have much impact in shifting the aggregate supply schedule. This raises the issue of the absence of a machine goods sector which accounts for continued reliance on external supply of essential capital goods and ensuing production bottlenecks when the availability of these imports are curtailed because of balance of payments difficulties. An important aspect of the strategy for dealing with the economic problems facing Guyana, therefore, would be the promotion of an industrial policy that can lead to the development of an internal capital goods sector if there is to be success in overcoming the existing problems of adjustment and growth.

Considering the diagnostic and macroeconomic policy issues surrounding the multiplier results and the simulation exercises, it can be stated that the relationship between inflation, real economic growth, and the balance of payments is a complex one. The multiplier results and the parameter estimates suggest that there is not much room to maneuver on the part of policy makers particularly when it comes to the use of demand management policies to dampen the adverse effects of certain shocks. The indications of limited success judging from the macroeconomic responses of output, the price level and the current account of the balance of payments to the mix of policy measures that have been tried also suggests that there is a small margin for error. Monetary and fiscal policies in the form of manipulations of the money supply—primarily through domestic credit guidelines—or the public sector deficit, for instance, have not been able to accommodate shocks in the economy in the sense of quickly moderating the adverse impacts. Part of the problem has been the way in which central bank policies have tended to accommodate public sector spending, thereby reducing monetary and fiscal policies into one operational policy instrument.

As the multiplier results indicate, there is a trade-off that may be exploited if there is a separation of fiscal and monetary measures since both the money supply and the public sector deficit affect the endogenous variables in the same direction. In practice, a prerequisite for exploiting this possibility is the separation of the close correspondence of the monetary and fiscal policy instruments and actions that has been characteristic of policy making in Guyana. At a minimum this would mean that the central bank should effectively maintain its relative autonomy vis-à-vis the operations of fiscal policy and thereby allow its actions and policies to be guided by the consideration of maintaining a stable economic environment rather than automatically accommodate fiscal policies.

Although the forecasting ability of the model in relation to ex-post forecasts may not be as good as could be expected given the rejection of the hypothesis of no structural change in parameter estimates for the *AS* and *AD* equations, the in-sample forecasts are reasonable for these equations. At the same time, while the hypothesis of no structural change was not rejected for the *B* equation, the in-sample forecasts for this equation is not as satisfactory. Specification tests also indicated problems in terms of the statistical significance of a number of variables, even though there is plausible economic reasoning to justify their inclusion in the model.

Even though the experience has shown that policy makers have not been able to do much at the level of adjustment processes, especially in relation to supply side policies that operate favorably at the level of business decisions, there is a pressing need for policy initiatives in this direction. In general, there has been a state of inertia in the behavior of the official economy in Guyana, coupled with active and fast moving markets in the unofficial economy, particularly the forward looking behavior of foreign exchange operations as well as in certain segments of the goods market. It is the latter tendencies which suggest that a possible course of action involves the pursuit of an industrial policy that deals with the economic structure in terms of developing particular industries and resource allocation between sectors, with the active involvement of the private sector. This requires the use of market forces which is complementary with overall economic policy, supporting and facilitating general fiscal and monetary policies and harmonizing programs in one sector with the others as opposed to centralized control over economic activity.

This recommendation is in contrast to a popular argument made in relation to LDCs which states that the private sector acts more as a deterring force rather than a promoter of the desired social and economic objectives within these countries. An important aspect of the historical performance of the private sector in many LDCs that is often neglected by the proponents of this viewpoint is that what constituted private enterprise was the exercise of market power by relatively few firms. The potential distortions of such non-competitive market situations and the likely divergences from efficiency criteria are well documented in the economic literature. Thus the question is not simply whether private enterprise is capable or not of initiating and promoting economic development, but what kind of market structure prevails and whether this can explain the detrimental effects identified. Indeed, the experience in the case of Guyana has shown that the replacement of private sector market power with public sector market power did not automatically lead to better results.

A necessary condition for the emergence of a viable economic system in Guyana is the reduction of the officially created bottlenecks and elimination of inefficiencies that exist in the public sector. However, it is important that the limits on what can be immediately achieved be recognized. For instance, while a general policy of public sector deficit reduction may be attempted by policy makers, the specific measures adopted have to be carefully weighed. Some simple arithmetic, for instance, indicates that if the policy is one of expenditure reduction then this cannot be achieved primarily through employment reduction in the public sector. Although the wage payments in the public sector has averaged between 300 and 400 million Guyana dollars per year between 1976 and 1984, even if all the workers were laid off, the deficit would still exist, particularly since the item that accounts for a major share of government expenditures is interest owed to domestic and foreign sources. Debt management policies would have to be an important part of the deficit reduction strategy.

The failure in the past of standard stabilization packages may also be explained with some of the quantitative results. The adoption of a balance of payments strategy which focuses on the exchange rate (a primary aspect in all the IMF programs since 1978), in particular, eliminating the overvaluation of the exchange rate through devaluation is seen to have serious repercussions for output in the immediate and intermediate periods judging from the impact and total multiplier effects. Thus, a unit increase in RE (devaluation) is seen to result in a reduced real output of G$222.8 million in the short term and G$174.9 million in the long term even though the current account position of the balance of payments would improve by G$220.1 million in the short term. In the long term the improvement in the current account position is much lower at G$54.4 million. It is in this sense that there is the need for stabilization policies that can address both the production problems that face the economy as well as the macroeconomic imbalance in the operations of the external sector.

A most important aspect of future policy making concerns the commitment of policy makers to the resolution of the current economic problems facing Guyana. Over the past two decades, the emphasis placed on political pragmatism with little apparent regard to a set of economic beliefs was not a successful strategy. The absence of tenable economic beliefs, for example, resulted in political priorities tending to dominate economic goals, with economic thinking having little influence on decision making. At the present time the extent of the economic problems dictate that not much can be achieved unless policies are enacted to utilize the population that has shown remarkable resourcefulness in coping with the rapid decline in economic conditions that has taken place.

Notes

1. T. Haavelmo, "The Probability Approach in Econometrics," *Econometrica* 12 (July 1944): 12–18.

2. This is because this type of data for macroeconomic variables generally exhibits a trending pattern which undermines the assumption of a random sample of a set of independent and identically distributed random variables.

3. Except for the AD equation where in addition to the degrees of freedom problem strong collinearity among some variables and TT, CIM and the 1 period lags of these variables resulted in their exclusion from the unrestricted model that was estimated.

4. The two stage least squares estimation technique was used. The choice of this method of estimation is explained later in the chapter.

5. Although this is a large sample test it has been found useful in small samples (see, R. Ramanathan, *Introductory Econometrics* (San Diego: Harcourt Brace Jovanich, 1989), and is used here because of the operational problems created for other tests for homoscedasticity such as the Goldfield-Quandt test and the Breusch-Pagan test when the sample size is relatively small.

6. This approach was first formalized by R. L. Brown, J. Durbin, and J. M. Evans, "Techniques for Testing the Constancy of Regression Relationships over Time," *Journal of the Royal Statistical Society* 37 (1975). Considering the regression model:

$$Y_t = X_t'\beta + u_t, \qquad t = 1, \ldots, T,$$

where Y_t, represents observations on the dependent variables, X_t, is a vector of nonstochastic regressors, β is a vector of regression coefficients and u_t is a disturbance term that follows a normal distribution with mean zero and variance σ_y^2. Since the question is whether the regression coefficients β are constant over different observations, *i.e.* the alternative model is:

$Y_t = X_t'\beta_t + u_t, \qquad t = 1, \ldots, T$, with the null hypothesis $H_0 = \beta_1 = \cdots = \beta_T$.

7. This information is provided by the Statistical Bureau in Guyana and it is obtained by summing the products of the length of each strike by the number of workers involved in the strike.

8. Two types of information are generally identified. First, there is 'prior information', which takes the form of the lists of endogenous and predetermined variables, information about which variables enter each equation, about which equations are exact relationships (identities) and which variables are regarded as determining all of which combine to indicate the normalization for each equation and the zero restrictions that exist. The second general type of information consists of information about the degree of correlation of disturbances within and across equations.

7

Conclusion

This study is intended as a step toward the construction of a policy oriented framework that can address contemporary problems such as low economic growth, persistent inflation, and substantial balance of payments deficits that are very much in evidence in a number of LDCs. A case study involving Guyana provides the context for the construction of an operational macroeconometric model that focuses on these issues and yields quantitative results which are assessed in terms of their potential for appropriate policy analysis.

The design of the model used in this study follows several stages. The first is related to the issue of model selection among competing theoretical frameworks. As the discussion on macroeconometric modeling in Chapter 2 suggests, this issue cannot be framed simply as one involving the use of statistical tests to determine the relevant theory since empirical work has shown in a number of instances that more than one theoretical model performs reasonably well with the same data. Under these circumstances one important guideline in the model building process is to strive for greater theoretical realism by constructing models that can take into account relevant historical detail and institutional constraints on economic behavior of interest.

The second stage involved an examination of the theory and practice of macroeconometric modeling for LDCs in order to identify the applicability and usefulness of this type of economic analysis for countries that faced short run stabilization problems as well as long run structural problems. An outgrowth of this discussion in Chapter 3 was the recognition that in general the economic problems facing LDCs were closely linked to interdependencies between the demand

and supply sides of these economies. Four basic questions are suggested to be as relevant for the LDCs as for the developed countries (where macroeconometric modeling has a longer tradition), in the model building process. These concerns are: whether the economy consists of interdependent markets or sectors, identifying the critical markets or sectors with reference to the structure and performance of the economy, ascertaining the links which exist within or between the critical markets or sectors, and identifying the mechanisms which form these links.

A description of Guyana's economy between 1960 and 1984 in Chapter 4 constituted the third stage of the modeling procedure. This chapter provides information on the performance of important macroeconomic aggregates, critical aspects of the economic structure, and the main institutional relationships that influence economic behavior. One important conclusion is that the production and decision processes affecting production choices, resource allocation decisions, and changes in technical and economic circumstances have been influenced significantly by the growth of the public sector during the period under study. An assessment of economic performance within the framework of the prevailing product and input market structures, the nature of entrepreneurial behavior, and the existing technical production relationships indicate the following: (a) An absence of technical and structural change which account for unsustained productivity increase. (b) A limited industrial base with the virtual nonexistence of a capital goods sector which creates a critical dependence on imports of capital and intermediate goods for the smooth functioning of the economy on the supply side. (c) An open economy that is extremely vulnerable to external developments on account of the minimal intersectoral linkages among domestic production sectors and the considerable influence exerted by export earnings (largely from primary products) on income and domestic activity. (d) The collapse of monetary and fiscal policy into one policy because of the accommodative role performed by the central bank to public sector spending.

The theoretical model developed in Chapter 5 had as its variables of interest the behavior of aggregate output, the price level, and the current account of the balance of payments. The analytical framework consists of an aggregate demand schedule, an aggregate supply schedule, and a current account balance of payments schedule which are derived from equilibrium conditions in the production sector, the expenditure and monetary sectors, and the current account position of the balance of payments, respectively. Taking into account the insights provided in Chapter 4, it was hypothesized that the three schedules were inelastic with respect to changes in the price level. One policy implication from this hypothesis was that demand management policies would have a greater impact on the price level than on output. The comparative static results derived from the model indicated that there was ambiguity about the direction of impact of changes in the exchange rate, the import price level, or in import capacity on output and the current account balance. In the case of changes in the money supply and in the public sector deficit, the comparative static results indicated a direct relationship with output and the price level, but an inverse relationship with the current account position.

The main findings in the estimation of the model were as follows: (1) Contrary to expectations, the aggregate demand schedule was found to be relatively elastic with respect to price level changes. This raised questions about the assumptions made about the elasticity of the IS and LM schedules in the theoretical model suggesting in fact that there was some sensitivity of investment to interest rates, and that the interest sensitivity of money demand to interest rates was not large enough to offset the impact of relative price changes on imports. The hypotheses of inelastic aggregate supply and current account balance schedules were empirically supported. (2) The direction of the multiplier effects of the important shock variables (external and policy induced) confirmed some of the theoretical conclusions but were inconsistent with others. With regard to the variables for which the comparative static results were ambiguous, the empirical results indicated that: an increase in the real exchange rate as well as the import price level was shown to have a negative impact on output and a positive impact on the current account position of the balance of payments; an increase in import capacity had an adverse effect on output as well as on the current account balance. The analytical results with regard to the impact of changes in the money supply were empirically supported since there was a positive impact on output and the price level and a negative impact on the current account position. The empirical estimates of the impact of an increase in the public sector deficit also supported the theoretical conclusion of a positive relationship with output and the price level, though in the short term the results indicated an improved current account position of the balance of payments contrary to the postulated inverse relationship. However, over a longer period—5 years—there is an adverse impact on the current account balance.

In general, the magnitude of the impact and long term multipliers were seen to be relatively small except for the import price level and the exchange rate variables. For instance, in the case of the former an index point increase would result in a G$3.7 million decline in output, while a unit increase in the exchange rate would cause a G$222.8 million decline in output.

The forecasting results of the model were seen to be reasonable with respect to in-sample tracking. However, the out-of-sample forecasts were relatively poor whether evaluated by measures such as Theil's inequality coefficient or root mean square error. A major reason for the latter result may be that the out-of-sample period (1981–1984) coincides with a deterioration of the available data due to data gathering problems largely related to the rise of parallel market activities.

The simulation exercise that addressed the counterfactual question as to what the effect of the same economic policies would be if the structure of the economy had remained unchanged indicated that the performance of the economy would have been much better in terms of the output and price level variables. This suggests that economic behavior did respond to the changes that occurred in spite of the evidence of a number of structural rigidities. The other simulation exercise involved an assessment of the short term elasticity of the aggregate supply schedule based on the impact of a 10 percent increase in the public sector deficit in 1983 which was consistent with the supply elasticity estimate derived from the estimates of the structural parameters in the model.

The interpretation of these results for economic policy focuses attention on (a) The relative ineffectiveness of demand management policies to alter aggregate output since shifts in the aggregate demand schedule in the context of an inelastic aggregate supply means that output response would be much smaller that price level changes.

(b) The need for an industrial policy that is geared toward the establishment of a domestic capital goods sector. The existence of a relatively elastic aggregate demand schedule suggests that policies that can shift the aggregate supply schedule to the right would be the key to substantial increases in output and a permanent reduction of inflation rates. But, as the empirical estimates indicate the policy variables examined in this study have a negligible shift effect on the aggregate supply schedule. It is significant that the greatest effect is exerted by the import capacity variable indicating the influence of imported inputs. It is in this context that a strong case exists for the fostering of a vibrant domestic machine goods sector as a prerequisite for eliminating major production bottlenecks that have helped to stall sustained increases in output even under favorable demand conditions. (c) The lack of feasibility of using a policy variable like the exchange rate to achieve multiple targets such as output expansion—largely in the export sector—and an improvement in the balance of payments position.

The empirical results indicate that a unit increase in the exchange rate (devaluation) will improve the current account position by G$220.1 million but at the same time will cause output to decline by G$222.8 million, and (d) The need to avoid collapsing monetary and fiscal policy into one policy. The multiplier effects indicate that both the public sector deficit and money supply changes affect output and the price level in the same direction but the current account of the balance of payments in opposite directions. In this sense, independent fiscal and monetary policy actions present greater potential for the achievement of multiple targets than is possible whenever the central bank is accommodative to public sector spending.

It is also important to point out areas for further work. One direction for improvement is to make the model completely dynamic so as to consider longer run issues in relation to growth rates and inflation rates. Further, a dynamic model would be important in addressing the issue of model stability. As suggested in the theoretical model, there are important policy implications if, for example, an external shock such as a foreign price level increase causes production to decline faster than absorption which would lead to permanent disequilibrium in the balance of payments position. The modeling of disequilibrium aspects of the economy—in the sense that there is no permanent balance between supplies and demands in certain goods and input markets—may also be another direction for future work. Another area for further work is the design of a more disaggregated model that would be able to address sectoral issues as well as policy concerns in relation to the problem of external debt. The application of alternative estimation techniques would also have to be considered as a direction of interest especially if the model is considered in non-linear form, and the availability of data permits other system estimation methods such as three-stage least squares. Finally, there is considerable scope for further testing of the model for other LDCs that share economic problems and institutional characteristics that are similar to those in Guyana.

Bibliography

Adams, G. *The Business Forecasting Revolution.* Oxford: Oxford University Press, 1986.

Agarwala, R. A. *An Econometric Model of India.* London: Frank Cass, 1970.

Anderson, L. C., and Carlson, K. M. "A Monetarist Model for Economic Stabilization." *Federal Reserve Bank of St. Louis Review* 52 (1970): 7–25.

Ando, A., and Modigliani, . " The 'Life-Cycle' Hypothesis of Saving: Aggregate Implications and Tests." *American Economic Review* 53 (1963): 35–84.

Artus, P.; Laroque, G.; and Michael, G. "Estimation of a Quarterly Econometric Model with Quantity Rationing." *Econometrica* 52 (1984): 1387–1414.

Baran, P. *The Political Economy of Growth.* New York: Monthly Review Press, 1957.

Barro, R. J., and Grossman, H. I. "A General Disequilibrium Model of Income and Employment." *American Economic Review* 61 (1971): 82–93.

Batten, D., and Hafer, R. "The Relative Impact of Monetary and Fiscal Actions on Economic Activity: A Cross-Country Comparison." *Federal Reserve Bank of St. Louis Review* 65 (1983): 5–12.

Behrman J. R., and Hanson, J. A. *Short-Term Macroeconomic Policy in Latin America.* Cambridge: Ballinger, 1979.

Bergman, L. "Extensions and Applications of the MSG Model: A Brief Survey." In *Production, Multi-Sectoral Growth and Planning*, edited by F. R. Førsund et al. Amsterdam: North-Holland, 1985.

Bergstrom, R. *The Construction and Use of Economic Models.* London: English Universities Press, 1967.

Bergstrom, R., and Wymer, D. "A Model of Disequilibrium Neoclassical Growth and its Application to the United Kingdom." In *Statistical Inference in Continuous Time Economic Models*, edited by R. Bergstrom. Amsterdam: North-Holland, 1976.

Bird, G. *International Macroeconomics.* London: MacMillan, 1987.

Brown, R. L.; Durbin, J.; and Evans, J.M. "Techniques for Testing the Constancy of Regression Relationships over Time." *Journal of the Royal Statistical Society* 37 (1975): 149–163.

Bruton, H. J. "Growth Models and Underdeveloped Economies." *Journal of Political Economy* 63 (1955): 322–336.

Cameron, R. ed. *Banking and Economic Development: Some Lessons of History.* New York: Oxford University Press, 1972.

Canto, V.; Joines, D.; and Laffer, A. *Foundations of Supply-Side Economics.* New York: Academic Press, 1983.

Cardoso, F. H. "Associated-Dependent Development: Theoretical and Practical Implications." In *Authoritarian Brazil: Origins, Policies, and Future,* edited by A. Stepan. New Haven: Yale University Press, 1973.

Carlson, K. M. "Inflation, Unemployment, and Money: Comparing the Evidence from Two Simple Models." *Federal Reserve Bank of St Louis Review* 60 (1978): 2–6.

Carter, N. G. "A Macroeconometric Model of Jamaica 1959–1966." *Social and Economic Studies* 19 (1970): 178–201.

Cebula, R. J. and Skogstad S. L. "A Note on the Domestic Monetary Policy Conditions of IMF Stand-by Assistance." *Indian Journal of Economics* 60 (July 1979): 109–117.

Central Bank of Guyana. *Annual Reports: 1961 to 1984.*

Central Bureau of Statistics. "ELSA - Indonesia Model." In *Preliminary Results of Econometric Models in the ELSA Project: Vol II.* Tokyo: Institute of Developing Economies, 1984.

Challen, D.W.; and Hagger, A.J. *Macroeconometric Systems, Constructions, Validations, and Applications.* New York: St. Martin's Press, 1983.

Chenery, H. B., and Bruno, M. "Development Alternatives in an Open Economy: The Case of Israel." *Economic Journal* 72 (March 1962): 79–103.

Chenery, H. B., and Strout, A. M. "Foreign Assistance and Economic Development." *American Economic Review* 56 (September 1966): 679–733.

Cheong, M., and Kim, Y. "Korea Model." In *Econometric Models of Asian Link*, edited by S. Ichimura and M. Ezaki. Tokyo: Springer-Verlag, 1985

Chiu, Y. "Taiwan Model." In *Econometric Models of Asian Link*, edited by S. Ichimura and M. Ezaki. Tokyo: Springer-Verlag, 1985.

Chow, G. "Tests of the Equality Between Two Sets of Coefficients in Two Linear Regressions." *Econometrica* 28 (1960): 591– 605.

Christ, C. *Econometric Models and Methods.* New York: Wiley, 1966.

Cline, W. R., and Weintraub, S. *Economic Stabilization in Developing Countries.* Washington, DC.: Brookings Institution, 1981.

Colman, D., and Nixson, F. *Economics of Change in the Less Developed Countries.* Oxford: Philip Allan, 1986.

Corbo, V.; Goldstein, M.; and Khan, M. ed. *Growth Oriented Adjustment Programs.* Washington: IMF and World Bank, 1987.

Corden, M. *The Relevance for Developing Countries of Recent Developments in Macroeconomic Theory*. Cambridge, Mass.: Harvard University, 1985.

Crockett, A. D. "Stabilization Policies in Developing Countries: Some Policy Considerations." *International Monetary Staff Papers* 28 (March 1981): 54–79.

De Grauwe, P. *Macroeconomic Theory for the Open Economy*. Hampshire: Gower, 1983.

Diaz-Alejandro, C. F. "A Note on the Impact of Devaluation and the Redistribution Effect." *Journal of Political Economy* 71 (1963): 577–580.

Dixon, P. B.; Parmenter, B.; Ryland, C.; and Sutton, J. *ORANI: A Multisectoral Model of the Australian Economy*. Amsterdam: North-Holland, 1977.

Domar, E. D. "Capital Expansion, Rate of Growth, and Employment." *Econometrica* (April 1946): 137–147.

Dornbusch, R. *Open Economy Macroeconomics*. New York: Basic Books, 1980.

Dos Santos, T. "The Crisis of Development Theory and the Problem of Dependence in Latin America." In *Underdevelopment and Development: The Third World Today*, edited by H. Bernstein. Harmondsworth: Penguin Books, 1973.

Downing, L. D., and Solis, J. F. "An Econometric Model for Nicaragua." In *Short-term Macroeconomic Policy in Latin America*, edited by J. Behrman and J. A. Hanson. Cambridge: Ballinger, 1979.

Engle, R. F.; Hendry, D. F.; and Richard, J. F. "Exogeneity." *Econometrica* 51 (1983): 277–304.

Epstein, R. J. *A History of Econometrics*. Amsterdam: North-Holland, 1987.

Fair, R. C. *Specification, Estimation, and Analysis of Macroeconometric Models*. Cambridge: Harvard University Press, 1984.

Fellner, W. "Individual Investment Projects in Growing Economies." In *Investment Criteria and Economic Growth, Proceedings of a Conference: Center of International Studies*. Cambridge: Massachusetts Institute of Technology, 1955.

Fisher, D. *Macroeconomic Theory: A Survey*. London: Macmillan, 1983.

Fleming, M. "External Economies and the Doctrine of Balanced Growth." *Economic Journal* 65 (June 1955): 241–256.

Førsund, F.R.; Hoel, M.; and Longva, S., ed. *Production, Multi-Sectoral Growth and Planning*. Amsterdam: North-Holland, 1985.

Foster, J. *Evolutionary Macroeconomics*. London: Allen and Unwin, 1987.

Frank, A. G. "The Development of Underdevelopment." *Monthly Review* 18 (September 1966): 17–31.

———. *Capitalism and Underdevelopment in Latin America: Historical Studies of Chile and Brazil*. New York: Monthly Review Press, 1967.

———. *Latin America: Underdevelopment or Revolution: Essays on the Development of Underdevelopment and the Immediate Enemy.* New York: Monthly Review Press, 1969.

Fransman, M., ed. *Machinery and Economic Development.* London: Macmillan, 1986.

Frenkel, J.; Gylfason, T.; and Helliwell, J. " A Synthesis of Monetary and Keynesian Approaches to Short-run Balance of Payments Theories." *Economic Journal* 90 (1980): 582–592.

Friedman, M. "The Role of Monetary Policy." *American Economic Review* 58 (1968): 1–17.

Gersovitz, M. "Estimation of the Two-Gap model." *Journal of International Economics* 12 (1982): 111-124.

Goldsmith, R. W. *Financial Structure and Development.* New Haven: Yale University Press, 1969.

Guitan, M. "Credit versus Money as an Instrument of Control." *International Monetary Fund Staff Papers* 20 (1973): 785– 800.

Gylfason, T., and Risager, O. "Does Devaluation Improve the Current Account." *European Economic Review* 25 (1984): 37– 64.

Haavelmo, T. "The Probability Approach in Econometrics." *Econometrica* 12 Supplement (July 1944): 1–115.

Hansen, L. P., and Sargent, T. "Formulating and Estimating Dynamic Linear Rational Expectations Models." *Journal of Economic Dynamics and Control* 2 (1980): 7–46.

Hanson, J. A. "Contractionary Devaluation, Substitution in Production and Consumption and the Role of the Labor Market." *Journal of International Economics* 14 (1983) 179–189.

Harrod, R. F. "An Essay in Dynamic Theory." *Economic Journal* 49 (1939): 14–33.

Hendry, D.F., and Richard, J-F. "The Econometric Analysis of Economic Time Series." *International Statistical Review* 51 (1983): 111–163.

Hirschman, A. "Devaluation and the Trade Balance: a note." *Review of Economics and Statistics* 31 (1949): 50–53.

———. *The Strategy of Economic Development.* New Haven: Yale University Press, 1958.

Hollander, S. *Classical Economics.* New York: Basil Blackwell, 1987.

Hope, K. R. *Economic Development in the Caribbean.* New York: Praeger, 1986.

Houthakker, H. S. "The Pareto Distribution and the Cobb-Douglas Production Function in Activity Analysis." *Review of Economic Studies* 23 (1955/56): 27–31.

Ichimura, S., and Ezaki, M., ed. *Econometric Models of Asian LINK.* Tokyo: Springer-Verlag, 1985.

Imaoka, H., and Meyanathan, S. "A Survey of Macroeconometric Models for Malaysia." In *Review of National Economies and Econometric Models in the ELSA Project: Vol. 1*, pp. 37–74. Tokyo: Institute of Developing Economies, 1984.

International Monetary Fund. *International Financial Statistics Yearbook*. Washington D. C.: International Monetary Fund (Various Issues).

International Bank for Reconstruction and Development. *World Tables*. 3rd ed. Baltimore: The John Hopkins University Press, 1983.

Johansen, L. *A Multi-Sectoral Study of Economic Growth*. Amsterdam: North-Holland, 1960.

———. *Production Functions*. Amsterdam: North-Holland, 1972.

Johnson, H. G., ed. *Further Essays in Monetary Theory*. London: Allen and Unwin, 1972.

Johnston, J. *Econometric Methods*. New York: McGraw-Hill, 1972.

Jorgenson, D. W. "The Development of a Dual Economy." *Economic Journal* 71 (1961): 309–334.

———. "The Theory of Investment Behavior." In *Determinants of Investment Behavior*, edited by R. Ferber. New York: Columbia University Press, 1967.

Kalman, R. E. "Theory of Modeling." In *Proceedings of IBM System Science Symposium*, pp. 53–69. Edited by Y. Nishikawa. Oiso, 1979.

———. "System- Theoretic Critique of Dynamic Economic Models." *International Journal of Policy Analysis and Information Systems* 4 (1980): 3–22.

———. "Identifiability and Problems of Model Selection in Econometrics." In *Advances in Econometrics*, edited by W. Hilderbrand. Cambridge: Cambridge University Press, 1983.

Keynes, J. M. *The General Theory of Employment, Interest, and Money*. London: Macmillan, 1936.

Khan, M. S. "Macroeconomic Adjustment in Developing Countries: A Policy Perspective." *World Bank Research Observer* 2 (January 1987): 23–42.

Khan, M., and Montiel, P. "Growth Oriented Adjustment Programs." *International Monetary Fund Staff Papers* 36 (1989): 279–306.

Kinoshita, S. "On Macroeconometric Model Building in ASEAN countries – The Case of Thailand." In *Review of National Economies and Econometric Models in the ELSA Project: Vol. 1*. Tokyo: Institute of Developing Economies, 1984.

Klein, L. R. "Remarks on the Theory of Aggregation." *Econometrica* 14 (1946): 303–312.

———. *Economic Fluctuations in the United States 1921–1941* New York: Wiley, 1950.

_____ . "What Kind of Macroeconometric Model for Developing Economies?" *Econometric Annual of the Indian Economic Journal* 13 (1965): 313–324.

_____ . *The Economics of Supply and Demand.* Baltimore: John Hopkins University Press, 1983.

Kmenta, J., and Ramsey, J. B. *Large-Scale Macro-Econometric Models.* Amsterdam: North-Holland, 1981.

Kooiman, P., and Kloek, T. "An Empirical Two Market Disequilibrium Model for Dutch Manufacturing." *European Economic Review* 29 (1985): 323–354.

Krueger, A. O. *Foreign Trade Regimes and Economic Development: Liberalization Attempts and Consequences.* Lexington, Mass.: Ballinger Press for the National Bureau of Economic Research,1978.

Krugman, P., and Taylor, L. "Contractionary Effects of Devaluation." *Journal of International Economics* 8 (1978): 445–456.

Kuznets, S. *Modern Economic Growth: Rate, Structure and Spread.* New Haven: Yale University Press, 1966.

Lal, D. *The Poverty of Development Economics.* London: Institute of Economic Affairs, 1983.

Lambert, Jean-Paul. *Disequilibrium Macroeconomic Models.* Cambridge: Cambridge University Press, 1988.

Leontief, W. W. *The Structure of the American Economy 1919– 1939.* New York: Oxford University Press, 1941.

Lewis, W. A. "Economic Development with Unlimited Supplies of Labor." *The Manchester School of Economic and Social Studies* 22 (May 1954): 139–191.

Lin, T., and Chou, W. "Hong Kong Model." In *Econometric Models of Asian Link*, edited by S. Ichimura and M. Ezaki. Tokyo: Springer-Verlag, 1985.

Little, I.M.D. *Economic Development: Theory, Policy and International Relations.* New York: Basic Books, 1982.

Long, F. "Patents In Guyana: The Case for Legal Reform–A Note." *Transition* 5 (1982) 71–77.

Loxley, J. *Debt and Disorder: External Financing for Development.* Boulder: Westview Press, 1986.

Lucas, R. E. Jr. "Econometric Policy Evaluation: A Critique." In *The Phillips Curve and Labor Markets*, edited by K. Brunner and A.H. Meltzer. Amsterdam: North-Holland, 1976.

_____ . *Models of Business Cycles.* Oxford: Basil Blackwell, 1987.

Mahalanobis, P. C. "Some Observations on the Process of Growth in National Income." *Sankhya* 12 (1953): Part 4.

Malinvaud, E. "Econometrics Faced with the Needs of Macroeconomic Policy." *Econometrica* 49 (1981): 1363–1375.

Mandle, J. "The Role of Agriculture in Self-Reliant Development." *Social and Economic Studies* 34 (1985): 153– 175.

Marwah, K. "An Econometric Model of Columbia: A Prototype Devaluation View." *Econometrica* 37 (1969) 228–251.

May, K. "The Aggregation Problem for a One-Industry Model." *Econometrica* 14 (1946): 285–298.

Maynard, G ., and Rijckegham, V. "Stabilization Policy in an Inflationary Economy - Argentina." In *Development Policy: Theory and Practice*, edited by G. Papanek. Cambridge: Harvard University Press, 1968.

McCallum, B. T. "Rational Expectations and the Estimation of Econometric Models: An Alternative Procedure." *International Economic Review* 17 (1976): 484–490.

McKinnon, R. "Foreign Exchange Constraints in Economic Development and Efficient Aid Allocation." *Economic Journal* (June 1964): 388–409.

McNees, S. K. "The Predictive Accuracy of Econometric Forecasts." *New England Economic Review* (September-October 1973): 3–27.

______ . "How Accurate are Economic Forecasts?" *New England Economic Review* (November-December 1974): 2–19.

______ . "The Recent Record of Thirteen Forecasts." *New England Economic Review* (September-October 1981): 5–21.

Meltzer, A. "On Keynes and Monetarism." In *Keynes and the Modern World*, edited by D. Worswick and J. Trevithick. Cambridge: Cambridge University Press, 1983.

Minford, P., and Peel, D. *Rational Expectations and the New Macroeconomics.* Oxford: Martin Robertson, 1983.

Ministry of Economic Development, Guyana Statistical Bureau. *Economic Survey*, (Various Issues).

Moore, E. J. "On System-Theoretic Methods and Econometric Modeling." *International Economic Review* 26 (February 1985): 87–106.

Muth, J. F. "Rational Expectations and the Theory of Price Movements." *Econometrica.* 29 (1961) 315–335.

Myint, H. "The Classical Theory of International Trade and Underdeveloped Countries." *Economic Journal* 68 (June 1958).

Narasimham, N. V. A. *Short-term Planning Model for India.* Amsterdam: North-Holland, 1956.

Nurkse, R. *Problems of Capital Formation in Underdeveloped Countries.* Oxford: Basil Blackwell, 1957.

O'Brien, P.J. "A Critique of Latin American Theories of Dependency." In *Beyond the Sociology of Development: Economy and Society in Latin*

America and Africa, pp. 7–27. Edited by I., Oxaal, T. Barnett., and D. Booth. London: Routledge & Kegan Paul, 1975.

Paul, L. "Export Simulations of the Guyanese Economy." (Ph.D. dissertation), Howard University, 1978.

Persad, U. "An Econometric Model of Trinidad and Tobago 1960– 1971." *Social and Economic Studies* 24 (1975): 389–419.

Pesaran, M. H. "Comparison of Local Power of Alternative Tests of Non-Nested Regression Models." *Econometrica* 50 (1982): 1287–1305.

_____ . *The Limits to Rational Expectations.* Oxford: Basil Blackwell, 1987.

Phelps, E. S. "Phillips Curves, Expectations of Inflation and Optimal Unemployment over Time." *Economica* 34 (1967): 254- -281.

_____., ed. *Micro-Economic Foundations of Employment and Inflation Theory.* Norton, 1970.

Phillips, A. W. "Stabilization Policy in Closed Economy." *Economic Journal* 64 (1954): 290–323.

_____ . "Stabilization Policy and the Time Forms of Lagged Responses." *Economic Journal* 67 (1957): 265–277.

Powell, A. A. "The Major Streams of Economy-Wide Modeling: Is Rapprochement Possible?" In *Large-Scale Macro-Econometric Models*, edited by J. Kmenta and J.B. Ramsey. Amsterdam: North- Holland, 1980.

Polak, J. J. "Monetary Analysis of Income Formation and Payments Problems." *International Monetary Fund Staff Papers* VI (1957/58): 1–50.

Polak, J. J., and Boissonneault, L. "Monetary Analysis of Income and Imports and Its Statistical Applications." *International Monetary Fund Staff Papers* VII (1959): 349–415.

Porter, R.C., and Ranney S.I. "An Eclectic Model of Recent LDC Macroeconomic Policy Analysis." *World Development* 10 (1982) 751–765.

Preston, R. S. "The Wharton Long Term Model: Input-Output within the context of a Macro Forecasting Model." *International Economic Review* 16 (1975): 3–19.

Pu, S. S. "A Note on Macroeconomics." *Econometrica* 14 (1946): 299–302.

Ramanathan, R. *Introductory Econometrics.* San Diego: Harcourt Brace Jovanovich, 1989.

Ranis, G., and Fei, J. C. "A Theory of Economic Development." *American Economic Review* 51 (1961): 533–565.

Rosenberg, N. *Perspectives on Technology.* Cambridge: Cambridge University Press, 1976.

_____ . *Inside the Black Box: Technology and Economics.* Cambridge: Cambridge University Press, 1982.

Rosenstein-Rodan, P. N. "Problems of Industrialization in Eastern and South-Eastern Europe." *Economic Journal* 53 (1943): 202–211.

Rostow, W. *The Stages of Economic Growth: A non-Communist Manifesto.* New York: Cambridge University Press, 1960.

Samuelson, P. "Comment on Leijhonhufvud." In *Keynes and the Modern World*, edited by D. Worswick and J. Trevithick. Cambridge: Cambridge University Press, 1983.

Santomero, A.M., and Seater, J.J. "The Inflation-Unemployment Trade-Off: A Critique of the Literature." *Journal of Economic Literature* 16 (1978): 499–544.

Sargent, T. "A Classical Macroeconometric Model for the United States." *Journal of Political Economy*. 84 (1976): 207– 232.

Schlicht, E. *Isolation and Aggregation in Economics*. Berlin: Springer-Verlag, 1985.

Scitovsky, T. "Two Concepts of External Economies." *Journal of Political Economy* LXII (April 1954): 143–151.

Seers, D. "The Limitations of the Special Case." *Bulletin of Oxford Institute of Economics and Statistics* 25: 2 (May 1963): 77–98.

Shapiro, S. S., and Wilk, M. B. " An Analysis of Variance Test for Normality." *Biometrika* 52 (1965): 591–611.

Shea, K. L. "Imported Inputs, Devaluation and Balance of Payments." *Southern Economic Journal* 43 (October 1976): 1106–1111.

Sims, C. "Evaluating Short-term Macroeconomic Forecasts: The Dutch Performance." *Review of Economics and Statistics* 49 (May 1967): 225–236.

———. "Policy Analysis with Econometric Models." *Brookings Papers on Economic Activity*. 1:82 (1982): 107–164.

Sneessens, H. *Theory and estimation of Macroeconometric Rationing Models*. New York: Springer-Verlag, 1981.

Soonthornsima, C. *A Macroeconomic Model for Economic Development of Thailand*. Institute of Public Administration, Bankok: Thammasat University, 1964.

Spanos, A. *Statistical Foundations of Econometric Modelling*. Cambridge: Cambridge University Press, 1986.

Stekler, R. "Forecasting with Econometric Models: An Evaluation." *Econometrica* 36 (1968): 437–463.

Stewart, F. *Technology and Underdevelopment*. London: Macmillan, 1977.

Stiglitz, J. "Distribution of Income and Wealth among Individuals." *Econometrica* 37 (1969): 382–397.

Taylor, J. B. " Econometric Implications of the Rational Expectations Hypothesis." *Econometrica* 48 (1980): 49–73.

Taylor, L. *Macro Models for Developing Countries*. New York: McGraw-Hill, 1979.

———. *Structuralist Macroeconomics: Applicable Models for the Third World*. New York: Basic Books, 1983.

Thomas, C. Y. "Foreign Currency Blackmarkets: Lessons from Guyana." *Social and Economic Studies* 38 (1989): 137–181.

Tobin, J. "The Interest-Elasticity of the Transaction Demand for Cash." *Review of Economics and Statistics* 38 (1956): 241–247.

______ . "Comment on Kaldor." In *Keynes and the Modern World*, edited by D. Worswick and J. Trevithick. Cambridge: Cambridge University Press, 1983.

Toida, M. "ELSA-Singapore Model." In *Preliminary Results of Econometric Models in the ELSA Project: Vol II.* Tokyo: Institute of Developing Economies, 1984.

UNCTAD. "Models for Developing Countries." In *The International Linkage of National Economic Models*, edited by R. Ball. Amsterdam: North-Holland, 1973.

Velasco, V. T. "A Macro-econometric Model of the Philippines." In *Preliminary Results of Econometric Models in the ELSA Project: Vol. II*, pp. 95–157. Tokyo: Institute of Developing Economies, 1984.

Walras, L. *Elements of Pure Economics.* Translated by William Jaffee. London: Allen and Unwin, 1954.

Watson, B. *Supplementary Notes on Foreign Investment in the Commonwealth Caribbean.* Kingston: Institute of Social and Economic Research, University of the West Indies, 1974.

Weisskopf, T. E. "An Econometric Test of Alternative Constraints on the Growth of Underdeveloped Countries." *Review of Economics and Statistics* 54 (1972): 67–78.

White, H. "Heteroscedasticity-constant covariance matrix estimation and a direct test for heteroscedasticity." *Econometrica* 48 (1980): 817–838.

Wickens, M. R. "The Efficient Estimation of Econometric Models with Rational Expectations." *Review of Economic Studies* 49 (1982): 55–67.

Wold, H. "Soft Modeling: The Basic Design and Some Extensions." In *Systems under Indirect Observation*, edited by K, Joreskog and H. Wold. Amsterdam: North-Holland, 1982.

Young, W. *Interpreting Mr. Keynes: The IS-LM Enigma.* Cambridge: Polity Press, 1987.

Index

For Product Safety Concerns and Information please contact our EU representative GPSR@taylorandfrancis.com
Taylor & Francis Verlag GmbH, Kaufingerstraße 24, 80331 München, Germany

www.ingramcontent.com/pod-product-compliance
Lightning Source LLC
LaVergne TN
LVHW011130300926
849160LV00008B/586

* 9 7 8 0 3 6 7 1 6 5 8 5 7 *